Neither on this Mountain Nor in Jerusalem

THE SOCIETY OF BIBLICAL LITERATURE
MONOGRAPH SERIES

Adela Yarboro Collins, Editor
P. Kyle McCarter, Jr., Associate Editor

Number 35
Neither on this Mountain Nor in Jerusalem
A Study of John 4

by
Hendrikus Boers

Hendrikus Boers

NEITHER ON THIS MOUNTAIN NOR IN JERUSALEM
A Study of John 4

Scholars Press
Atlanta, Georgia

NEITHER ON THIS MOUNTAIN NOR IN JERUSALEM

by
Hendrikus Boers

Library of Congress Cataloging in Publication Data

Boers, Hendrikus.
　Neither on this mountain nor in Jerusalem : a study of John 4 /
Hendrikus Boers.
　　p. cm. -- (Monograph series / Society of Biblical Literature
; no. 35)
　　Bibliography: p.
　　ISBN 1-555-40220-8 (alk. paper). ISBN 1-555-40221-6 (pbk. : alk.
paper)
　　1. Bible. N.T. John IV--Criticism, interpretation, etc.
I. Title. II. Series: Monograph series (Society of Biblical
Literature) ; no. 35.
BS2615.2.B564　　1988
226'.5066--dc19
　　　　　　　　　　　　　　　　　　　　　　88-4622
　　　　　　　　　　　　　　　　　　　　　　CIP

Printed in the United States of America
on acid-free paper

To William A. Beardslee:

friend, colleague,
mentor

Christel and the Samaritan Woman
by Giovanni Francesco Barbieri Guercino

Permanent Collection of
The High Museum of Art
Atlanta, Georgia

CONTENTS

ABBREVIATIONS

(Italics indicate periodicals; Roman characters serials)

AB	Anchor Bible
Aug	*Augustinianum*
BArchy	*Biblical Archaeology*
Bib	*Biblica*
BTB	*Biblical Theology Bulletin*
BTod	*Bible Today*
BTS	*Bible et terre sainte*
BZ	*Biblisches Zeitschrift*
CB	*Cultura biblica*
CBQ	*Catholic Biblical Quarterly*
EBib	Etudes bibliques
ED	*Euntes Docete*
ER	*Ecumenical Review*
ExpTim	*Expository Times*
GThT	*Gereformeerd Theologisch Tijdschrift*
HeyJ	*Heythrop Journal*
HNT	Handbuch zum Neuen Testament
HPR	*Homiletic and Pastoral Review*
HTKNT	Herders theologischer Kommentar zum Neuen Testament
JBL	*Journal of Biblical Literature*
JEThS	*Journal of the Evangelical Theological Society*
KEKNT	Kritisch-exegetischer Kommentar über das Neue Testament
LB	*Linguistica Biblica*
NCB	New Century Bible
NovT	*Novum Testamentum*
NRT	*Nouvelle revue théologique*
NTD	Das Neue Testament Deutsch
NTS	*New Testament Studies*
RSB	*Religious Studies Bulletin*
RSR	*Recherches de science religieuse*
SacDoc	*Sacra Doctrina*
SEA	*Svensk Exegetisk Årsbok*
SJT	*Scottish Journal of Theology*
ThDiss	Theologischen Dissertationen
THKNT	Theologischer Handkommentar zum Neuen Testament

Abbreviations

Th	*Theology*
VD	*Verbum domini*
VT	*Vetus Testamentum*
ZDPV	*Zeitschrift des deutschen Palästina-Vereins*
ZNW	*Zeitschrift für die neutestamentliche Wissenschaft*

LIST OF SYMBOLS

NP   narrative program

F   function, an action changing a circumstance into its opposite

[ ]   the limits of the function

S   subject, either acting or of a circumstance

=>   the action of an acting subject

$\leq$ the circumstance of a subject conjoined with an object

$\geq$ the circumstance of a subject disjoined from an object

O   object

( )   the limits of a circumstance

->   the change from one circumstance to its opposite

PREFACE

The present study has two main parts. In the first A.J. Greimas' semiotic theory is used to investigate the text of John 4, and in the second the results of the semiotic investigation are implemented in an interpretation of the chapter. I discovered Greimas' theory after many years in search of a means of moving beyond the surface of a text to what makes it give expression to meaning. It has always been my interest to discover a kind of metaphysics of New Testament texts. I want to know what holds a text together from its inside. In the sense of Goethe's *Faust*, I am interested in trying to understand "was die Welt im Innersten zusammenhält" (282-83). My endeavors have never been as far-reaching as Faust's: "Philosophie, Juristerei und Medizin" (354-55), but have been limited to "leider [nur] Theologie" (356), and increasingly to the New Testament. Nevertheless, within that more limited area my objectives remain,

> Daß ich erkenne, was die [Texten]
> Im Innersten zusammenhält,
> Schau' alle Wirkenskraft und Samen,
> Und tu' nicht mehr in Worten kramen. (382-386)

In due course it had become more and more clear to me that it was impossible to understand, especially Paul, unless one approached him from behind his texts — but how could one do that?

The work of the "religionsgeschichtliche" School provided the first fruitful avenue of approach. Especially worth mentioning is Richard Reitzenstein's chapter on "Paulus als Pneumatiker" in *Die hellenistischen Mysterienreligionen*.[1] It is the best interpretation of Paul that I know. Reitzenstein does not "trade with words," but reveals the "efficacy" and the "seeds" of Paul's thought.

---

[1] Richard Reitzenstein, *Die hellenistischen Mysterienreligionen nach ihren Grundgedanken und Wirkungen* (Stuttgart: Teubner, 1910; reprint of the 3rd ed. of 1927: Darmstadt: Wissenschaftliche Buchgesellschaft, 1956). ET: *Hellenistic Mystery Religions: Their Basic Ideas and Significance* (trans., John E. Steely; Pittsburgh: Pickwick Press, 1978).

And then, through the study of linguistics, I discovered a means through which I might attain my objectives in New Testament studies in the semiotics of A.J. Greimas, especially in the generative grammar of linguistic expression he and J. Courtés presented in *Sémiotique. Dictionnaire raisonné de la théorie du langage.*[2] Greimas' theory of language provides a complete grammar for the study of texts. What makes this grammar an effective tool for the investigation of texts is that it is not restricted to syntax, but includes semantics as well. Greimas' theory of language provides the means of investigating what holds a text together syntactically as well as semantically; i.e., what provides cohesion, by linking the various elements of the text together, and what constitutes its coherence, the meaning which comes to expression in it. Part One of this study is an exhaustive analysis of the text of John 4 by means of Greimas' theory in order to understand how meaning comes to expression in it. The analysis will proceed in such a way that the text itself determines what features of Greimas' theory are used. In that regard the study is at the same time a test of the effectiveness of the theory.

In Part Two the results of the investigation are applied in an interpretation of John 4. In that part too the text remains dominant. I do not engage in dialogue with scholarship on the chapter, even though that scholarship is the framework in which my interpretation takes place, but remain focused throughout on the text itself. Scholarship on John 4 is represented by extensive quotations of the relevant material in footnotes and by brief introductory discussions, at the beginning of each section, of the main issues that have emerged in the history of recent interpretation.

For readers who are not familiar with this kind of investigation, I propose reading Chapter 2 of Part One first. The abstract

---

[2] A.J. Greimas and J. Courtés, *Sémiotique. Dictionnaire raisonné de la théorie du langage* (Paris: Hachette, 1979), specifically p. 160, but developed in many details throughout the work. ET: *Semantics and Language* (trans., Larry Crist, Daniel Patte, and others; Bloomington: Indiana University Press, 1982) 134.

Written as a semiotic encyclopedia (note the French title), the work is as much the presentation of a semiotic theory as if it had been written as a single discourse. Each entry has a number of cross-references. One should treat the work as the presentation of a semiotic theory in paradigmatic, rather than syntagmatic form. This allows each reader to construct her or his own syntax as she or he strings together the various entries while reading. One can also do so in written form by combining various entries into a single structure. I did so with the generative trajectory by introducing the details from the relevant entries into a single structure on large sheets, based on the graphic outline of the trajectory on p. 160 (ET 134).

level at which it commences is soon involved in a process of increasing concretization which should help the reader recognize the degree to which the analysis disclosed internal features of the text. That should be an encouragement to follow how those features were uncovered in the analysis.

Contrary to what one may expect from the cold logic of semiotics, in the course of this investigation over a period of about six years the Samaritan woman became for me a real person, characterized especially by the inquiring independence with which she leads Jesus forward in doing the will of his Father. Pleasant was my surprise when I came across Guercino's mid-17th century painting of her. With an inquiring look, uninhibited by self-consciousness, she attends to the words of Jesus. It is the woman of "Neither on this Mountain nor in Jerusalem."

In conclusion, I would like to express gratitude to Jean Delorme of the *Centre pour l'Analyse du Discours Religieux* for encouraging me to consider Greimas' theory as a means of finding solutions to the issues in New Testament interpretation that concerned me. And then, I am greatly indebted to an anonymous reader for the *SBL Monograph Series*, whose penetrating engagement with the manuscript, ending in many pages of sometimes sharp, but always constructive, criticism helped me enormously by demanding that I explain a lot of what seemed self-evident to me. In place of the customary disclaimer I would like to emphasize to you, the reader, that she/he is largely responsible for the degree of intelligibility which this manuscript shows. At the 1987 SBL meeting in Boston, one day after I received the finally edited copy of the manuscript from Adela Yarbro Collins, Daniel Patte identified himself as that reader, "who made you work so hard."

HENDRIKUS BOERS
DECEMBER 1987

PART ONE

A SEMIOTIC INVESTIGATION OF JOHN 4

Introduction

In the following inquiry semiotic analysis is allowed to come into operation only inductively, i.e., not as something given, but as something that emerges in due course as the investigation of the text demands the application of analytical procedures to clarify its structure. I hope in this way to avoid letting semiotic analysis appear as the application of a method that is alien to the text, and to make it possible for the reader to recognize that it is as relevant for the clarification of a text as an analysis of the syntax of a sentence can be for its understanding. Our guide in this exploration will be the generative trajectory proposed by A.J. Greimas and J. Courtés in *Sémiotique. Dictionnaire raisonné de la théorie du langage* to which I referred in the preface.

This inquiry will not be complete with the analysis alone. When the analysis of a text is concluded, the way for the interpretation of its meaning has been prepared, but the actual interpretation has not yet begun. The objective of the analysis is to arrive at the highest degree of abstractness by breaking the text up into its most general constituents in terms of universal principles and the structural relationships between them. The task of clarifying the meaning of a particular text should then be to see if the analysis of its structure can contribute to an understanding of what it has to say — which is at the same time a decisive test for the analysis, and by implication for the method used.

The analysis should be followed by a description of the generative trajectory of the specific text from its deepest level, as revealed by the analysis, to its concrete manifestation in the actual text. It is very much like analyzing the grammatical structure of a difficult sentence in a foreign language in terms of its syntax and the meanings of its individual words, in order to proceed to an interpretation of its meaning. A native speaker executes this process completely intuitively. A grammatical or semiotic analysis of a difficult passage, which includes a syntactic and a semantic component, should be able to help clarify its meaning, but also to show how an intuitive meaning is derived, and thus function as a control of the correctness of an intuitive reading.

In this study reference will be made more than once to the importance of intuitive readings, even to the extent that intuition functions as a control of the analysis. If it is not possible to recognize by intuition the validity of a reading proposed by the analysis, that reading is probably incorrect; the analysis itself probably contributed to the proposed meaning of the text. To the degree that it did so, the analysis was not really analytical.

The first step in the analysis of a text is to establish minimal units of meaning. In a text, unlike, for example, a proverb, meaning is expressed in larger units than sentences. There are exceptions in our text which can serve to illustrate the point; for example, the parenthesis "Jews and Samaritans do not associate." The explanation is universal; its meaning does not depend on the surrounding text. On the other hand, it clarifies a situation in the text. The meaning of the situation to which it refers depends on what is explained by the parenthesis. The dependence is not reciprocal. "Jews and Samaritans do not associate" has meaning as a single sentence.

The woman's question, however, "How do you, a Jew, ask of me, a Samaritan woman, a drink of water?" has no meaning except as part of the story. Meaning in John 4 comes to expression by the way in which the entire text is structured, i.e., by the way the individual words are linked syntactically in phrases, sentences, paragraphs and finally in the story as a whole. Our first task will thus be to clarify in a preliminary way the structure of the text as a whole, by noting its relationship to what precedes and what follows, and the way the internal parts relate to each other.

Some Preliminary Observations Concerning the Structure of John 4

Verses 1-4 form a transition from the previous story about the relationship between Jesus and John with regard to the number of their respective disciples. Verses 5-6 form the introduction to the story of Jesus and the Samaritans; its completion is marked by the indication of time, "it was about the sixth hour" (v 16), and then the action begins, "A woman from Samaria came to draw water" (v 7).

The entry of the Samaritan woman (v 7) signals the beginning of a first sequence and her leaving (v 28) its completion.

However, within this sequence there is a significant break when Jesus changes the subject abruptly from the issue of water (vv 7-15) to that of the woman's husband(s) (vv 16-18). The first sequence thus appears to be broken up into at least two subsequences, verses 7, 9-15 (v 8 is parenthetic) and verses 16-26, 28-29 (v 27 is again parenthetic). The coming of the Samaritan villagers to Jesus (v 30) signals a new sequence. This sequence is interrupted by the appearance of the disciples (vv 31-38), but taken up again in verses 39-40a and completed with the villagers' confession of Jesus as the savior of the world (v 42). This second sequence is comprised of verses 30, 39-42.

Verse 43 signals the beginning of a new story. Note, however, that verse 44, "Jesus himself testified that a prophet does not have honor in his fatherland," does not fit at all with Jesus' experience in Galilee as stated in the very next verse, "When he came to Galilee, the Galileans received him, having seen all he did in Jerusalem." Verse 44 is probably less, if at all, a comment on Galilee than on the experience Jesus had just had in Samaria, on the amazing reception which "the prophet" had in what was not his fatherland.

The sequence with the disciples is superimposed and *may* have been added subsequently (vv 8, 27, 31-38). The sequence with the Samaritans (the woman and the villagers) is complete without the involvement of the disciples; the discussion with the disciples actually interrupts the sequence with the Samaritans after verse 30, which is taken up again in verses 39-40a. Note also that in the transition from the preceding narrative (vv 1-4) and in the introduction (vv 5-6) only Jesus is mentioned; he alone arrives at the Samaritan village ("he arrived" v 4). Also in the conclusion it is only Jesus who stays with the Samaritans ("he stayed" v 40).

In a preliminary way, thus, we arrive at a story of Jesus and the Samaritans. Verses 5-6 comprise the introduction. It has two main sequences, namely, Jesus and the Samaritan woman (vv 7, 9-26, 28-29) and Jesus and the Samaritan villagers (vv 30, 39-42). Onto this story has been superimposed the story of Jesus and the disciples (vv 8, 27, 31-38), which is not necessarily a later addition. We have also noted a possible break in the sequence of Jesus and the Samaritan woman between verses 15 and 16. The first subsequence, verses 7, 9-15, appears to be relatively stable, having water as its topic. In the second subsequence, verses 17-26, 28-29, there appears to be two topics, the woman's husband(s) (vv 16-18), and the right place of worship (vv 20-25), with verse 19 forming a transition from the one to the other.

We can also note that the theme of the transition in the second sequence concerning the Samaritan woman, i.e., the question of the identity of Jesus (prophet), is taken up again in verses 25-26 in his claim to be Messiah. This suggests another, a third topic in the sequence, i.e., the question of the identity of Jesus. In this case, however, it is a topic that transcends all the sequences with the Samaritans. This topic also appears in the first subsequence, when Jesus claims that he can provide the water of life (v 10), in the woman's question to Jesus, "Are you greater than our father Jacob?" (v 12), in the woman's presumption that Jesus may be the messiah (v 29) which is accepted by the villagers (cf. v 39), and finally in the Samaritans' recognition of Jesus as the savior of the world (v 42).

The cohesion of the story is provided by the development from the woman's suggestion that Jesus may be the messiah (v 29) to the villagers' recognition that he is truly the savior of the world (v 42); that it signifies progress in understanding is made explicit by the villagers' statement to the woman, "we no longer believe through your talk, because we ourselves have heard and know that he is truly the savior of the world" (v 42).

It is also possible to posit progress in the woman's own understanding of who Jesus was, from complete scepticism in verse 12, to the affirmation that he is a prophet in verse 19, again to scepticism in verse 25, and then to the presumption that he may indeed be the messiah in verse 29. The progress in her understanding, however, is paradigmatic; i.e., it is not presented as a single narrative sequence, but as a series of scenes, like entries in an encyclopedic dictionary which progressively deepen the insight.

From this it is clear that the identity of Jesus is a very important topic in the story. At the same time, however, it does not provide the story with syntactic cohesion, but signals paradigmatic overlays as one moves from scene to scene. The paradigmatic development in the sequence of Jesus and the woman, however, does not overcome the incoherence which results from the way in which topics are taken up and then dropped to pass on to others in this part of the story. The three main topics in the sequences with the woman are: who gives whom water to drink (vv 7, 9-15), the woman's husband(s) (vv 16-18), and the right place to worship (vv 20-25).

It is worth noting that, although the first subsequence has a single topic and the second has two, there is a remarkable degree of structural similarity between them. In both subsequences Jesus requests something of the woman; water in the first subsequence (v 7), and the fetching of her husband in the second (v 16). In both cases, for different reasons, she does not do what Jesus requests; in the first for cultural reasons (v 9) and in the second because of her complicated relationships to men (vv 17-18).

This leads in each case to a change in topic. In the second, the change of topic is clear; it is from the woman's husband(s) to that of the right place to worship (vv 20-23). But in the first also, there is a change in topic even though the word, water, remains the same. The water Jesus requested of the woman is not the same as that which he proposes giving her (vv 10, 13-14).

Actually the change of topic is more abrupt in the first case than in the second. In the latter, the issue of the woman's husband(s) leads her to the recognition of Jesus as a prophet. This motivates her proposal of the topic of the right place of worship (v 20), even though, according to verse 25, she was of the opinion that only Messiah could speak authoritatively about such matters. In the case of the first subsequence the transition is so abrupt that the woman does not even recognize that Jesus has switched topics. This is made all the more difficult by the fact that he keeps using the same word. She thinks that he is still talking about drinking water (vv 11-12, 15). It should also be noted that, although the recognition of Jesus as a prophet provides a transition from the discussion of the woman's husband(s) to that of the right place of worship, materially there is more cohesion between this new topic and the reason for her ignoring Jesus' request for a drink of water in the first subsequence, namely, the opposition between Jew and Samaritan (cf. vv 9 and 20). Thus we may suggest that the structural similarity between the two subsequences — Jesus requesting something of the woman which she does not heed, followed by a change of topic — suggests that the syntactic break in each case may not be accidental, but intended.

These preliminary observations reveal that John 4 has a very intricate structure in which syntactic and paradigmatic features cross over; as the story moves forward syntactically it reaches back paradigmatically to earlier features that are unconnected syntactically. An example is the issue of Jews and Samaritans. After having been brought up in verse 9, it is suddenly present again in verse 20, but then does not seem to have further significance in the story.

It would now be helpful if one could have at one's disposal a grammar of discourse by means of which it would be possible to get a proper hold on the discourse syntax of the narrative, and of the way in which paradigmatic features interrelate structurally apart from their syntactic binding in the text. Such a grammar should include a syntactic as well as a semantic component.

The generative trajectory of discourse proposed by A. J. Greimas and J. Courtés, to which I referred above, promises to be such a grammar of discourse.

GENERATIVE TRAJECTORY		
	syntactic component	semantic component
Semio-narrative structures	deep level FUNDAMENTAL SYNTAX	FUNDAMENTAL SEMANTICS
	surface level SURFACE NARRATIVE SYNTAX	NARRATIVE SEMANTICS
Discourse structures	DISCOURSE SYNTAX	DISCOURSE SEMANTICS
	Discoursivization actorialization temporalization spatialization	Thematization Figurativization

By distinguishing, on the one hand, between a syntactic component and a semantic component, and on the other, between a discourse structure and a semio-narrative structure, it becomes possible to get hold of the various features of the text's structure individually. In the case of the semio-narrative structures it is possible to differentiate further between a surface and a deeper level, i.e., between the level of the actual text, and that of the principles underlying its organization. It is not my intention to provide a theoretical discussion or justification of this proposed grammar here from which the analysis of the text could then proceed deductively. Rather my intention remains to derive whatever we can say theoretically about such a grammar inductively from the text of John 4, using the Greimas/Courtés proposal as a guide. My translations of the Greimas/Courtés terminology in the analysis are not rendered abstractly in terms of the theory itself, but concretely in terms of the function they fulfil in the analysis — which is the sole final justification for the existence of the theory.

A list of the symbols used in the investigation is provided above, after the table of contents and the list of abbreviations. The lists of subjects, objects, and narrative programs in appendixes 1 - 4 should also be useful.

Chapter 1

ANALYSIS OF JOHN 4: FROM THE CONCRETE LEVEL OF THE TEXT TO ITS ABSTRACT STRUCTURE AND MEANING

Introduction

In our analysis of John 4 we will consider its syntactic and semantic components separately. Since the syntax does not exist without the meaning, and inversely, the meaning comes to expression through the syntax, one cannot avoid involving semantic features in the syntactic analysis, and inversely, syntactic features in the semantic analysis. In each case, however, the focus will be purely on the syntax and the semantics, respectively. In the syntactic analysis the focus will be on how the syntax contributes to the expression of meaning in the text by structuring the components of its meaning; in the semantic analysis the focus will be on what the meaning is that comes to expression by means of the syntactic structuring of its components.

A. THE SYNTACTIC COMPONENT

An obvious place to begin the analysis is the (semio-)narrative syntax, specifically at the surface level, i.e., the surface narrative syntax, because that comes closest to our intuitive reading of a text, our perception of the flow or course of the narrative.

1. *The Surface Narrative Syntax of John 4*

a. *The Sequence with the Woman* (vv 6-7, 9-29)[1]

In terms of the surface narrative structure the first subsequence with the woman (vv 7, 9-15) does not seem to get very far; she remains insensitive to Jesus' request for a drink of water (v 7) because of her cultural outlook (v 9). The second subsequence (vv 16-26, 28-29) also begins with failure. The woman claims that she cannot fulfil his request because she does not have the ability to do so; she does not have a husband (v 17a). In both cases Jesus tries further persuasion to get her to co-operate in his attempt to get through to her, although in each case he gives up the attempt to get her to do what he asked in the first

---

[1] Verse numbers are given here only as a guide. The structural integration of the text makes it impossible to separate the sequences and subsequences completely, as can be seen in the outlining of the narrative programs below.

place. In the first subsequence the attempt at persuasion is explicit: "If you knew the gift of God and who it is that said to you, give me to drink, *you would ask him* to give you water of life" (v 10). In the second it is implied by her recognition of him as a prophet. The effect of Jesus' persuasion is that the woman invites him to talk to her concerning the question of the correct place of worship, i.e., she "empowers" him to do so, something she had not been willing to do in the first subsequence in which she remained sceptical about his ability to carry out the program of action he had proposed (v 10, cf. vv 11-12). With regard to the first subsequence, however, it is not altogether clear whether Jesus did not nevertheless proceed to his program of action in the sense that what he *said* about the water of life was in effect *giving* the water of life, or whether in his explanation he was merely continuing his attempt to persuade her to allow him to give her the water of life (vv 13-14). Whatever the case may be, his attempt appears to have failed when it becomes clear that the woman thinks he is still talking about drinking water.

Now the reason for the break in the sequence with the woman becomes clear. It is that the first subsequence failed, a failure which led to a new attempt (in the second subsequence) at persuading her to co-operate with him in his attempt to get through to her. This new attempt succeeds at least to the degree that the woman's previous scepticism about Jesus' ability (vv 11-12) is now replaced by her recognition that he is a prophet (v 19). This in turn leads to her proposing a topic for discussion (v 20) which is closely related to that which had prompted him to suggest to her that she should allow him to give her the water of life (v 9, cf. 10). At the end of the entire sequence she even wonders if Jesus may not be the messiah (v 29), which appears to be at least an openness to his claim that he was Messiah whom she expected to clarify "everything" (vv 25-26). However, her wondering is not in response to what he said with regard to the question of the right place to worship (vv 21-24), but because he told her "everything I did" (v 29), referring to the conversation about her husband(s) (vv 16-18). The conclusion of the entire story, when the Samaritans contrast their own insight into the identity of Jesus with hers (v 42), seems to confirm that she never reached the mark. As will become clear in due course the opposite is true. The Samaritans' remark expresses the supreme irony of the passage; it establishes the complete success of the woman's mission to the villagers. In terms of success, Jesus' program appears to have had three stages marked by the three (sub)sequences of the story involving the Samaritans: verses 7 and 9-15, failure; verses 16-26, and 28-29, partial success; and verses 30, and 39-42, final achievement.

The narrative schema as a means of analysis

The above partial analysis of John 4 can be formalized in terms of the narrative schema proposed by Greimas as a means of analyzing the narrative trajectory ("parcours narratif").

NARRATIVE SCHEMA			
A Need	B Preparedness	C Performance	D Sanction
A subject of a circumstance, disjoined from a desirable object, or conjoined with an undesirable object	An active subject, willing or obliged, and able (having the power), to overcome the need, specified in A, by a performance	The active subject performing the action transforming the circumstance specified in A into its opposite	Recognition of the success or failure of the performance, or of the achievement of a desired value

The course or "trajectory" of a narrative may be analyzed into one or more such narrative schemas comprising the four phases; three in terms of which a program of action can be differentiated, preceded by a fourth representing the situation of need or lack which the program of action is called upon to remedy.

This narrative schema is not merely the formalization of what is said in the text, but a structure which can clarify what happens syntactically. This is similar to our expectation of a sentence. We expect that it normally should have a noun phrase and a verb phrase or, in traditional terms, a subject and a predicate, even if, as in an exclamation, only the predicate is given. All four phases of the narrative schema do not have to be actually represented in the text; nevertheless they are presupposed by those that are represented. So, for example, if one has only the *performance* of an action in a text, it presupposes a *need* which the performance has to satisfy, and a subject who is *prepared* to carry it out; it also anticipates a *sanction* indicating whether it is a success or a failure.

The first sequence of Jesus with the woman can be schematized in three programs of action proposed by Jesus as follows:

i. *First subsequence with the woman* (vv 6-7, 9-15)

A (need)	B (preparedness)	C (performance)	D (sanction)
6	7 (9)		(9)
(9)	10 (11-12)		(11-12)
(11-12)		13-14	15

The parentheses indicate a verse which functions in more that one phase of the narrative schema; it will be noted that those verses occur more than once in the schematic presentation of the sequence. So, for example, the woman's statement in verse 9, "How do you, a Jew ask a drink of me, a Samaritan woman?" She gives a negative *sanction* to Jesus' proposed program of action with which he hopes his need of a drink of water can be satisfied. The negative sanction concerns the *preparedness* of her and Jesus to engage in the course of action. At the same time this negative sanction becomes the expression of a new *need* which Jesus then proposes to remedy with a new program of action, verse 10, to which the woman once more gives a negative sanction, denying that Jesus has the ability to carry out his proposed program, verses 11-12. It will be noted that the situation with verses 11-12 is similar, giving expression first to phase D, the woman's negative sanction of Jesus' ability to give her the water, and at the same time A (need) in another program, the woman's lack of understanding of what Jesus proposes, which Jesus tries to remedy in verses 13-14, with the woman's sanction in verse 15 revealing that he did not succeed.

Jesus requests a drink of water from the woman (v 7); he proposes a program of action to her and tries to elicit her willingness to carry it out as part of the preparedness of a subject to perform an action. It should be noted that this is really a subprogram providing Jesus with the means (preparedness) to quench his thirst. This presupposes Jesus' thirst which is not explicitly stated. The statement in verse 6 that he was tired from the journey and sat on the well expresses a more general need, but a drink of water is evidently a crucial element in it.

The woman ignores his request with a statement that has the form of an anti-program which opposes not specifically her giving him a drink of water, but in a more general sense, the association between a Jewish man and a Samaritan woman (v 9). As such it represents her unpreparedness to engage in the program Jesus had proposed, but since Jesus leaves it at that it also spells the failure of his proposed program (negative sanction or failure). Even more important, as an anti-program it represents a new need, the attribution of a positive value to non-association between Jew and Samaritan, which Jesus' proposed program would have eliminated by implication. The new program which he now proposes specifically opposes this need; his program would absolve the negative value, non-association between Jew and Samaritan. In this way the course of the narrative has moved from a specific, rather innocent, level of a request for a drink of water, to the level of a principle which plays a dominant role in the rest of the narrative. The program which Jesus has in mind now no longer concerns the issue of a drink of water, but the principle which his request for a drink of water had unmasked. This change in level is marked by the change in the meaning of the term, water, and also in who would now be the active subject carrying out the program; it is no longer the woman, but Jesus.

The sequence once more moves into the phase of preparedness, i.e., of the second proposed program of action. Jesus, the new active subject who is to carry out the proposed program, obviously has the willingness to do so and claims also to have the ability, but he tries to persuade the woman to authorize him to go ahead with it (v 10). The woman, not recognizing who he is, but also not recognizing the true nature of the program, refuses him the authorization (vv 11-12). Her refusal represents a double need, failure to recognize who Jesus is, and failure to understand his program, i.e., failure to attach the correct meaning to it. The first does not function immediately as a need to be satisfied in a program of action, but it will function as such in the first part (vv 16-19) of what we have identified as the second subsequence with the woman. Her failure to recognize the nature of Jesus' program functions here as the need for the program in which Jesus now engages, namely, to clarify to her the true nature of his proposed program to give her water (vv 13-14). For the moment at least, he abandons the program of giving her water of life. Thus her failure to understand the program, and to authorize Jesus to proceed with it, spells the failure of the program.

Two things have become clear as a result of our understanding of the way in which the double need represented by the woman's reaction to Jesus' offer functions in the narrative schemas of this part of the discourse: 1. There is no reason to consider Jesus' explanation of the meaning of his program as already engaging in it; the explanation is exactly what it appears to be, the attempt to satisfy the woman's need to have a proper understanding of his program. We should thus expect the actual giving of the water of life to be something other than merely talking about it. 2. It appears that there is a far closer connection between what we have identified as the first and the second subsequences of Jesus with the woman in the sense that the beginning of the second subsequence's program of action is intended to satisfy a need that had come to expression in the first subsequence, namely, the woman's failure to recognize who Jesus was by arguing that he could certainly not be greater than Jacob (v 12).

But first let us return to the last part of the first subsequence. Jesus proceeds to the program of instruction to satisfy the woman's need to understand correctly his program of giving her water of life (vv 13-14) without any further preparation. He obviously has the willingness to do so; he proceeds as one who has the ability, and evidently does not consider it necessary to request the woman's authorization. The program once more fails when the woman asks Jesus to give her his miraculous water so that she would not need to come to the well again to draw water (v 14). She still attributes false values to the water about which Jesus spoke, thus giving a negative sanction to his program. She thinks of a different program, the miraculous provision of drinking water, which would supersede Jacob's miracle. As we will see, however, her statement is ironic: She will indeed abandon her quest for drinking water from the well, but not in the way she expresses it here.

What we have identified as the first subsequence of Jesus with the woman can be summarized analytically in terms of the three narrative schemas outlined above:

1.   The first concerns a program of action to satisfy a need of Jesus, his thirst. He authorizes (preparedness) the woman to carry out this program by asking her for a drink of water, but she reacts negatively to this (negative sanction) by accepting the "obligation not to" engage in the program (preparedness) imposed by the convention of non-association between a Jewish man and a Samaritan woman. The woman's unwillingness to engage in Jesus' proposed program effectively causes it to fail.

2.   The new program which Jesus suggests presupposes a different need since it is now Jesus who is to give water to the woman. The need which the new program has to satisfy is thirst for water of life; it is the woman's negative sanction of the program which Jesus had originally proposed which brought this new need to expression. Jesus now asks the woman to authorize him (preparedness) to engage in a new program, but she declines (negative sanction), pointing out that he does not have the ability to carry it out (preparedness). The woman's refusal to au-

thorize Jesus, effectively preventing him from engaging in the program — at least for the time being — causes it too to fail.

3. The woman's unwillingness to authorize Jesus to carry out the second program which he proposed manifests a double need, lack of understanding of the nature of water of life, and of Jesus' ability. To this second need Jesus will respond in what we have identified as the second subsequence with the woman, thus forming a close link between the two subsequences. Here in the last part of the first subsequence, he responds to the first need, failure to understand the nature of water of life. There is no preparedness phase; Jesus immediately moves to the performance of the program of action, instructing the woman concerning the water of life. Her reaction, misunderstanding water of life as spring water miraculously provided, is once more a negative sanction of Jesus' performance. He obviously failed to correct the woman's misunderstanding.

This third narrative schema could be considered as a subschema of the second in the sense that a correction of the woman's misunderstanding of the nature of water of life could have served to overcome her unwillingness to authorize (preparedness) Jesus to carry out his second proposed program of action. His failure to correct her misunderstanding thus means a complete failure of the second program at this point. In the second subsequence he makes a new beginning by now concentrating first on the issue of his ability (preparedness), which represents the one aspect of the double need which became manifest in the woman's unwillingness to authorize him to engage in the second proposed program. In that regard it still concerns the phase of preparedness of the second program.

With regard to the relationship between the first and second subsequence of Jesus and the woman, it is important to note also that the topic for discussion which the woman proposes to Jesus in the second (preparedness), the question of the right place to worship (need), has affinity with the convention which obliged her to ignore Jesus' initially proposed program in the first subsequence, and which we considered above to have brought to expression the need for the second proposed program in the first subsequence with the woman, thirst for water of life. The way in which that need is addressed in Jesus' performance which follows in the second subsequence, however, teaching concerning true worship of the Father in the spirit, along with other considerations, indicates that it no longer serves merely as the phase of preparedness as in the previously proposed program, but constitutes the main program of the new subsequence. In that regard the second subsequence has advanced beyond the first.

What we have identified as the first subsequence with the woman thus fails in every respect. Apart from Jesus' original need for drinking water, the woman has revealed three needs. These are represented by: 1. the positive value which she attributes to the non-association between Jew and Samaritan, 2. her misunderstanding of Jesus' program of giving her water of life, and 3. her lack of understanding who Jesus is. In the next subsequence two of these needs are going to be addressed specifically: the identity of Jesus in verses 25-26, and 29, and the issue of the relationship between Jew and Samaritan in verses 20-24. In this second subsequence Jesus is more successful than in the first. Before proceeding to the analysis of the rest of the surface narrative structure of John 4, however, it would be useful to indicate how the four phases of the narrative can be analyzed in even greater detail in terms of their narrative programs, in anticipation of their complete analysis in the next section below on "The Syntactic Deep Structure." In that way the connection between the "surface narrative syntax" and the "fundamental syntax" will become clear.

Narrative programs as means of further analysis

If we take as an example the program of action which Jesus proposed to the woman, that she give him a drink of water, we can analyze it further in terms of a statement concerning an action in which the woman is to engage and a statement concerning a circumstance in which Jesus would find himself, having a drink of water, as a result of the action of the woman. This can be formalized as follows:

$$NP = F[S_1 => (S_2 \leq O)]$$

in which NP refers to the narrative program to which the statement gives expression, F (function) to the entire incident, S_1 to the acting subject, in this case the woman, $=>$ to the action of the acting subject, S_2 to the subject of the circumstance, in this case Jesus, $\leq$ to the conjunction[2] of the subject of circumstance conjoined with an object, O, which is in this case the drinking water. The brackets indicate the extent of the expression of the action and the parentheses the extent of the expression of the circumstance. A narrative program can be defined as a function

---

[2] The usual symbol for conjunction is ∩; for disjunction ∪. I use $\leq$ and $\geq$, respectively, because they are available on the extended ASCII (American Standard Code for Information Interchange) keyboard.

in which an enunciation of an action ("énoncé de faire") governs an enunciation of a circumstance ("énoncé d'état"). It is easy to recognize that, in this narrative program, the expected result of the woman's action, if she were to have performed it, presupposes a circumstance in which Jesus was without, or disjoined from, the object, drinking water. It is the situation of need which Jesus' proposed program of action for the woman was to have eliminated. This situation could be formalized as an expression of a circumstance as $(S_2 \geq O)$, in which $\geq$ refers to the situation of disjunction. (For a complete listing of the subjects, objects, and narrative programs referred to in this inquiry, see the appendixes.)

The program of action can be written out more fully as
$$F[S_1 => (S_2 \geq O) \rightarrow (S_2 \leq O)]$$
thus showing not only the resulting circumstance but also the one from out of which it is transformed. $\geq$ refers to the disjunction of the subject of circumstance from the object. There is a certain redundancy to this fuller formulation because the initial circumstance $(S_2 \geq O)$ can without difficulty be inferred from the resultant circumstance $(S_2 \leq O)$. It does, however, provide greater clarity.

Jesus' action of proposing the program to the woman can also be analyzed in terms of a narrative program in which Jesus conjoins the woman with the program, written as follows:
$$F[S_2 => (S_1 \leq O_2)],$$
in which O_2 represents the program of action given immediately above. This demands of the woman an act of the will which can be analyzed in terms of her conjunction with the modal object, willingness, written
$$NP = F[(S_1 \geq O_m) \rightarrow (S_2 \leq O_m)]$$
in which O_m represents the modal object of an attitude of the will. The woman, conjoined with a program of action in which she is the proposed subject of the action, adopts an attitude of the will.

The logical structure of discourse (willingness, obligation, authorization, and ability to perform an action)

This modal object, willingness, is quite complex. According to our text the woman does not specifically refuse to carry out the program, but neither does she agree to it; i.e., she makes no decision. However, she also does not carry out the program so that her undecidedness nevertheless remains negative; she does not have the will to carry out the program. This situation can be clarified by means of the logical square showing the possibilities open to her. With that we are moving for a while to the deeper syntactic level of the principles underlying the surface structure. The possibilities open to the woman can be presented as follows:

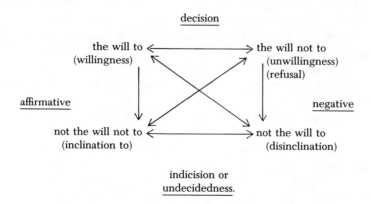

in which the diagonal axes represent contradiction, the horizontal axes contraries (above) and subcontraries (below), and the vertical axes implication. It is important to note that both contraries cannot be the case at the same time, but that both subcontraries can.

The logical square indicates all the logical possibilities of the woman's attitude of will. On a similar square, functioning as a semiotic square, it is possible to show which positions the woman actually occupies and the moves she makes.[3] According to our text she remained on the negative side of the axis of the subcontraries (*undecidedness*); she does not have the will to engage in the program, (*disinclination*). If Jesus had persisted, she could have hardened this disinclination into a decision not to engage in the program. In that case she would still not have the will to engage in it, but would now be reinforced with outright *unwillingness*; or he could have persuaded her to change her mind (will) into a decision to engage in it, (*willingness*), in which case it would imply that she does not have the will not to, (*incli-*

---

[3] My understanding of the semiotic square is slightly different from that of Greimas. In my usage the semiotic square is completely coordinate with the traditional logical square. The main difference compared with Greimas concerns the lines of implication which run vertically upwards from the subcontraries to the contraries in Greimas' interpretation. In my interpretation they run from the contraries to the subcontraries, as in the logical square. This makes it possible to coordinate completely the logical and semiotic structures of the analyzed texts. The differences are reconcilable.

nation to). All of this will be discussed more fully in the section "The Syntactic Deep Structure" below.

Returning to our actual text, since Jesus apparently abandoned the program himself, the woman was never compelled to leave the position of negative undecidedness, i.e., of disinclination. The analysis nevertheless shows that although she did not make a decision, she was faced with all the possible attitudes of the will, so that her very *inactivity* inevitably involved her in some kind of *act* of the will.

Before proceeding to the analysis of the surface narrative syntax of the second subsequence of Jesus and the woman, it would be useful to clarify the rather complex situation that has been disclosed in connection with the preparation phase of the narrative schema in a text. Our analysis so far has revealed the following three aspects of the qualification of an acting subject — a *willingness* to engage in the program ("vouloir faire") which Jesus tried to solicit from the woman by asking her to give him a drink of water, and which he himself revealed when he suggested that she ask him to give her the water of life; an *authorization* to carry out a program ("pouvoir faire"), which Jesus gave to the woman when he asked her for a drink of water, and which he suggested to her for his own program of providing her with water of life, "you would have asked him . . ." (v 10); finally, the ability to carry out the program ("savoir faire"), which the woman is assumed to have had, i.e., the ability to give Jesus the drinking water if she had decided to do so, and which Jesus claimed to have had for his program of giving her water of life (v 10), but which she disputed, misunderstanding his program, and posing over and against his claim of having such an ability Jacob who proved to have had it by miraculously providing drinking water.

There is also a fourth aspect of preparedness, *obligation* ("devoir faire"), which is closely related to *authorization* ("pouvoir faire"). Even though it does not come to expression at the surface level of the text, it is present at a deeper level in the sense that by asking Jesus for the water of life, authorizing him to give it to her, the woman permits him, i.e., allows that he has "no obligation not to" do so ("ne pas devoir ne pas faire"). Permission, negation of the obligation not to, does not necessarily mean authorization which requires affirmation of the action. Jesus does not want the woman merely not to stand in the way of his proposed action; he wants her approval of it. Inversely, the absence of an authorization is not tantamount to obliging someone not to engage in an action, but merely does not support engagement in it. Authorization allows for, and depends on, the willingness of the acting subject; obligation subjects the will of the acting subject. The relationship between willingness and obligation can be presented on a logical square as follows:

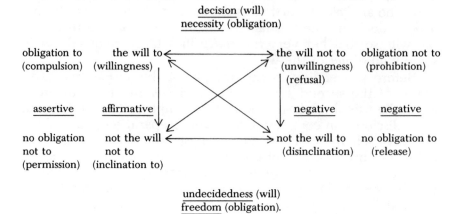

decision (will)
necessity (obligation)

| obligation to (compulsion) | the will to (willingness) | the will not to (unwillingness) (refusal) | obligation not to (prohibition) |

assertive   affirmative   negative   negative

| no obligation not to (permission) | not the will not to (inclination to) | not the will to (disinclination) | no obligation to (release) |

undecidedness (will)
freedom (obligation).

It is easy to recognize that the interrelationships are very complex. It is not possible here, nor is it necessary, to consider every detail since they are not all relevant to our text. It will be noted that having the will to engage in a program conforms with having the obligation to do so, but in such a way that it is not possible to change to any other position on the square of the will. The same applies to the will not to and the obligation not to.

Furthermore, "the will to" is as contrary to "the obligation not to" as it is to "the will not to," and in the same way "the will not to" is as contrary to "the obligation to" as it is to "the will to." It is possible for "the will to" and "the obligation to" to be the case at the same time since they are in conformity with each other, and similarly "the will not to" and "the obligation not to." However, while it is not possible for contraries on the same square to be true at the same time, e.g., "the obligation to" and "the obligation not to," it is possible for contraries between the squares to be the case at the same time, "the obligation to" and "the will not to" and "the will to" and "the obligation not to."

Every position on the axes of the sub-contraries can be true at the same time. We have noted that there is a limited freedom of the will when both positions on the side of the contraries are the case, e.g., the obligation to and the will to. There is a freedom to will as long as it is in conformity with the obligation. The only way in which there can be freedom of the will to take in

any position is when both sub-contraries on the square of obligation are the case, i.e., when there is neither an obligation not to
nor an obligation to. Thus if there is complete freedom of the
will in a text it implies that both subcontraries on the square of
obligation are the case.

Obligation can be due either to internal factors in the active
subject of the program, for example, a sense of responsibility or
compassion, or to external factors, for example, effective pressure from another or others, or from social convention. In our
text no participant in the events ever limits the freedom of
choice of others. In that regard, even though obligation or its
absence is never expressed at the surface level of the text, it is
clear that at a deeper level this implies that the sub-contraries of
obligation are both the case, i.e., that there is neither the obligation not to nor the obligation to engage in any program. It is a
kind of zero expression in the sense of being self-evidently present without needing to be explicitly mentioned.

In one case, however, the pressure of social convention does
determine the obligation not to engage in a program: the woman's statement that it is not proper for a Jewish man to ask a
Samaritan woman for a drink of water is a concession to social
convention of the obligation not to engage in the program proposed by Jesus. As such it does not imply the will not to engage
in the program, but it does imply not having the will to, i.e.,
remaining on the negative side of undecidedness. Her position
will become even clearer when we consider the other aspect of
preparation for which obligation has implications, namely, the
power to engage in a program.

Between obligation and the power or authority to perform
an action there is also a complex set of relationships as the diagram below reveals. If no obligation exists one may have the authority to perform an action and also not to do it, i.e., one may
be free to do either. If, however, the authority to perform an
action is an implication of the obligation to do so — obligation
implies authorization — then no authority not to is also implied,
as the diagram shows. The broken lined arrows indicate implications between the square of obligation and that of authority.
Note the double implication between obligation to and having
no authority not to, and between obligation not to and no authority to.

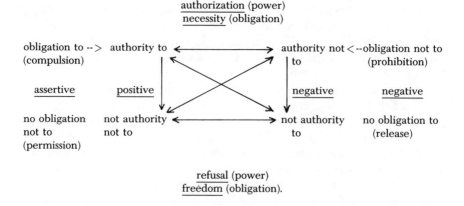

The authority to does, however, imply no obligation not to, and so also the authority not to implies having no obligation to. Since obligation includes authority, and obligation not to includes authority not to, all the relationships on the square of authority also apply in the case of either of the contraries of the square of obligation. Note that none of this applies in the case of the sub-contraries of the square of obligation.

We can now clarify the situation with the woman not giving Jesus drinking water by analyzing it in terms of the phase of preparation. When Jesus asks her for a drink of water, he, in effect, authorizes her, i.e., allows her to do so. She contradicts his authorization, not because of an unwillingness, but because of the obligation laid upon her by the social convention of non-association between Jews and Samaritans. Jesus' authorization, which appeals to her willingness to engage in the proposed action, is contradicted by the more powerful social obligation not to engage in it. She does not feel free to accept his invitation to engage in the action, notwithstanding his authorization, because her will is bound by social convention.

In the discussion above all four aspects of preparedness have been taken in the sense of the active subject, for example, the willingness to engage in an action; all of these aspects do, however, also apply to the subject of the circumstance. So, for example, when Jesus asks the woman for a drink of water, he also expresses the willingness to be conjoined with the object, drinking water. Similarly, when he proposes to the woman to ask him to give her water of life, it implies suggesting to her a willingness to be the subject of the circumstance of being conjoined with water of life. All of this merits a full discussion of the four aspects of preparation in terms of expressions of circumstance (or being), and of their interrelationships, but enough has been said now about those matters for the time being.

We return now to our text. In our analysis of the first subsequence of Jesus and the woman a very intricate relationship with the second subsequence became clear. In the first subsequence the woman revealed three needs: that represented by her anti-program of non-association between Jew and Samaritan, her misunderstanding of Jesus' program of providing water of life, and her failure to recognize who Jesus was. In the second subsequence we find two of these explicitly addressed. The woman recognizes that Jesus does have an ability at least comparable with that of Jacob. She says, "I see that you are a prophet" (v 19), and at the end of the entire sequence wonders, "Maybe he is the messiah" (v 29). Both of these, according to the text, occur as a result of Jesus having demonstrated miraculous knowledge to her — although the question of Messiah first comes up in connection with the issue of the conflicting positions on the right place of worship for Jews and Samaritans. The issue of the opposition between Jew and Samaritan occupies the second part of the second subsequence (20-21, 23-25) in the form of the question of the right place to worship. The question may be considered to be another way of raising the issue of the association between Jew and Samaritan. The only need which Jesus does not appear to address in the second subsequence is the woman's misunderstanding of his program of providing water of life, but one may ask whether it is not involved in one or the other of the two already mentioned, or both of them. The offer of water of life was made in reaction to the woman's proposal that Jews and Samaritans do not associate, and her failure to appreciate who Jesus was is intricately involved in his offer and clarification of the water of life. A final answer to the question of these interrelationships will have to wait for the analysis of the semantic component of the narrative, since it has to do with the question of what giving the water of life means. Does it, for example, mean to resolve the conflict between Jew and Samaritan which comes to expression both in the woman's proposal that Jews and Samaritans do not associate, and in the counterclaims concerning the right place of worship?

The close relationship between the two subsequences may raise the question whether it is still appropriate to consider them as such, i.e., as subsequences. We might instead ask if they do not simply belong to one single sequence of Jesus and the woman. The following considerations, however, suggest that they are distinguishable subsequences, because the second places the development on a different level.

1. We have already noted their parallelism in structure. Jesus requests something of the woman which she does not perform, and a change of topic follows. This pattern occurs in both subsequences.

2. In every respect the section which we have identified as the first subsequence ends in failure; it does not carry the story forward. Instead it appears to be preparatory in the sense that it poses the issues that are addressed in the second subsequence, which in turn prepares for the final sequence with the Samaritan villagers.

ii. *The Second subsequence with the woman* (vv 16-21, 23-26, 28-29)

The syntactic structure of the second subsequence can be formalized in the following three parts.

Second subsequence, first part (vv 16 -19)

A (need)	B (preparedness)	C (performance)	D (sanction)
(12)	16-17a	17b-18	(19)

The fact that Jesus knows everything about the woman's so-called husbands should leave no doubt that his request that she fetch her husband (v 16) was not intended as a proposed program of action. In this subsequence it functions as preparation for Jesus' own program, proving to the woman that he knows all about her so-called husbands (vv 17b-18). Her reaction to his performance, the recognition (sanction) that Jesus is a prophet (v 19) because of his miraculous knowledge, makes it clear that the need which Jesus' action satisfied was her ignorance about his ability, expressed in her disbelief that he could claim to be "greater than our father Jacob" (v 12). When the woman said that she had no husband (v 17a), Jesus took that as an opportunity in the sense of her authorizing him to reveal that he knows everything about her husbands. The woman had become ready to listen to him. There is a sense in which Jesus tricked the woman with his request that she fetch her husband into giving him the authority to proceed (preparation) with his act of revelation (performance) which she does when she asks him about the right place to worship.

The first part of this subsequence moves directly into the second.

Second subsequence, second part (vv 20-21, 23-25)

A (need)	B (preparedness)	C (performance)	D (sanction)
(20)	(19-20)	21-24	(25)

The woman's sanction of Jesus' action by attributing to him the ability of a prophet (v 19) functions in this new part as the recognition of a know-how which qualifies him (preparation) to discuss religious matters. As a result, she empowers Jesus to discuss the contrary positions of Jews and Samaritans concerning the right place to worship (v 20). It is clearly part of a larger issue which recalls her earlier reminder that a Jewish man does not speak to a Samaritan woman (v 9). Actually she does more than allow Jesus the authority to speak on the subject; she assumes the role of the assigner ("destinateur"), assigning the task to Jesus who accepts the role of assignee ("destinataire").[4] With that a significant point has been reached in the development of the narrative; the woman who had previously appealed to the convention that Jews and Samaritans do not associate, herself now puts the issue forward for discussion.

Her new formulation of the issue functions at the same time as the expression of a need, and she authorizes Jesus (preparedness) to engage in a program of instruction (performance) as the means of eliminating that need, i.e., unclarity about who is right, Samaritan or Jew. In his reply Jesus moves beyond the question of who is right, maintaining that the truth lies beyond both positions (vv 21-24). The woman's response that it is Messiah who will clarify the issue (v 25) is effectively a negative sanction of Jesus' performance. The text does not give an indication why she remained unpersuaded, but her subsequent presumption that he may be the messiah, not because he announced "all these things" to her, but because he told her "everything" she did (v 29), reveals that with regard to Jesus' identity she had in reality not yet moved beyond the position she had reached after what he had told her about her husbands (vv 17b-18). Is she as incapable of understanding him now as she had been when he was speaking of water of life? Is this because she cannot move beyond the alternatives of "this mountain" or Jerusalem? Ironi-

---

[4] Unfortunately, there is no term in normal English usage for the person who gives the assignment or does something equivalent, but many for the one who receives the assignment; even a commissioner is a person who receives, not one who gives, a commission. The term "sender" is a satisfactory translation of the French "destinateur," but it is not really descriptive of the role. Under the circumstances I propose "assigner" and "assignee," terms that are limited in current usage to the legal profession, but used here in this extended meaning.

cally she is of course correct: What she expected of Messiah was precisely what Jesus=Messiah had just done.

The final part of this subsequence can be formalized as follows:

Second subsequence, third part (vv 26, 28-29)

A (need)	B (preparedness)	C (performance)	D (sanction)
(25)		26(17b-18)	28-29

The need in this part is clearly the negative sanction of Jesus' previous performance (vv 21-24) by the woman (v 25). Jesus immediately moves to another performance to remove this lack of understanding (v 26), to which the woman responds with an extremely ambiguous sanction (vv 28-29). She recognizes that Jesus may indeed be the messiah. She does so as a sanction, not of the performance on the basis of which Jesus made the claim, i.e., resolving the issue between Jews and Samaritans concerning the right place to worship (vv 21-24), but of his earlier performance in which he disclosed miraculous knowledge about her (vv 17b-18, cf. v 29).

What the woman *does not sanction* here may be the most important, namely, what lies between her mandating Jesus to discuss the issue of the right place to worship (v 20) and her withdrawal of the mandate by implying that only Messiah is able to accept it (v 25). In her recognition that Jesus may be the messiah (v 29), she, so to speak, gives a sanction on both sides of Jesus' performance with regard to this central issue. Her sanction thus creates a great tension in the text, a kind of vacuum, a need which is ready to draw in its own resolution. The performance which could fill this need would have to be of a kind which could fill the vacuum created by the tension between practically all the woman's responses, but most specifically between, at the one side of what creates the vacuum, her recognition that Jesus is a prophet whom she mandates to discuss the issue which separates Jews and Samaritans (vv 19-20), and at the other side, her withdrawal of this mandate because it could only be accepted by Messiah (v 25). Thus, in effect, she screens off his resolution of that issue (vv 21-24) from her subsequent recognition that he may be the messiah (v 29). Abandoning her jar as she hurriedly leaves for the village (v 28) would seem to signify a certain bewilderment, conforming with the confused, but searching, quality of her reaction to the encounter with Jesus. As we will see, however, it has another, very different, meaning.

The pressure creating the vacuum between the woman's

mandating Jesus to discuss the issue of the right place of worship (v 20) and her refusal to allow him that mandate as Messiah (v 25) pushes back to the earlier issue, the social convention of non-association between Jew and Samaritan which obliged the woman not to respond to Jesus' request for a drink of water. It reinforces the pressure produced by the immediate issue seeking a resolution, namely, that of the right place of worship which reaffirms the separation between Jew and Samaritan. All of this reveals once more the very tight syntactic structure of the narrative notwithstanding the appearance of great looseness, i.e., of a series of loosely connected, almost unrelated, sequences.

The need or lack to which Jesus' performance in the final sequence (vv 30, 39-42) responds thus appears very complex. It is, as already stated, like a vacuum which wants to draw in its own solution. The vacuum is created by the woman's coming right up to the recognition that Jesus is the one who can resolve what has become manifest as the central issue, the separation of Jews and Samaritans, but then letting go of it, taking it up again on the other side by denying Jesus that competence, yet recognizing him as possibly the messiah because he had told her everything she had done. The lack or need is of a double nature. What needs to be addressed primarily is the separation of Jews and Samaritans as it comes to expression in verses 9 and 20, the non-association of a Jewish man and a Samaritan woman and the contradictory views of Jews and Samaritans on the right place to worship. Resolution of that issue by Jesus would at the same time resolve the issue of his preparedness, i.e., by resolving the issue convincingly (calling forth a positive sanction) he would also settle the question of his identity. That is the second, related, lack which needs to be satisfied, namely, that Jesus' identity concerns basically the issue of the relationship of Jews and Samaritans and not miraculous knowledge about the woman.

There is a sense in which everything up to this point concerned primarily the phases "need" and "preparedness." This observation explains also the introduction at this stage of the discussion with the disciples, now that the story is about to enter fully into the phase of "performance." That discussion functions to clarify what is about to happen. We will return to it later.

The second subsequence of Jesus and the woman, like the first, can be summarized analytically in terms of the three narrative schemas outlined above.

1.   The need which the first part of this sequence satisfies is the woman's lack of understanding who Jesus is, at least in terms of his ability compared with Jacob (v 12). His request that she

fetch her husband cannot be understood as the actual authorization of a program of action, but as a manipulation by means of
which he, in effect, receives from her for the first time authorization (preparedness) (vv 16-17a) to proceed with the performance of a program of action in which he proves to her his
miraculous knowledge about her affairs (vv 17b-18). She sanctions his performance by attributing to him the ability of a
prophet (v 19). Recognition of ability (preparedness) after a performance is a form of sanctioning the performance. What is
most important is that the need which the performance had to
satisfy has been met, the first step towards success in the
narrative.

2.   When the woman then brings up the topic of the right
place to worship she seems to be assigning it to Jesus, i.e., she
authorizes (preparedness) him to satisfy the need for a resolution of the issue involved (v 20), prompted by her prior recognition of his ability as a prophet (preparedness) (v 19). Jesus in any
case proceeds to the performance of the presumed assignment
by pointing out that true worship of the Father is in spirit and
truth (vv 21-24). That the topic did indeed express a need is confirmed by the woman when she remarks that it is Messiah who
will announce everything (v 25). The remark is however at the
same time a negative sanction of Jesus' performance, suggesting
that he does not (after all?) have the ability (preparedness) to
carry it out successfully.

3.   The woman's remark about Messiah, insofar as it denies
Jesus the ability to carry out the performance resolving the issue
of the right place to worship, gives expression to a continued
need (v 25); she still does not recognize who Jesus really is. Once
more without a preparedness phase Jesus moves to the performance which is to satisfy this need; he claims to be Messiah (v 26).
The woman's reaction is ambiguous; she does not sanction his
performance negatively, but neither does she positively. Instead
she sanctions the performance in which he proved to her his
miraculous knowledge about her, but in terms which apply to
Jesus' two immediately previous performances, speculating that
he may be the messiah (vv 28-29).

Up to this point, thus, the woman sanctioned positively only
one performance of Jesus, the proof that he had miraculous
knowledge about her, and thus also only one need has been satisfied, the woman's lack of understanding with regard to who
Jesus was, and that only to the degree that Jesus is now comparable with Jacob. In the sense of Jesus' true identity that need
also remains unsatisfied. Not a single one of the five needs that

have come to expression in the narrative so far has been fully satisfied: Jesus' thirst for a drink of water, the woman's thirst for water of life, her lack of understanding the nature of water of life, and of who Jesus is (even though some progress has been made), and the issue of Jew and Samaritan in terms of both the association between them and of the right place to worship. Jesus did engage in actions to satisfy a number of these needs, but, to the degree that none of them were sanctioned positively, they remain unsatisfied.

A connection is established between the sequence with the woman and the next two sequences with the disciples and with the Samaritan villagers by the fact that the needs that have come to expression in the sequence with the woman are taken up again in these last two sequences. The first three needs concerning water are taken up in the sequence with the disciples, not directly, but in terms of food, the equivalent of water. The issues of Jews and Samaritans and of the identity of Jesus are taken up in the sequence with the Samaritan villagers. In that regard the sequence with the woman functions as a preparation for the final two sequences by bringing to expression a complex of needs that are to be resolved in them.

b. *The Final Sequence with the Samaritans* (vv 30, 39-42)

The sequence of Jesus and the Samaritans can be formalized as follows:

Final sequence (vv 30, 39-42)

A (need) (9, 20)	B (preparedness)	C (performance)	D (sanction)
	30, 40ab	40c	41-42
(11-12, 19, 25, 29, 39)			

It is not difficult to recognize that, when the Samaritans seek Jesus (v 30) and ask him to stay with them (v 40ab), they are authorizing him to proceed with the resolution of both issues: that of the Samaritans and the Jews (vv 9, 20) and of his identity (vv 11-12, 19, 25, 29, 39). These issues have reached a peak in the woman's recognition that Jesus may be the messiah, even if in the clearly mistaken sense of a miracle worker. Jesus stays with them for two days (v 40c). Not much of a performance, one might say, except for everything that happened before that to heighten the meaning of the event. In reality, however, in the Gospel of John, to stay with Jesus is lexically the equivalent of the synoptics' eating bread in the kingdom of God (cf. Lk 13:29; 14:15). In Jesus' eschatological speech in chapter 14, the culmination of all the events is expressed in his statement to the disciples, "in order that where I am, you will also be" (14:3). In the beginning of the Gospel an incident similar to that of the Samaritans is described with great simplicity: when Andrew and the other disciple, having heard John the Baptist announce that Jesus was the lamb of God who takes away the sins of the world (1:36, cf. v 29) follow Jesus, they ask him, " 'Rabbi, where do you stay?' He says to them, 'Come and see!' They came then and saw where he stayed, and they stayed with him that day" (1:38).

When Jesus stays with the Samaritans on their invitation, he goes to them — the reversal heightens the significance — to bring about what he announced to the two disciples as the culmination of his activity, that they should be where he is. There can be almost no question that the only appropriate sanction for them was that he was "truly the savior of the world" (v 42). With that, at the same time, they more than sanctioned his resolution of the issue which divided Jews and Samaritans; he a Jew — the savior of the world, but nevertheless a Jew — "stays" with them two days.

This calls for a comment on verse 22 which causes difficulty in its present context, but may fit as a later affirmation which misunderstands the story as an affirmation of the correctness of the Christian position over and against Jews as well as Samaritans. In the present context, however, especially of Jesus' resolution of the opposed views of Jews and Samaritans concerning the right place of worship, the assertion that "you worship what you do not know, but we worship what we know, for salvation is from the Jews" stands out disruptively. It reaffirms the very conflict which Jesus resolved by rejecting the religious alternatives of either on this mountain or in Jerusalem in favor of true worship of the Father in spirit and truth (vv 21, 23-24), by affirming the correctness of what has the appearance of the Jewish position, but is in reality Christian. This insistence on being right is understandable as a partisan religious point of view which looks back at the conclusion of the story as a demonstration of the correctness of the Christian point of view. It is as the Christian savior that Jesus, who is indeed a Jew, is recognized by the Samaritans as the savior of the world (v 42). It is incongruous with the immediate context in which it is placed, and is almost certainly a later, unfitting, addition to the story.

In the discussion of the final sequence with the Samaritans it became unavoidable to touch on issues of meaning at a number of points which really belong in the analysis of the semantic component of the text. We will take these issues up again systematically when we come to that part of the analysis. That such issues arise here in the analysis of the surface syntax merely goes to show to what degree all aspects of the narrative gravitate towards each other in the conclusion of the story, creating a great density.

c. *The Sequence with the Disciples* (vv 8, 27, 31-38)

The sequence with the disciples has two clearly distinguishable parts, one in which the disciples play the role of acting subject wanting to give Jesus food to relieve his hunger (vv 8, 27, 31-34), and the other in which Jesus clarifies the anti-program which he proposed in verse 34. Jesus' anti-program is a program which opposes the disciples' program, and in which Jesus himself plays the active role, i.e., of reaper of the harvest (vv 35-38). It is worth noting that the disciples' program parallels that originally proposed by Jesus to the woman when he asked her for a drink of water (v 7b), but which he abandoned when she opposed it with the remark that a Jewish man and a Samaritan woman do not associate (v 9). The lack which had been manifested in the woman's statement called for an entirely different program which relegated Jesus' initially proposed program to relative insignificance.

The same relationship is evident between the program in which the disciples were engaged and the anti-program which Jesus now proposes. This anti-program evidently concerns everything in which Jesus had been engaged from the point when the woman told him that it was contrary to established convention for a Jewish man to ask a Samaritan woman for a drink of water. The sequence with the disciples is a comment on Jesus' entire program, and in effect on the initially proposed program of a drink of water, explaining why it was abandoned. It does so by moving on two different levels, the level of an actual program (that of the disciples — vv 8, 27, 31-34) and the level of commentary on a program (that of Jesus — vv 35-38). On the first level Jesus' initially proposed program to the woman is repeated in a parallel performance, whereas the second explains why it is abandoned in favor of an anti-program. The woman's response provided Jesus with other nourishment, doing the will of the one who sent him and completing his work (v 34). This nourishment made the drink of water irrelevant, and equally so the disciples' food. The completion of the work evidently refers to what Jesus was at the point of doing, i.e., going to the Samaritan village and staying with the villagers for two days.

The first part of the sequence with the disciples can be formalized as follows:

Disciples' sequence, first part (vv 8, 27, 31-34)

A (need)	B (preparedness)	C (performance)	D (sanction)
(7)	8, 31, 33		27 (32, 34)
	32	34	

The need which the disciples' program was intended to satisfy is related to that which made Jesus, in the beginning of the narrative, ask the woman for a drink of water (v 7). The related needs of a drink and of food thus tie together the program Jesus initially proposed to the woman and the disciples' program. Both are subprograms, intended to provide Jesus with the means to quench his thirst and to satisfy his hunger, i.e., giving him the ability to do so (preparedness). That the disciples went to the village (v 8a — preparedness) to buy food (v 8 — performance) is formulated in a way which presupposes that they also had a mandate, i. e., had been authorized to do so (preparedness). Actually, going to the village (v 8a) is a subprogram, preparing the disciples (phase B) to engage in the main program, to buy food (v 8b). The mandate belongs to phase B of the subprogram. In both cases one may be able to assume that Jesus was the assigner, the woman and the disciples the assignees. It is inappropriate to introduce psychological speculation here concerning what Jesus may have intended. According to the text one has to conclude that Jesus himself had been persuaded by circumstances to change over to an anti-program, in the case of the woman by a complete reversal — "If you knew. . ., *you* would have asked *him*, and *he* would have given *you* water" (v 10) — and, in the case of the disciples, by an anti-program which bypasses the means provided by their subprogram to enable Jesus to engage in his program of satisfying his hunger.

The situation which the disciples encounter when they return (v 27) already forebodes a negative sanction of their program; they remain out of the picture while Jesus is still engaged in conversation with the woman. When they try to bring their subprogram to a conclusion by giving Jesus the means to satisfy his hunger, they encounter his anti-program, a program that is opposed to theirs; he has other food to eat (v 32), i.e., he already has the means to satisfy his hunger. They interpret this as a program parallel to theirs, i.e., as a complementary program; someone else brought him food (v 33). Jesus then sanctions their program negatively by informing them of his anti-program which obviates theirs; his food is to do the will of the one who sent him and to bring that work to completion (v 34). What he is talking about is obviously not merely the means, but the performance itself of satisfying his hunger.

In the second part of the sequence Jesus then elaborates further on that anti-program. What is important to note here is the difference in the relationship, on the one hand, between the disciples' program and this elaboration of the anti-program, and, on the other, Jesus' initially proposed program to the woman and the anti-program of water of life which he then proposed to her. The need in the case of the program of water of life was expressed in the woman's statement that a Jewish man does not ask a Samaritan woman for a drink of water. In Jesus' elaboration of his anti-program in the sequence with the disciples, the need is formulated entirely differently. It is not immediately the issue of the separation of Jews and Samaritans, as one might expect. If it were, it would be parallel also in that respect to Jesus' first proposed anti-program in the sequence with the woman. In the elaboration of his anti-program in the discussion with the disciples it is the need that the work which has begun be brought to a conclusion: "The fields are white for the harvest" (v 35). This agrees with our conclusion concerning the sequence with the Samaritans. The need which had been created by the woman's responses up to this point created a vacuum which was ready to draw in its own solution.

But there is another equally important feature to note. The anti-program which Jesus proposes to the disciples stands over and against the program of physical nourishment, not as a reaction to the negative sanction of the latter program, but as a substitution for its need, physical hunger, of the need for nonphysical nourishment. The anti-program here thus stands over and against the program of physical nourishment, not only at the one point of the sanction, but also in every phase of the narrative schema. In that regard the discussion with the disciples not only explains what is about to happen, confirming our analysis of the sequence with the Samaritans, but also why Jesus had given up the program of physical nourishment, which includes by implication also the request for a drink of water. The woman's response, because it revealed a nonphysical thirst, demanded a program that ran counter to that of physical thirst, not only with regard to its performance, but in every respect, because it had to satisfy a counter-need.

The last two negative sanctions of the disciples' program, in verses 32 and 34, represent the immediate need which his anti-

program has to satisfy. This second part of the sequence with
the disciples can be formalized as follows:

Disciples' sequence, second part (vv 35-38)

A (need)	B (preparedness)	C (performance)	D (sanction)
(32, 34), 35	(32, 34),(35b?)		36
			34
	38a		
(38b)		(38b) 38c	

The need expressed in the negative sanction of the disciples'
program (vv 32, 34) also functions as a qualification of Jesus; it is
his obligation to eat this food.

There is a double ambiguity in this part of the narrative. According to verse 38 the disciples are to be the reapers. Jesus sent
them to harvest where they did not sow (v 38a — preparation);
others worked (38b — performance of a previous program creating the need which the disciples' reaping was to satisfy) and
they, the disciples, are to enter into the work of those others
(38c — performance). The ambiguity which this verse creates
lies in its interpretation of verse 35b, "Look up and see the
fields; they are white for the harvest," as preparation of the disciples to be the active subject in the coming harvest. In the final
sequence of the narrative (verses 39-42), however, Jesus alone is
the active subject. This final sequence takes verse 35b as part of
the description of a need. The fields are ready to be reaped and
Jesus as qualified active subject brings in the harvest. Verse 38
has to be taken as referring to another program in which the
disciples were to have been involved as reapers of fields that
were prepared for harvesting by others. That verse evidently
does not fit in the present narrative syntax.

The situation with the saying (proverb?) of verse 37 is equally
ambiguous. It could be a mere comment on verse 36, but
equally well a transition preparing for verse 38. The fact that it
is parenthetic leaves it very loosely structured, making it difficult to determine its function syntactically. As a comment, it is
not of decisive importance to know to what it refers. The same is
not true of verse 38. This verse clearly lies beyond the context of
the present story, apparently referring to a later Samaritan mission. As such it may be a later addition to the story by the same
hand which introduced the statement affirming the correctness
of the Jewish position in verse 22, with which it could also be in
conformity.

In the rest of the sequence there is no actual performance.
Verse 35 is the description of the need, whereas verse 36 is the

sanction of the performance in anticipation of its completion. An important question for the interpretation of this text has always been who fills the role of the sower. Our analysis of the sequence with Jesus and the Samaritans has shown that the harvest is the Samaritans' coming to the recognition that Jesus is the savior of the world. That leaves little doubt that the sower must be the woman. It is she, notwithstanding herself, who has made the issue of the separation between Jew and Samaritan ripe for the harvest, first by raising the question with Jesus, and then by motivating the Samaritans to go out to meet Jesus. Thus, even though, in their sanction, the villagers say they no longer need her talk because they themselves have seen and know that Jesus is truly the savior of the world (v 42), Jesus in his sanction here in verses 36-37 suggests in advance that the Samaritan woman rejoices with him in the achievement of his program, because she is the sower who prepared the harvest which he is about to reap.

Although we analyzed the final sequence with the Samaritan villagers before the sequence with the disciples it appears useful to discuss the two together here, with the disciples' sequence coming before that with the villagers. As we indicated above, all five of the needs that came to expression but remained unsatisfied in the two sequences with the woman are met in these two sequences. In the disciples' sequence the three needs in connection with water are satisfied before the two principal needs can be addressed: the issue of the Jews and Samaritans and, in a final way, the question concerning the identity of Jesus. The sequence with the disciples, thus, at the level of the text, appears as a superimposed story line compared with the main story line of Jesus and the Samaritans (the woman and through her the villagers) but, at the level of the narrative schemas, it appears very much part of the narrative as an integral whole. What distinguishes the disciples' sequence is merely the change of characters, the actors who play the role of discussion partners with Jesus, a feature of the discourse syntax which lies close to the surface of the text. The role which the disciples play is very much the same as that of the woman in the first part of the story.

A feature of the disciples' sequence that still stands out, however, is Jesus' comment about the harvest which is ready and the sower who rejoices with the reaper in the fruit of the harvest (vv 35-36). As a comment on the main story line it cannot be integral to it. It is also free from a necessary involvement with any of the actors in the actual story; it could have been formulated as a parenthesis by the author. In the mouth of Jesus it sheds light on the character of this actor, which in turn affects its meaning. However, Jesus does not make the comment as a participant in the story. In making the comment he fills the role of someone who stands effectively beyond the events, commenting on them. And as far as the disciples are concerned, the readers are as much addressed in the comment as they are. In that regard they fill the role more of spectators than of participants in the story; the comment is as little integral to the rest of the disciples' sequence as it is to the narrative as a whole.

The two final sequences can be summarized as follows:

1.   The first part of the disciples' sequence consists of the disciples' program and Jesus' anti-program which sanctions the former negatively. The need which the disciples' program has to satisfy is related to the program which Jesus initially proposed to the woman, i.e., to give him a drink of water; both concern physical hunger and thirst. The disciples' offering Jesus food, or thinking that someone else brought him some, is a subprogram enabling Jesus to satisfy his hunger (preparedness). Jesus' refusal, two times, has the form of an anti-program which sanctions negatively the program for which the disciples wanted to prepare Jesus.

In Jesus' anti-program he maintains that he has other means (preparedness) of satisfying his hunger (need), which is to do the will of the one who sent him and to complete that task (performance). This performance satisfies hunger in a double sense; hunger to do the will of the one who sent him, which also satisfies the hunger for which the disciples' program was intended as a preparation. As such, Jesus' anti-program is a parallel to the program for the satisfaction of the double need, physical thirst and thirst for the water of life.

2.   In the comment about the harvest, the need is the readiness of the fields to be harvested, followed almost immediately by the sanction that the harvest is already being gathered to the joy of sower and reaper alike, without the performance being stated explicitly. The proverb in verse 37 reinforces this sanction.

The exhortation of the disciples to raise their eyes to see that the fields are ready for the harvest is ambiguous; since they are not involved in the reaping of the harvest, it cannot be considered as preparing them for the performance of reaping, but as a reinforcement of the statement of need. In the sense of verse 38, however, according to which the disciples are sent out to reap the harvest, it should be considered as part of their preparation, along with the specific statement to that effect in which

Jesus assigns them to that task. The second part of verse 38 formulates the performance to which the disciples are assigned.

3. In Jesus' proposed anti-program he satisfies both his physical hunger and his hunger to do the will of the one who sent him, as parallels to his physical thirst and thirst for the water of life (see 1. above). In his clarification of this anti-program, i.e., in the disciples' sequence as a whole, he is also engaged in a program (a performance) of satisfying the need for an understanding of the food about which he speaks, which is parallel to the woman's need for an understanding of the water of life. That performance is not sanctioned in the disciples' sequence, but it is sanctioned in the final sequence when the villagers recognize him as the savior of the world.

4. In the final sequence it is the Samaritan villagers who act as the assigner who assigns Jesus the program of staying with them (preparedness), which he does for two days (performance). This is sanctioned by them with the recognition that he is the savior of the world. Their sanction makes clear that his performance satisfied three needs. First, the question of his identity, which was at issue from very early on in the narrative, is resolved. Secondly, they sanction his resolution of the issue of Jews and Samaritans when they recognize him, a Jew, staying with them, Samaritans, as the savior of the world. With that, they also sanction his doing the will of the one who sent him and completing that work, which is the satisfaction of his hunger. Thirdly, in that way the Samaritans also sanction the satisfaction of his related need, thirst, which made him originally ask the woman for a drink of water. The water of life which Jesus offered the woman is water with which he himself also quenches his thirst. The unity of savior and saved comes to expression in Jesus' statement that "whosoever drinks of this water will not thirst again" (v 13).

Conclusion

Our analysis so far has shown a series of narrative schemas in terms of which the sequences and subsequences of John 4 could be analysed, and also some connections between the schemas, most typically in the sense that one narrative schema produces or brings to expression a need for which another provides the program of action to satisfy the need. It now becomes necessary to try to uncover the logic which underlies these narrative schemas, and also their interrelationships. We have already taken note of the logic which underlies willingness, obligation, and ability to carry out a program, as aspects of the phase of preparation. We now need to give further and more systematic attention to the entire logical schema which underlies the surface narrative structure.

2.   *The Syntactic Deep Structure*

In the analysis of the surface narrative syntax of John 4 we were able to establish the remarkable structural integrity of the text by determining how certain parts of it can be analyzed in terms of interrelated phases of different narrative schemas. The coherence of a text, the integrity of its meaning, is determined at an even deeper, more abstract, syntactic level by its logical coherence, to such a degree that a text that does not show cohesion at its concrete, surface level may still make perfectly good sense. In this section I would like to investigate the logical structure of our text by analyzing it at the most abstract level in terms of the traditional logical square, showing all the circumstances and relationships that are logically *possible*. At a slightly more concrete level, I will also analyze the text in terms of the semiotic square, showing which of the logical possibilities are *actualized* in the text and, at an even more concrete level, how one relationship is transformed into its contrary; for example, how the circumstance of ignorance about the identity of Jesus in which a subject finds itself is transformed into its contrary, understanding, by a qualified acting subject which may be another, but may also be identical with the subject of the circumstance itself. Such an analysis will reveal, for example, that when Jesus asks the woman for a drink of water, he merely asks her, as an acting subject, to provide him with the means, the ability, to quench his thirst, i.e., transform his circumstance of thirst into its opposite. The woman can only function at the phase of preparedness in the program to satisfy Jesus' need to quench his thirst. Satisfying his need for a drink of water does not quench his thirst. Jesus himself is the only active subject who, adequately qualified, can perform the act which eliminates his need to quench his thirst, i.e., transform his circumstance of thirst into its opposite. It is an appropriately abbreviated form of speech to say that Jesus asked the woman for a *"drink* of water." In reality she can give him only the water; he himself has to take the drink, even if she were to have to assist him physically in the act.

This may appear to be a splitting of hairs. Whether that is indeed the case will depend on whether such a detailed analysis renders meaningful results. It should be borne in mind that such a determination can be made only after the detailed analysis has been made. If it does not render meaningful results one can abandon the analysis in the final version of one's work. As will become clear in this case, the detailed analysis of what is involved in Jesus' request for a drink of water provides decisively important insights into the meaning of the water of life and the parallel "other food" to which Jesus refers when the disciples cannot understand why he refuses the food they offer him (vv 33-34).

a. *The Quenching of Thirst* (vv 7, 9)

In our analysis of the first sequence with the woman, we noted that it was possible to analyse the various phases of the narrative schema in terms of narrative programs. The program of action which Jesus proposed to the woman was formalized in terms of the following narrative program:

$$NP = F_1[S_1 => (S_2 \leq O_1)]$$

in which NP refers to the narrative program, F_1 to the entire program of action, S_1 to the acting subject, in this case the woman, $=>$ to the action of the acting subject, S_2 to the subject of the circumstance, in this case Jesus, $\leq$ to the subject of circumstance being conjoined with an object, O_1, which is in this case the drink of water. The brackets indicate the extent of the expression of the action and the parentheses the expression of the circumstance. We also noted that this program of action presupposed a situation of need, i.e., Jesus in need of, or not having, a drink of water, which could be formalized as $(S_2 \geq O_1)$, in which $\geq$ refers to the circumstance of disjunction. We also noted that the program could be written more fully as

$$NP = F_1[S_1 => (S_2 \geq O_1) -> (S_2 \leq O_1)]$$

It is easy to recognize that logically the contradiction or negation of $(S_2 \leq O_1)$ is $(S_2 \geq O_1)$; the contradiction or negation of conjunction is disjunction, and vice versa. Thus it is possible to introduce these two circumstances and their interrelationship on a semiotic square,[5] leaving vacant for the time being those corners of the square not expressed, although implied, in the text.

[5] As I indicated in footnote 3 of section 1, "The Surface Narrative Syntax of John 4," above, my use of the semiotic square is slightly different from that of Greimas. In my usage the semiotic square agrees completely with the structure of the traditional logical square, the main difference compared with Greimas being with regard to the lines of implication, which run vertically upwards from the subcontraries to the contraries in Greimas' interpretation. The differences are reconcilable.

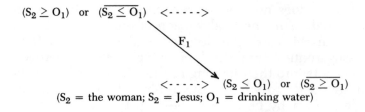

$(S_2 \geq O_1)$ or $(\overline{S_2 \leq O_1})$ $<\!-\!-\!-\!-\!->$

F_1

$<\!-\!-\!-\!-\!->$ $(S_2 \leq O_1)$ or $(\overline{S_2 \geq O_1})$

$(S_2$ = the woman; S_2 = Jesus; O_1 = drinking water)

$(\overline{S_2 \leq O_1})$ is the negation of $(S_2 \leq O_1)$, and $(\overline{S_2 \geq O_1})$ the negation of $(S_2 \geq O_1)$.

Jesus, however, does not merely ask the woman for a drink of water, but that she give him to drink, i.e., he is in need of having a drink of water to quench his thirst. His need is of a double nature: he not only lacks a drink of water $(S_2 \geq O_1)$, but is also thirsty $(S_2 \leq O_2)$, with O_2 representing the thirst which needs to be satisfied, i.e., quenched $(S_2 \leq \bar{O}_{2'})$. Thirst $(S_2 \leq O_2)$ implies the lack of quenching $(S_2 \geq \bar{O}_{2'})$, as does the lack of water $(S_2 \geq O_1)$.

The logic involved in each of these needs can be presented respectively on the following squares:

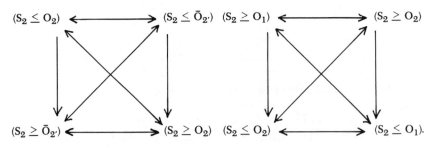

$(S_2 = $ Jesus; $O_1 = $ drinking water; $O_2 = $ thirst; $\bar{O}_{2'} = $ quenching)

This means that quenching $(S_2 \leq \bar{O}_{2'})$, which implies the elimination of thirst $(S_2 \geq O_2)$, also implies having a drink of water $(S_2 \leq O_1)$. Thus two logical squares can be combined into a single one which makes this clear.

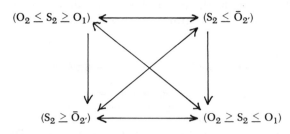

$(S_2 = $ Jesus; $O_1 = $ drinking water; $O_2 = $ thirst; $\bar{O}_{2'} = $ quenching)

In order to achieve this at the level of performance, however, two separate actions are required. To quench his thirst Jesus has to engage in the following action:

$$F_{1b}[S_2 => (S_2 \geq \bar{O}_{2'}) -> (S_2 \leq \bar{O}_{2'})],$$

which implies the elimination of or disjunction from his thirst ($S_2 \geq O_2$), which is what quenching thirst has as its effect; but it also implies having a drink of water ($S_2 \leq O_1$), which is not an effect of the quenching of thirst, but a presupposition for it. This becomes clear when one considers that he cannot transform the lack of quenching his thirst ($S_2 \geq \bar{O}_{2'}$) into the quenching of it ($S_2 \leq \bar{O}_{2'}$) as long as he does not have a drink of water ($S_2 \geq O_1$), which implies the lack of quenching his thirst ($S_2 \geq O_2$). Thus, before he can quench his thirst by his program of action, F_{1b}, he has to be relieved of not having a drink of water, by the transformation of ($S_2 \geq O_1$) into ($S_2 \leq O_1$), which is the program he proposed to the woman:

$$F_1[S_1 => (S_2 \geq O_1) -> (S_2 \leq O_1)],$$

"Give me (water) to drink" (v 7). It should be noted that the outcome of the woman's program of action, Jesus having a drink of water ($S_2 \leq O_1$), does not imply the quenching of his thirst ($S_2 \leq \bar{O}_{2'}$), but the inverse is true; if the quenching of his thirst is the case ($S_2 \leq \bar{O}_{2'}$), the implication is that he has drinking water ($S_2 \leq O_1$), as we have already established above.

The two performances can be presented on a square as follows:

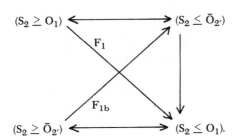

$$(S_2 = \text{Jesus}; O_1 = \text{drinking water}; \bar{O}_{2'} = \text{quenching})$$

The circumstance ($S_2 \leq \bar{O}_{2'}$) implies the existence of the circumstance ($S_2 \leq O_1$) as the outcome of F_1. Thus, F_{1b} cannot take place unless F_1 is also performed, but since ($S_2 \leq O_1$) does not imply the existence of ($S_2 \geq \bar{O}_{2'}$), F_1 can take place even if F_{1b} does not. This can be presented on a logical square as follows: Jesus quenching his thirst, F_{1b}, implies, under the circumstances, that the woman provided him with the water, F_1, but not the inverse.

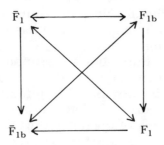

The analysis of John 4 at the deeper level of the underlying syntactic principles reveals that the action which Jesus requested of the woman is actually a subprogram intended to provide him with the ability to carry out his own program of action, the quenching of his thirst. At this level the program of action requested of the woman belongs to the preparedness phase of the narrative schema which has, as its performance phase, Jesus' action of quenching his thirst. The need which the woman's action was to have satisfied is not Jesus' thirst, but his lack of the means to quench it.

At the surface level of the actual text, however, the two programs have become abbreviated into a single one in which the focus is entirely on the program of action Jesus proposed to the woman as if it is the main program, with Jesus' thirst as the need which it is to satisfy. Jesus' drinking the water to quench his thirst never enters into the picture as a separate performance, except as a kind of "zero" program that has no particular significance at this stage of the narrative. Our analysis of this part of the text above in terms of a single narrative schema thus remains valid. It is nevertheless important to take note of it. In terms of the generative structure or trajectory of the text, it is a transformation or conversion, to use Greimas' term, from out of its deep structure, which can include features not actualized in the text.

Even though the quenching of Jesus' thirst does not come into focus as a feature of the actual text of John 4, it can nevertheless be recognized as important when we consider that the circumstance of the satisfaction of hunger is of great importance in the discussion with the disciples. In Jesus' explanation of the water of life, the quenching of thirst is of decisive importance: "Everyone who drinks of this water will not thirst again; whoever drinks of the water which I give her/him, will never again thirst" (vv 13-14a).

b. *Non-association of Jews and Samaritans* (v 9c)

We already discussed above at the level of the underlying principles how the social convention of non-association between Jew and Samaritan prevented the woman from engaging in the program which Jesus had proposed to her. The obligation not to engage in the program which the convention imposed on her implied that she neither had the will, nor did she accept Jesus' authorization, to do so. There is also a logic involved in Jesus' contravention of this social convention. It is our task now to try to discern all which that involves.

It should be noted that the parenthesis, "for Jews and Samaritans do not associate" (v 9c) — missing in some manuscripts — interprets the woman's statement in 9b as an instance of a rule that is broader than what may have been implied or intended. That it is a breach of convention for a Jewish man to ask a Samaritan woman for a drink of water does not have to mean that Jews and Samaritans in general did not associate; the convention could have prohibited only association between the sexes of the two groups. On the other hand, although the woman's statement emphasizes that she is a Samaritan *woman*, it may have been based on the more general rule, as stated in the parenthesis; the fact that she was a woman merely meant that Jesus was breaching the convention at a particularly sensitive point. In our analysis below we will assume the minimum application of the rule, that a Jewish man does not associate with a Samaritan woman, bearing in mind, however, that it probably did have broader application.

The reasoning applied by the convention is that, since Jewish men do not associate with Samaritan women, Jesus, being a Jewish man, is not supposed to associate with the Samaritan woman. However, by associating with the woman ($S_{3a} \leq O_{3a'}$), Jesus as a particular Jewish man not only violated the convention; he negated it ($\overline{S_3 \geq O_{3a}}$). The logic can be formalized as follows:

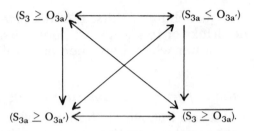

$$(S_3 = \text{Jewish men}; S_{3a} = \text{a particular Jewish man [Jesus]};$$
$$O_{3a} = \text{association with Samaritan women}; O_{3a'} = \text{a particular Samaritan woman})$$

The woman suggests to Jesus that the convention $(S_3 \geq O_{3a})$ applies to him as well $(S_{3a} \geq O_{3a'})$, in which $O_{3a'}$ represents association with a Samaritan woman.

Actually, Jesus had already dissociated himself from the rule by asking the woman for a drink of water, which meant associating with her $(S_{3a} \leq O_{3a'})$. In that way he negated the rule. If a single Jewish man associates with a Samaritan woman the convention is already broken, $(S_{3a} \leq O_{3a'})$ implies $(\overline{S_3 \geq O_{3a}})$. That is what makes his act so intolerable from the point of view of the convention.

From the above it becomes clear that Jesus had actually already engaged in a very important program of action. As a Jew, the rule $(S_3 \geq O_{3a})$ also applied to him $(S_{3a} \geq O_{3a})$, but by asking the woman for a drink of water, he transformed himself from that circumstance to its contradiction $(S_{3a} \leq O_{3a})$, which can be written as the following narrative program, substituting Jesus' own symbol, S_2, as subject for that of a particular Jew, S_{3a}:

$$F_2[S_2 => (S_2 \geq O_{3a'}) \rightarrow (S_2 \leq O_{3a'})].$$

On the semiotic square this has the following effect: by associating with the woman $(S_2 \leq O_{3a'})$ Jesus negated the convention of non-association between Jewish men and Samaritan women $(S_3 \geq O_{3a})$:

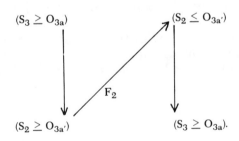

$$(S_2 = \text{Jesus}; S_3 = \text{Jewish men}; O_{3a} = \text{association with Samaritan women};$$
$$O_{3a'} = \text{association with a particular Samaritan woman})$$

Although Jesus broke the convention, the woman refuses to confirm his action; she reminds him of the convention. This is what sets the entire narrative on its main course of action. It is the woman's refusal to confirm Jesus' performance, not her refusal of his proposed program of action for her, which sets the narrative on its course. This agrees with the understanding of the incident provided by Jesus' discussion with the disciples concerning his refusal of the food they offered him (vv 31-34), as we concluded above.

c. *The Water of Life* (vv 10-15)

In his response to the woman's refusal Jesus now models a new program of action on the one he had previously proposed to her, switching the active subject and the subject of the circumstances around and changing the meaning of the object, water, from drinking water, O_1, to water of life, O_{1b}. So the initially proposed program,

$$F_1[S_1 => (S_2 \geq O_1) -> (S_2 \leq O_1)],$$

now becomes,

$$F_3[S_2 => (S_1 \geq O_{1b}) -> (S_1 \leq O_{1b})].$$

From our previous analysis of the underlying syntactic principles, we already know that this involves at least two programs, Jesus giving the woman the water, and the woman "drinking" it, based on the following two sets of logical relationships:

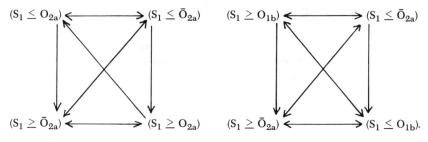

(S_1 = the woman; O_{1b} = the water of life; O_{2a} = thirst for the water of life;
$\bar{O}_{2a}$ = quenching thirst for the water of life)

If the woman were to quench her thirst with the water offered by Jesus it would be by the following program:

$$F_{3b}[S_1 => (S_1 \geq \bar{O}_{2a}) -> (S_1 \leq \bar{O}_{2a})].$$

We can now indicate on the following semiotic squares which of these possibilities are brought to expression, or presupposed by the text:

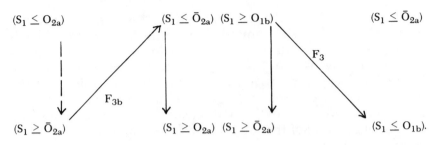

$(S_1 = $ the woman; $O_{1b} = $ the water of life; $O_{2a} = $ thirst for the water of life; $\bar{O}_{2a} = $ quenching thirst for the water of life)

Jesus' program, F_3, presupposes that the woman does not have water of life $(S_1 \geq O_{1b})$, which implies that her thirst for it is not quenched $(S_1 \geq \bar{O}_{2a})$, but not that she thirsts for it $(S_1 \geq O_{2a})$. If she were to drink the water, though, as Jesus expects according to verse 14,

$$F_{3b}[S_1 => (S_1 \geq \bar{O}_{2a}) -> (S_1 \leq \bar{O}_{2a})],$$

she would by implication be relinquishing such a thirst $(\overline{S_1 \leq \bar{O}_{2a}})$. It thus appears that even though his offer of the water of life does not *imply* thirst for it, Jesus *assumes* it to be the case, and therefore offers the water. The logic behind Jesus' offer thus commences, not with the recognition that the woman does not have water of life $(S_1 \geq O_{1b})$, but that she has a thirst for it $(S_1 \leq O_{2a})$ which implies the need for, the disjunction from, the quenching of it $(S_1 \geq \bar{O}_{2a})$. "If you knew the gift of God and who it is that says to you, 'Give me to drink,' you would ask him to give you water of life" (v 10). His statement indicates that he thinks she does thirst for the water of life, but equally, that she is probably not aware of it. That this is the case is confirmed by the conversation which follows in which Jesus speaks of never thirsting again (v 14), but the woman still thinks of drinking water (v 15).

The woman does not show the slightest inclination to engage in the program of action F_{3b}, drinking the water Jesus offers, but challenges him with the statement that he is certainly not greater than "our father Jacob" (vv 11-12), to which we will give our attention below. Jesus responds to the challenge by the introduction of yet another program which explains the incomparable nature of water of life: "Everyone who drinks of this water will thirst again; whoever drinks of the water I give will never thirst again, but the water I give will become to her/him a fountain springing up to eternal life" (vv 13b-14). The water of life is no mere object, O_{1b}, but is itself also the active subject, S_4, of a program of continuous provision of itself and of the quenching of thirst for it, which implies never thirsting again, as the semiotic square will show. The program of action of the water of life is of a double nature:

$$F_{3e}[S_4 => (O_{1b} \geq S_{1a} \geq \bar{O}_{2a}) -> (O_{1b} \leq S_{1a} \leq \bar{O}_{2a})]$$

in which S_{1a} is whoever drinks of the water offered by Jesus.

The program of action of the water of life effects a double transformation as the following semiotic square reveals:

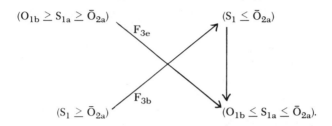

(S_{1a} = whoever drinks the water of life; O_{1b} = water of life;
$\bar{O}_{2a}$ = quenching of thirst for the water of life)

The program of the water of life, F_{3e}, duplicates Jesus' program of giving the water, $F_3[S_2 => (S_1 \geq O_{1b}) -> (S_1 \leq O_{1b})]$, as well as that of the one who drinks it, as the woman is expected to do, $F_{3b}[S_1 => (S_1 \geq \bar{O}_{2a}) -> (S_1 \leq \bar{O}_{2a})]$. The woman quenching her thirst, F_{3b}, implies the program of the water of life, F_{3e}.

The woman's challenge that Jesus is not greater than "our father Jacob" is based on the following reasoning. If one does not have the ability to perform an action, it implies that the circumstance which is the result of such an action cannot be produced. But, if one were to produce the intended circumstance, it would imply that one had the ability to do so, as the following logical square makes clear:

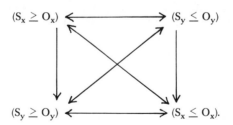

(S_x = subject of action, i.e., Jacob or Jesus; S_y = subject of circumstance;
O_x = ability to perform the action; O_y = the desired object of the circumstance)

It is worth noting that the subcontraries can both be true at the same time. A person can have the ability to perform an ac-

tion ($S_x \leq O_x$) and yet leave the action unperformed, i. e., leave
the subject of the circumstance disjoined from the object ($S_y \geq O_y$). The woman is such a person, who, although she has the ability to perform the action, i.e., she has the means of drawing
water ($S_1 \leq O_4$), does not provide Jesus with water ($\overline{S_2 \leq O_1}$).
When Jesus now offers the water of life, which she still under-
stands as drinking water, she points out that he does not have
the means, the ability, to do so in the sense in which she does:
"You do not have something with which to draw the water, and
the well is deep" (v 11). The only alternative she can think of is
the ability which Jacob had, but she does not believe that Jesus is
the equal of or, in an exaggerated sense, greater than Jacob (vv
11c-12a). The following semiotic square clarifies her reasoning.
Jesus does not have miraculous ability ($S_2 \geq O_{4a}$) such as Jacob,
which implies that he cannot effect the miraculous provision of
spring water ($S_y \leq O_{1'}$), but because Jacob did provide water ($S_y \leq O_{1'}$) it implies that he did have the ability ($S_5 \leq O_{4a}$):

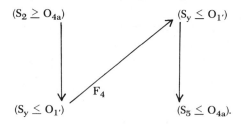

$$(S_2 \geq O_{4a}) \qquad\qquad (S_y \leq O_{1'})$$

$$F_4$$

$$(S_y \leq O_{1'}) \qquad\qquad (S_5 \leq O_{4a}).$$

(S_2 = the woman; S_5 = Jacob; S_y = subject of circumstance; O_{4a} = miraculous
ability; $O_{1'}$ = spring water)

In our text S_y is concretely Jacob, his sons and their livestock,
who benefit from the miraculous supply of water. By providing
the drinking water miraculously for himself, his sons and their
livestock by the following action,

$$F_4[S_5 => (S_y \geq O_{1'}) -> (S_y \leq O_{1'})],$$

Jacob proves by implication that he has the ability to do so
($S_5 \leq O_{4a}$). Jesus, who lacks the means such as the woman's, ($S_2 \geq O_4$), cannot provide water unless he is "greater than" Jacob,
something about which she is sceptical. Jesus, in her reasoning,
also does not have the miraculous ability of Jacob ($S_2 \geq O_{4a}$). It
should be noted that, at the level of logical principles, ($S_2 \geq O_{4a}$)
is not the contradiction of ($S_5 \leq O_{4a}$), because it is not the same
subject. But ($S \geq O_{4a}$) would be the contradiction of ($S \leq O_{4a}$). It is
in her reasoning that the woman has Jesus fill the position of S in

($S \geq O_{4b}$) and Jacob in the case of ($S \leq O_x$). Logically, in the case of Jacob, ($S_5 \leq O_{4a}$) and ($S_5 \geq O_{4a}$) are contradictions, which can be expressed by means of the following semiotic square:

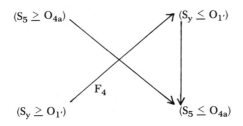

(S_5 = Jacob; S_y = the subject of circumstance; $O_{1'}$ = spring water; O_{4a} = miraculous ability)

The implication of Jacob's performance is that he has the ability to carry out the miraculous performance ($S_5 \leq O_{4a}$). What remains to be seen is whether Jesus can perform a similar act to contradict his not having such an ability ($\overline{S_2 \geq O_{4a}}$). As already indicated, the woman exaggerates her argument. Jesus does not have to be greater than Jacob, i.e., have greater ability than Jacob, to perform such an act; he merely needs to have an equal ability.

Jesus nevertheless accepts the woman's exaggerated challenge by claiming that the water which he offers is superior to that offered by Jacob. His reasoning is ambiguous to the degree that he makes two points at the same time: (i) in comparison with Jacob's water the water which he offers is continuously self-replenishing in the person who drinks it, thus providing uninterrupted quenching of thirst, and (ii) it is of a completely different kind than that of Jacob.

Jesus told the woman, "if you knew . . . who it is that said to you, 'give me to drink,' you would have asked him to give you water of life" (v 10), thus claiming the ability to provide this kind of water, which we will identify with the symbol, O_{4b}. When the woman then poses Jacob's miracle over and against his claim, he argues that his water is different, as a means of also arguing that his ability is different.

The basis of Jesus' reasoning is that water of life (O_{1b}) and Jacob's spring water ($O_{1'}$) are not only contraries, but the one implies negation of the other. The water of life which Jesus offers implies that it is not the spring water which Jacob provided.

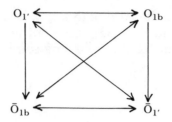

$(O_{1'} = $ spring water; $O_{1b} = $ water of life)

On that basis Jesus claims that the ability to provide the water of life which he has in mind is not the same as Jacob's miraculous ability:

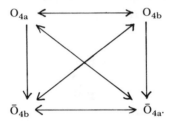

$(O_{4a} = $ Jacob's miraculous ability; $O_{4b} = $ ability to provide water of life)

Thus he could maintain that if Jacob's performance,
$$F_4[S_5 => (S_y \geq O_{1'}) -> (S_y \leq O_{1'})],$$
implies his miraculous power to provide spring water $(S_5 \leq O_{4a})$, as the woman's reasoning (clarified by the previous semiotic square) showed, then his (Jesus') performance,
$$F_3[S_2 => (S_1 \geq O_{1b}) -> (S_1 \leq O_{1b})],$$
implies that he has the power to provide water of life $(S_2 \leq O_{4b})$ by the following reasoning:

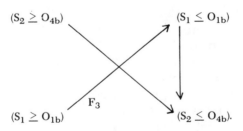

$(S_1 = $ the woman; $S_2 = $ Jesus; $O_{4b} = $ ability to provide water of life; $O_{1b} = $ water of life)

Providing the woman with the water of life $(S_1 \leq O_{1b})$ implies having the ability to do so $(S_2 \leq O_{4b})$. However, insofar as O_{1b} is contrary to $O_{1'}$, and O_{4b} contrary to O_{4a}, Jesus' ability to provide the water of life ($S_2 \leq O_{4b}$) cannot be compared with Jacob's miraculous ability to provide living water ($S_5 \leq O_{4a}$), but is contrary to it. With that Jesus moves the discussion beyond the issue of Jacob's miraculous provision of water.

This reasoning escapes the woman; she thinks Jesus merely claims to have a greater ability than Jacob's by providing spring water in an even more miraculous way, because she has not recognized that the water Jesus promises is not comparable with Jacob's. Her mistaking Jesus' water of life for another even greater version of Jacob's spring water implies also a mistaking the ability which Jesus claims for merely a stronger version of Jacob's ability. In this she reveals a double lack of understanding; lack of understanding of the nature of water of life, which we will identify with the symbol $O_{1b'}$, and lack of understanding of Jesus' ability to provide water of life, represented by $O_{4b'}$. Her lack of understanding would be represented by the following two formalized statements of circumstance: ($S_1 \geq O_{1b'}$) and ($S_1 \geq O_{4b'}$).

d. *The Right Place to Worship* (vv 16-26, 28-30)

Remarkably, Jesus now proceeds, not to dispel the woman's lack of understanding, but to provide her with proof that he has an ability of the same type as Jacob, by revealing to her his miraculous knowledge about her husbands in the following performance:

$$F_{4a}[S_2 => (S_1 \geq O_{4a'}) -> (S_1 \leq O_{4a'})],$$

in which $O_{4a'}$ represents Jesus' miraculous knowledge about the woman's husbands. The implication is that Jesus has a miraculous ability similar to that of Jacob. Revealing to the woman a miraculous knowledge about her husbands ($S_1 \leq O_{4a'}$) implies an ability equivalent to that of Jacob ($S_2 \leq O_{4a''}$), as the following square makes clear:

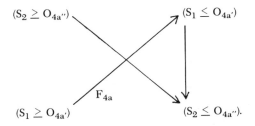

(S_1 = the woman; S_2 = Jesus; $O_{4a'}$ = miraculous knowledge of the woman's husbands; $O_{4a''}$ = duplication of Jacob's miracle)

The woman does not sanction Jesus' miraculous ability, but infers from his performance an ability of the type which Jesus had been claiming when he offered her the water of life. She formulates it as the ability of a prophet. By the following reasoning, the revelation of Jesus' miraculous knowledge $(S_1 \leq O_{4a'})$ implies in her understanding that he has the ability of a prophet $(S_2 \leq O_{5a})$:

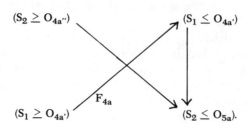

$$(S_2 \geq O_{4a''}) \qquad (S_1 \leq O_{4a'})$$

$$F_{4a}$$

$$(S_1 \geq O_{4a'}) \qquad (S_2 \leq O_{5a}).$$

$(S_1$ = the woman; S_2 = Jesus; $O_{4a'}$ = miraculous knowledge of the woman's husbands; $O_{4a''}$ = duplication of Jacob's miracle; O_{5a} = ability of a prophet)

The woman moved forward in her logic by taking $(S_2 \leq O_{5a})$ as the implication of $(S_1 \leq O_{4a'})$ and the contradiction of $(S_2 \geq O_{4a''})$. She then reinforces this inference by proposing a topic of discussion, the disagreement between Samaritans and Jews concerning the right place of worship. It is a topic which requires more than the ability to perform miracles. In the woman's understanding, the ability to perform the kind of miracle Jesus had just demonstrated qualified him as someone who had the ability of a prophet, indeed of Messiah as she herself suggests in verse 24, "Messiah, when he comes, will announce everything." This topic functions as a disengagement or shifting out of the course of the narrative into a different level of narrative, from the narrative in which she and Jesus are personally engaged to discussion of the more general topic concerning the right place to worship. In Jesus' reply he maintains this disengagement from the immediate narrative, except when he says "an hour comes *and now is*" (v 23). We will give specific attention to this when we discuss the discourse syntax below.

Jesus replies that true worshippers will worship the Father neither on "this mountain," nor in Jerusalem, but in spirit and truth (vv 21, 23). There are many features in his very complex statement which will need to be discussed when we come to the semantic component below. With regard to the syntactic component it is necessary to discuss only the program of action and the circumstances of the subjects that are involved. The action to which Jesus refers when he says that the true worshippers will worship neither on this mountain nor in Jerusalem, but the Father in spirit and truth, is the following:

$$F_{7a}[(S_6 => (O_8 \leq S_6 \geq O_{8a}) -> (O_8 \geq S_6 \leq O_{8a})]$$

in which S_6 represents worshippers, O_8 worshipping either on this mountain or in Jerusalem, and O_{8a} worshipping the Father in spirit and truth. There is a tautology in Jesus' statement, true worshippers worshipping in truth, which we can reformulate to eliminate the tautology as follows: "worshippers worship the Father in the spirit and in truth," meaning that true worship is to worship the Father in the spirit. Posing the worshipping of the Father in spirit and truth against either "on this mountain" or "in Jerusalem" involves the following logical structure:

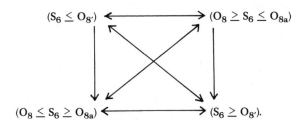

$(S_6 = $ worshippers; $O_{8'} = $ worship on this mountain or in Jerusalem;
$O_8 = $ the alternatives, either on this mountain or in Jerusalem;
$O_{8a} = $ worship of the Father in spirit and truth)

Note that accepting the alternatives of worshipping either on this mountain or in Jerusalem ($S_6 \leq O_8$) does not have to mean (does not imply) actually doing either ($S_6 \geq O_{8'}$); one can accept the alternatives but do neither: the subcontraries ($O_8 \leq S_6 \geq O_{8a}$) and ($S_6 \geq O_{8'}$) can both be the case. On the other hand, worshipping either on the mountain or in Jerusalem ($S_6 \leq O_{8'}$) does imply accepting them as alternatives ($S_6 \leq O_8$). Furthermore, negation of the alternatives ($\overline{S_6 \leq O_8}$), which is equivalent to ($S_6 \geq O_8$), implies worshipping neither on this mountain nor in Jerusalem ($S_6 \geq O_{8'}$).

But Jesus is not merely proposing a logic; he insists that this is now happening, "an hour comes *and now is*" (v 23), represented by the following semiotic square:

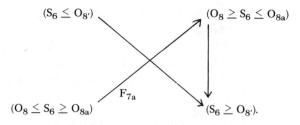

(S$_6$ = worshippers; O$_8$ = the alternatives, either on "this" mountain or in Jerusalem; O$_{8'}$ = worship on "this" mountain or in Jerusalem; O$_{8a}$ = worship of the Father in spirit and truth)

The significance of all of this is that what Jesus rejects is not one or the other of the alternatives. He does not engage in the controversy, but rejects the very fact of posing them as alternatives. Jesus does not pose a third alternative over and against the existing two, but true worship over and against all alternatives of the type, "either on this mountain or in Jerusalem."

With the woman's response, "I know that Messiah comes...; when he comes he will announce everything to us" (v 25), she shifts the conversation back into the narrative in which she herself is involved by telling Jesus that she would rather wait for Messiah's clarification:

$$F_8[S_7 => (S_y \geq O_{8b'}) -> (S_y \leq O_{8b'})],$$

in which S$_7$ represents Messiah, S$_y$ "us" to whom Messiah announces "everything," and O$_{8b'}$ the announcement of everything.

Jesus had actually given her the clarification which she expects of Messiah in the following performance:

$$F_7[S_2 => (S_1 \geq O_{8b}) -> (S_1 \leq O_{8b})],$$

in which O$_{8b}$ represents Jesus' clarification of the nature of true worship, but the woman does not accept this clarification. In appealing to Messiah as the one who would announce everything, the woman expresses her doubt about what Jesus had said concerning the right place to worship. Her doubt is based on the same logic as that by which she challenged his offer of the water of life. Having told him that he did not have the ability of Jacob to provide "living water," she now denies him the ability of Messiah to reveal the truth about worship. Her reasoning is based on the following logic:

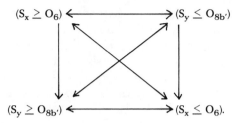

$(S_x = $ revealer; $S_y = $ recipient of revelation; $O_6 = $ ability to reveal; $O_{8b'} = $
revelation, i.e., the "announcement of everything")

Only if the subject of action has the ability to do so (O_6) can
there be a revelation $(O_{8b'})$: $(S_y \le O_{8b'})$ implies $(S_x \le O_6)$.
On the basis of this logic the woman reasons as follows:

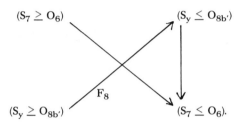

$(S_7 = $ Messiah; $S_y = $ recipient of revelation; $O_6 = $ ability to reveal; $O_{8b'} = $
revelation, i.e., the "announcement of everything")

Messiah, when he comes, will announce everything to the recipients of revelation $(S_y \le O_{8b'})$, which implies that he would have
the ability to do so $(S_7 \le O_6)$.

In her appeal to Messiah the woman denies Jesus the ability
to reveal truth to her because he is not Messiah, but this judgment is based on her not accepting what Jesus said about the
right place of worship as revelation. Her reasoning is as follows:

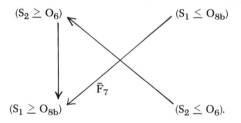

$(S_1 = $ the woman; $S_2 = $ Jesus; $O_6 = $ messianic ability to reveal truth;
$O_{8b} = $ revelation of truth about worship)

$\bar{F}_7$ represents the denial of Jesus' clarification of the nature of

true worship as revelation. She refuses to sanction his performance. Her denial of Jesus' ability to reveal truth ($S_2 \geq O_6$) implies
her denial of his performance, $\bar{F}_7$, as the revelation of truth
about worship. She ignores what Jesus said, because that is what
Messiah would reveal. In terms of the Evangelist's irony, of
course, she has spoken the truth, but not in the sense in which
she understood it: it is Messiah who would "announce everything," but that is precisely what Jesus had just done.

In response to the woman's statement, Jesus now makes explicit the ironic truth of what she said by claiming that he is
Messiah, $S_2 = S_7$, and so also that what he told her about true
worship is the announcement of "everything" which the woman
expects from Messiah, $O_{8b} = O_{8b'}$. His claim involves the following reasoning:

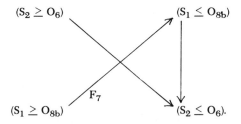

$$(S_2 \geq O_6)$$

$$(S_1 \leq O_{8b})$$

$$F_7$$

$$(S_1 \geq O_{8b})$$

$$(S_2 \leq O_6).$$

(S_1 = the woman; S_2 = Jesus; O_6 = messianic ability to reveal truth;
O_{8b} = revelation of truth about worship)

The truth about worship having been revealed to the woman (S_1
$\leq O_{8b}$) implies that Jesus has the ability ($S_2 \leq O_6$) which she attributed to Messiah ($S_7 \leq O_6$). Announcing the truth about worship is the epiphany of Jesus as Messiah.

The woman does not respond to this, but leaves her water jar
and, going to the village, she wonders if Jesus may not indeed be
the Messiah. She does not do so, however, on the basis of what
he said about the right place of worship, but reverts back to his
having told her everything about herself with performance F_{4a}
(v 29). By reverting back to Jesus' miraculous ability, the woman
reveals that she does not understand that Jesus' miraculous ability points beyond itself. She attributes to Jesus a misconceived
messianic ability as the performer of miracles in the following
performance, in which $O_{6'}$ represents her misconception of
Jesus' ability as that of a messiah:

$$F_{9b}[S_1 => (S_2 \geq O_{6'}) -> (S_2 \leq O_{6'})]$$

Her reasoning is as follows:

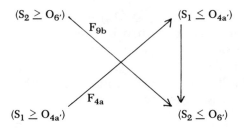

$(S_1$ = the woman; S_2 = Jesus; $O_{4a'}$ = miraculous knowledge;
$O_{6'}$ = misconceived ability to reveal truth)

She sanctions Jesus' performance of F_{4a}, revelation of his miraculous knowledge about her husbands, by recognizing him as having the ability of the messiah $(S_2 \le O_{6'})$, a sanction which she denied him for his performance of F_7, revelation of the truth about worship.

But note the word play: Messiah would announce everything (*hapanta*), and Jesus told her everything she did (*panta hosa epoiēsa*). Ironically, even as she refers to the wrong performance, F_{4a}, she hints at the correct one, F_7.

Just before the woman leaves, the disciples return and express surprise that Jesus is speaking to a woman, but do not engage in the conversation (v 27). Only when she leaves do they talk to Jesus. The understanding in the narrative is that the woman's being in company with Jesus excludes the disciples from being in his company. That understanding can be expressed logically as follows:

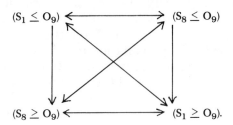

$(S_1$ = the woman; S_8 = the disciples; O_9 = the company of Jesus)

The woman's being in the company of Jesus $(S_1 \le O_9)$ excludes the disciples $(S_8 \ge O_9)$, and the disciples' entering the company of Jesus $(S_8 \le O_9)$ implies that the woman has left his company $(S_8 \ge O_9)$.

e. *The Satisfaction of Hunger* (vv 31-34)

When the woman leaves, returning to the village (v 28),

$$F_{11}[S_1 => (O_9 \leq S_1 \geq O_{9a}) -> (O_9 \geq S_1 \leq O_{9a})],$$

in which O_{9a} represents return to the village, the disciples engage in conversation with Jesus (vv 31-38),

$$F_{12}[S_8 => (S_8 \geq O_{9'}) -> (S_8 \leq O_{9'})],$$

involving the following interrelationships, with $O_{9'}$ representing engagement in discussion with Jesus:

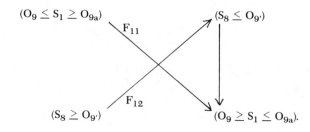

$(S_1$ = the woman; S_8 = the disciples; O_9 = the company of Jesus;
$O_{9'}$ = discussion with Jesus; O_{9a} = presence in the village),

The understanding in the development of the narrative is that F_{11} has priority over F_{12}, the disciples' joining in conversation with Jesus ($S_8 \leq O_{9'}$) implies, i.e., presupposes, that the woman is disengaged from his company ($S_1 \geq O_9$). On the basis of the same logic, after the disciples left the company of Jesus to go to the village the woman joined his company. The logic remains the same, but the actions through which the prior circumstances were enacted are reversals of F_{11} and F_{12}. It is easy to recognize that the reversal of F_{11} presupposes the reversal of F_{12}, i.e., the reversal of F_{12} has priority over F_{11}: the disciples left the company of Jesus before the women joined his company.

The disciples offer Jesus the food they have brought, but Jesus refuses it with the explanation that he has other food to eat about which they do not know (vv 31-32). It would facilitate our analysis if we now simply recall the double square in connection with the provision of water and the drinking of it, but substituting food, O_{10}, for drinking water, O_1, hunger, O_{11}, for thirst O_2, and satisfaction of hunger, $\bar{O}_{11'}$, for quenching of thirst, $\bar{O}_{2'}$. According to the logic of the first square the satisfaction of Jesus' hunger ($S_2 \leq \bar{O}_{11'}$) implies absence of hunger ($S_2 \geq O_{11}$), but also, according to the disciples reasoning, represented by the second square, that he has food ($S_2 \leq O_{10}$).

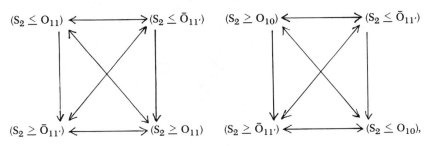

$(S_2 = \text{Jesus}; O_{10} = \text{food}; O_{11} = \text{hunger}; \bar{O}_{11'} = \text{satisfaction of hunger})$

The logic of the two squares on which the disciples reasoning is based can be combined in a single one:

$(O_{11} \le S_2 \ge O_{10}) \longleftrightarrow (S_2 \le \bar{O}_{11'})$

$(S_2 \ge \bar{O}_{11'}) \longleftrightarrow (O_{11} \ge S_2 \le O_{10}).$

$(S_2 = \text{Jesus}; O_{10} = \text{food}; O_{11} = \text{hunger}; \bar{O}_{11'} = \text{satisfaction of hunger})$

In the reasoning about water, the assumption had been that for Jesus to quench his thirst,

$$F_{1b}[S_2 => (S_2 \ge \bar{O}_{2'}) \rightarrow (S_2 \le \bar{O}_{2'})],$$

the woman would have had to give him a drink of water,

$$F_1[S_1 => (S_2 \ge O_1) \rightarrow (S_2 \le O_1)].$$

Similarly, the disciples now assume that they have to give Jesus food,

$$F_{13}[S_8 => (S_2 \ge O_{10}) \rightarrow (S_2 \le O_{10})],$$

so that he can satisfy his hunger,

$$F_{13a}[S_2 => (S_2 \ge \bar{O}_{11'}) \rightarrow (S_2 \le \bar{O}_{11'})].$$

We can present the two performances in connection with food on the following square:

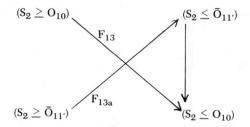

$(S_2 = \text{Jesus}; O_{10} = \text{food}; \bar{O}_{11'} = \text{satisfaction of hunger})$,

in which it is once more assumed that F_{13a} presupposes F_{13}.

When Jesus tells the disciples that he has other food to eat, O_{10b}, they think of it as a different supply of the same type of food they have to offer, but brought by someone else, $O_{10'}$, similar to the woman thinking that Jesus' water of life, O_{1b}, was just another, more miraculous version of Jacob's spring water, $O_{1'}$.

There is, however, a noteworthy difference here compared with the discussion concerning water of life. It is now Jesus himself who satisfies his hunger in contrast with his offering water of life to the woman to quench her thirst. This is something which will require our attention when we discuss the semantic component of our text.

It is also important to note that, for Jesus, satisfaction of hunger for the type of food which the disciples have to offer, $\bar{O}_{11'}$ (vv 31-32), is included in the satisfaction of hunger for the food about which he speaks, i.e., "to do the will of the one who sent me, and to complete his work" $\bar{O}_{11a'}$ (v 34), i.e., satisfaction of hunger for the food about which Jesus speaks ($S_2 \leq \bar{O}_{11a'}$) implies that hunger for the food which the disciples have in mind is also satisfied ($S_2 \leq \bar{O}_{11'}$). In Jesus' reasoning, satisfaction of the hunger to do the will of God also satisfies physical hunger. The logic of his reasoning can be presented as follows:

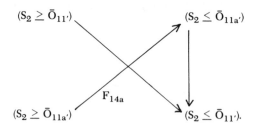

$(S_2 = \text{Jesus}; \bar{O}_{11a'} = \text{satisfaction of hunger for Jesus' "other" food};$
$\bar{O}_{11'} = \text{satisfaction of hunger})$,

in which satisfaction of the hunger to do the will of God ($S_2 \leq$ $\bar{O}_{11a'}$) by the following performance,

$$F_{14a}[S_2 => (S_2 \geq \bar{O}_{11a'}) -> (S_2 \leq \bar{O}_{11a'})],$$

implies also the satisfaction of physical hunger ($S_2 \leq O_{11'}$), but without a separate performance, such as F_{13a} assumed by the disciples,

$$F_{13a}[S_2 => (S_2 \geq \bar{O}_{11'}) -> (S_2 \leq \bar{O}_{11'})].$$

That is what makes the performance of

$$F_{13}[S_8 => (S_2 \geq O_{10}) -> (S_2 \leq O_{10})],$$

Jesus' receiving food from the disciples, unnecessary.

There is, in a sense, agreement between the woman and Jesus in that water of life and Jesus' food, O_{1b} and O_{10b}, would, respectively, quench thirst for drinking water and satisfy hunger for the kind of food which the disciples brought, O_2 and O_{11}. The very important difference is that, in this, the woman confused water of life, O_{1b}, and drinking water, O_1, whereas for Jesus it was satisfaction of hunger for the food about which he spoke, $\bar{O}_{11a'}$, which also satisfied hunger for the disciples' food, $\bar{O}_{11'}$, without identifying the food about which he spoke, O_{10b}, with that of the disciples, O_{10}.

From the above it is clear that at the level of the underlying syntax of the discourse there may be a closer connection between Jesus' request for a drink of water and his offer of water of life than appears at the surface level of the text, especially since Jesus no longer pursues the quest for a drink of water after the woman's reply prompted him to offer her the water of life. His thirst for drinking water was also satisfied without the expected performance of F_{1b}:

$$F_{1b}[S_2 => (S_2 \geq \bar{O}_{2'}) -> (S_2 \leq \bar{O}_{2'})]$$

This too will require our attention when we discuss the semantic component of the text. Does doing the will of him who sent Jesus also quench his thirst? What connection is there between the woman's appeal to the non-association between a Jewish man and a Samaritan woman, on the one hand, and the contrary positions of Jews and Samaritans concerning the right place to worship, on the other? Does resolving of the latter issue mean doing the will of the one who sent Jesus?

f. *The Harvest* (vv 35-38)

In his conversation with the disciples Jesus then proceeds to a discussion which, at the syntactic level, does not seem to have much of a connection with the preceding discussion about food. Almost cryptically he points out that the fields are ready for harvesting, the reaper already takes his reward and gathers fruit for eternal life, and the sower rejoices with the reaper (vv 35-36). The only connection to be made with the entire preceding text is a temporal one. That the reaper *now already* takes his reward (v 36) appears to refer to the same time as that to which Jesus refers when he says, "an hour comes, and now is, when the true worshippers will worship the Father in spirit and truth" (v 23). The discussion of the harvest as such, however, remains syntactically unconnected from the rest of the text.

The statement that the fields are ready for harvesting involves a very obvious logic that the reapers bringing in the harvest ($S_{10} \leq O_{12a}$) presupposes, i.e., implies, that the harvest is ready ($S_9 \leq O_{12}$):

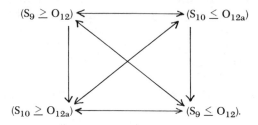

(S_9 = the fields; S_{10} = the reaper; O_{12} = readiness for harvesting; O_{12a} = the harvest)

The logic is that the reapers cannot bring in the harvest,
$$F_{15a}[S_{10} => (S_{10} \geq O_{12a}) -> (S_{10} \leq O_{12a}),$$
before the harvest has gone into readiness,
$$F_{15}[S_9 => (S_9 \geq O_{12}) -> (S_9 \leq O_{12})],$$
because ($S_{10} \leq O_{12a}$) implies ($S_9 \leq O_{12}$) as the outcome of the performance of F_{15}.

The following square shows the relationship between the performances:

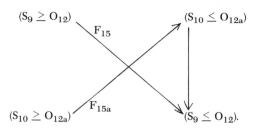

(S_9 = the fields; S_{10} = the reaper; O_{12} = readiness for harvesting; O_{12a} = the harvest)

Then Jesus makes a distinction which is very simple, but not as obvious as in the previous reasoning. The sower, S_{11}, and the reaper, S_{10}, are not identical, which can be clarified by the following logic:

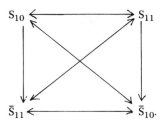

(S$_{10}$ = the reaper; S$_{11}$ = the sower)

Jesus leaves no doubt that the sower is not the reaper. He nevertheless maintains that the sower rejoices with the reaper, which involves the following reasoning:

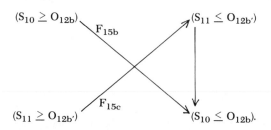

$(S_{10} = $ the reaper; $S_{11} = $ the sower; $O_{12b} = $ rejoicing in the harvest;
$O_{12b'} = $ rejoicing with the reaper in the harvest)

The understanding is that the sower's rejoicing in the fruit of the harvest,
$$F_{15c}[S_{11} => (S_{11} \geq O_{12b'}) \to (S_{11} \leq O_{12b'})],$$
presupposes the rejoicing of the reaper,
$$F_{15b}[S_{10} => (S_{10} \geq O_{12b}) \to (S_{10} \leq O_{12b})],$$
because $(S_{11} \leq O_{12b'})$ implies $(S_{10} \leq O_{12b})$ as the outcome of F_{15b}.

Before we move to a discussion of the last sequence of the narrative, Jesus' encounter with the Samaritan villagers, there is a characteristic feature of the previous part of the narrative which we need to note. Up to this point the performances were maximally two at a time, e.g., Jesus quenching his thirst, F_{1b}, implying that he already has acquired drinking water, F_1, which appeared on the performance square as follows:

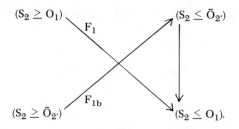

$$(S_2 = \text{Jesus}; O_1 = \text{drinking water}; \bar{O}_{2'} = \text{quenching})$$

In one case only was the relationship different, namely, when Jesus satisfied his hunger to do the will of the one who sent him $(S_2 \leq \bar{O}_{11a'})$ by the performance of F_{14a}. In this case his reasoning implied that he also satisfied his hunger for the kind of food brought by the disciples, $(S_2 \leq \bar{O}_{11'})$, without the expected performance of satisfying physical hunger, F_{13a}, having taken place. This appeared on the performance square as follows:

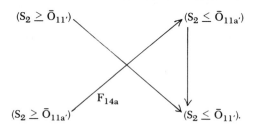

$$(S_2 = \text{Jesus}; \bar{O}_{11'} = \text{satisfaction of hunger};$$
$$\bar{O}_{11a'} = \text{satisfaction of hunger for Jesus' "other" food})$$

The various performances in this earlier part of the narrative, at the level of the deep syntax, are generally unrelated to each other beyond two performances at a time. In that regard the woman's sanctioning of Jesus' performance of revealing to her his miraculous knowledge about her husbands, F_{4a}, by attributing to him a misconceived ability of the messiah, F_{9b}, constitutes an unusual case. It concerns two incidents that are syntactically unconnected, but are related paradigmatically insofar as they both concern performances by Jesus, revealing miraculous knowledge about the woman's husbands, F_{4a}, and revealing to her the truth about worship, F_7. The former is sanctioned twice by the woman, first by the attributing to Jesus the ability of a prophet (v 19), and then of a messiah (v 29), but she seems to deny him a sanction for the latter. The second sanction, recognizing Jesus as the messiah, is not appropriate as a sanction of Jesus' disclosure of miraculous knowledge about her husbands to the woman, F_{4a}. It remains within the framework of the miraculous. But that same sanction, correctly conceived, would have been appropriate for the second performance, revealing to her the truth about worship, F_7. This unusual connection between the two performances is reinforced by the keyword, "everything," which Messiah would announce (v 25), and which Jesus told the woman about herself (v 29). What makes this all the more significant is that this sanction of the woman also connects up these two scenes with the final sequence, because it is her sanction which produces the Samaritan villagers' initial belief in Jesus.

g. *The Savior of the World* (vv 39-42)

In contrast with the general unconnectedness of the various performances in the first part of the narrative at the level of the deep syntax, the final sequence is constituted by a series of at least seven interconnected performances:

i.   The series begins with the woman's arrival in the village and her sanctioning Jesus' performance of revealing to her his miraculous knowledge about her husbands, F_{4a}, by attributing to him a misconceived messianic ability to reveal truth (vv 28-29, cf. 39). It forms the transition from the sequence of Jesus and the woman, but at the same time, as indicated immediately above, connects up the final sequence with two syntactically unrelated scenes in that earlier sequence.

The woman's sanction comes in the form of bearing witness about Jesus to the Samaritan villagers, and can be formalized as follows:

$$F_{16}[S_1 => (S_{12} \geq O_{7b'}) -> (S_{12} \leq O_{7b'})],$$

in which S_{12} represents the Samaritan villagers, and $O_{7b'}$ her witness about Jesus.

The relationship of the woman's witness to her leaving the company of Jesus and arriving in the village is clarified by the following performance square. The woman's witness to the villagers ($S_{12} \leq O_{7b'}$) presupposes, i.e., implies, that she has left Jesus, and arrived in the village ($O_9 \geq S_1 \leq O_{9a}$), i.e., F_{11} presupposes that F_{16} has taken place.

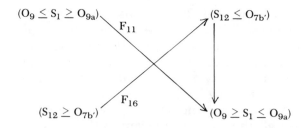

$(S_1 =$ the woman; $S_{12} =$ the villagers; $O_{7b'} =$ the woman's testimony;
$O_9 =$ the company of Jesus; $O_{9a} =$ presence in the village)

    ii.   As a result of the woman's witness, the villagers believe in Jesus in the sense of what she said (v 39a):

$$F_{16b}[S_{12} => (S_{12} \geq O_{7c}) -> (S_{12} \leq O_{7c})],$$

in which O_{7c} represents belief in Jesus in the sense of the woman's testimony.

    It should be noted that $(S_{12} \leq O_{7c})$, the Samaritan villagers believing in Jesus in the sense of the woman's witness, which is the result of performance, F_{16b}, and $(S_{12} \leq O_{7b'})$, the woman witnessing about Jesus to the Samaritan villagers, the result of F_{16}, are cognitive performances affirming a circumstance which is assumed to exist already, $(S_2 \leq O_{6'})$, i.e., Jesus having the (misconceived) ability of a messiah because of his miraculous knowledge of the woman, attributed to him by the woman with performance F_{9b}. Sanctions recognize (or deny) an existing circumstance; they do not transform one circumstance into another, as if Jesus was transformed from the circumstance of not having the ability of a messiah into having it. Indeed, as our analyses have shown, the circumstance of having the relevant ability is always presupposed by the performance for which it is necessary. In terms of the surface narrative syntax, phase C of the narrative schema, the actual performance of the action, always presupposes phase B, preparedness, which includes the ability to perform the action.

    The following performance square clarifies the relationship between the woman giving witness about Jesus, F_{16}, and the Samaritan villagers believing in him, F_{16b}:

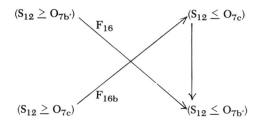

$(S_{12} = $ the villagers; $O_{7b'} = $ the woman's testimony; $O_{7c} = $ belief in Jesus in the sense of the woman's testimony)

$(S_{12} \leq O_{7c})$ presupposes, i.e., implies, $(S_{12} \leq O_{7b'})$ which is the outcome of the woman's performance, F_{16}.

iii. Believing in Jesus the Samaritan villagers go out to meet him (v 30, cf. 40a), represented by the following performance:

$$F_{17}[S_{12} => (S_{12} \geq O_9) -> (S_{12} \leq O_9),$$

in which O_9 signifies being in the company of Jesus in accordance with our earlier designation.

This performance presupposes $(S_{12} \leq O_{7c})$, their having come to believe in Jesus, as the following square illustrates:

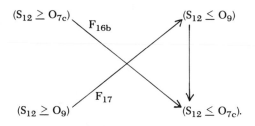

$(S_{12} = $ the villagers; $O_{7c} = $ belief in Jesus in the sense of the woman's testimony; $O_9 = $ the company of Jesus)

iv. Having arrived with Jesus the villagers ask him to stay with them (v 40b):

$$F_{18}[S_{12} => (S_2 \geq O_{13}) -> (S_2 \leq O_{13})],$$

in which O_{13} represents the request that Jesus stay with them.

In the sense of the narrative schema of the surface syntax, it is an authorization of Jesus to stay with them, and, as such, part of phase B (preparedness) for the performance of Jesus which is to follow.

The relationships between the performances are as follows. In order to be able to ask Jesus to stay with them $(S_2 \leq O_{13})$, the Samaritans have to be in his company $(S_{12} \leq O_9)$.

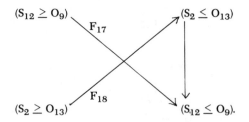

$(S_2 = \text{Jesus}; S_{12} = \text{the villagers}; O_9 = \text{the company of Jesus};$
$O_{13} = \text{invitation to stay with the Samaritan villagers})$

v.   Having been empowered to do so, Jesus stays with the Samaritan villagers for two days (v 40c):

$$F_{18a}[S_2 => (S_2 \geq O_{13'}) -> (S_2 \leq O_{13'})],$$

in which $O_{13'}$ represents the stay with the villagers.

The relationships between the performances are as follows. Jesus stays with the villagers on their invitation. Staying with them $(S_2 \leq O_{13'})$ presupposes having been asked, i.e., authorized by them $(S_2 \leq O_{13})$.

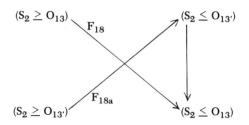

$(S_2 = \text{Jesus}; O_{13} = \text{invitation to stay with the Samaritan villagers};$
$O_{13'} = \text{staying with the villagers})$

vi.   Jesus' stay with the Samaritan villagers results in their no longer believing in him in the sense of the woman's testimony, but that he is the savior of the world (vv 41-42):

$$F_{19}[S_{12} => (O_{7c} \leq S_{12} \geq O_{14a'}) -> (O_{7c} \geq S_{12} \leq O_{14a'})],$$

in which $O_{14a'}$ represents belief in Jesus as the savior of the world. The relationship between their coming to believe in Jesus as the savior of the world and his staying with them is as follows. No longer believing on the basis of the woman's witness and the belief that he is the savior of the world $(O_{7c} \geq S_{12} \leq O_{14a'})$ are based on, i.e., presuppose, Jesus' staying with them $(S_2 \leq O_{13'})$.

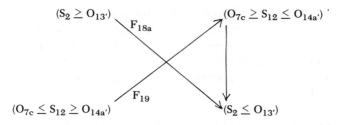

$(S_2 = \text{Jesus}; S_{12} = \text{the villagers}; O_{7c} = \text{belief in Jesus in the sense of the woman's witness}; O_{13'} = \text{staying with the villagers for two days}; O_{14a'} = \text{recognition of Jesus as the savior of the world})$

The villagers' faith ($S_{12} \leq O_{14a'}$) sanctions an existing circumstance, revealed to them by Jesus' performance of staying with them. They do not sanction Jesus' staying with them, even though his staying with them is presupposed by their sanction. Jesus' staying with them presupposes the circumstance which they sanction, namely, that he is the savior of the world. It is a circumstance for which no performance is stated. The villagers do not sanction a performance by Jesus, but his qualification as savior of the world ($S_2 \leq O_{14a}$), in which O_{14a} represents the qualification of being the savior of the world. It was with that qualification that Jesus stayed with the villagers. In that way he was able to act as the savior of the world, making it possible for them to recognize him as such. The relationship between the villagers' sanction and Jesus' qualification as savior of the world can be presented as follows on a semiotic square:

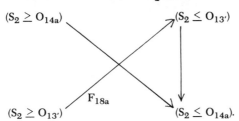

$(S_2 = \text{Jesus}; O_{13'} = \text{staying with the villagers for two days}; O_{14a} = \text{ability of the savior of the world})$

As indicated above, no performance for Jesus' achieving the status of savior of the world is given, i.e., it is assumed that he already has that status.

It will be noted that this square duplicates the structure of the performance square which clarifies the relationship between the Samaritan villagers' invitation that Jesus stay with them and his staying with them. Both squares concern the readiness of Jesus, authorization ($S_2 \leq O_{13}$) and ability ($S_2 \leq O_{14a}$), to carry out the performance of staying with the Samaritan villagers as savior of the world. It is as savior of the world that Jesus stays with them. In terms of the narrative schema, he has the ability and the willingness to stay with them, but he needs their authorization, i.e., invitation, in order to accomplish his mission successfully.

The interrelationships between this final series of performances can be presented in the following interrelated squares. It is for purely graphic reasons that only the relevant parts of the squares are shown. Similarly, the horizontal inversion of the first square at the bottom has no significance beyond graphic limitations.

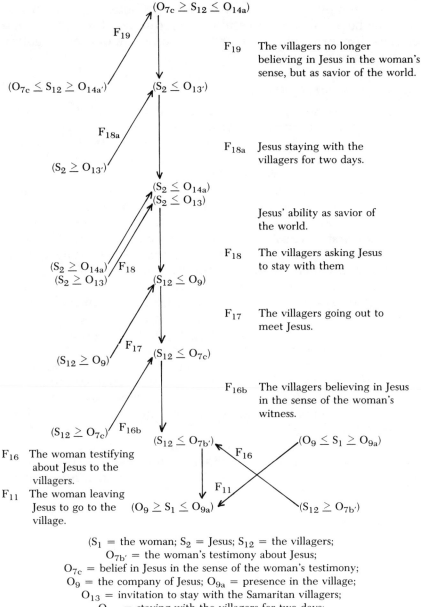

$(S_1$ = the woman; S_2 = Jesus; S_{12} = the villagers;
$O_{7b'}$ = the woman's testimony about Jesus;
O_{7c} = belief in Jesus in the sense of the woman's testimony;
O_9 = the company of Jesus; O_{9a} = presence in the village;
O_{13} = invitation to stay with the Samaritan villagers;
$O_{13'}$ = staying with the villagers for two days;
O_{14a} = ability of the savior of the world;
$O_{14a'}$ = recognition of Jesus as the savior of the world)

Having moved to the most abstract syntactic level of our text we now have to return to a more concrete level, what Greimas calls its discourse syntax,[6] in order to complete our investigation of the syntactic component.

3. *The Discourse Syntax*

In this final section of the syntactic component of John 4 we will consider what happens syntactically at the discourse level of the text, i.e., how the abstract subjects and objects, the situations in which they find themselves and the actions in which they engage come to expression in the text; by what means does the author "enact" the subjects and objects in their relationships grammatically in the text. It is important to reemphasize that this "enactment" does not refer to an actual process in time, as if an author first has abstract subjects, objects, etc. in mind, which she or he then makes concrete in the text. Abstractions are not entities with which an author operates, but means of analysis, in this case grammatical analysis, used by an investigator to give intelligible expression to what she or he understands about her or his subject matter. Everything discussed as features of the syntactic (similarly the semantic) component of the text is present in the text at the same time, similar to the way in which subjects and predicates, word cases and tenses, are present in a text, making it possible to distinguish them by abstraction, i.e., by giving them appropriate syntactic designations. The way in which the subjects and objects and their interrelationships come to expression as a discourse in our text is not by abstract reasoning, as in, for example, a philosophical or sociological discussion, but through actors who are engaged with each other in space and time. They are actorialized, spatialized and temporalized, to use Greimas' terms.

a. *The Actors*

The text is not a direct communication between the author and the reader(s), but stands in its own framework of actorial relationships: Jesus, the woman, the disciples, Jacob, the Samaritans, etc., with the author standing back in disengagement from what transpires, engaging only occasionally, for example, when he explains that Jews and Samaritans do not associate (v 9), or when he introduces the saying about the sower and the reaper not being the same person as a means of unfolding the meaning

---

[6] See under "Syntaxe discursive" and "Discours" in *Sémiotique*, "Syntax, Discursive" and "Discourse" in the English translation.

of Jesus' statement that the sower rejoices with the one who harvests (vv 36-37). The effect of this disengagement of the author
from the narrative is that what comes to expression in the text is
an effect of the interaction among the actors in the text. The
reader(s) are similarly disengaged. Interaction between author
and reader(s) is at a minimum. (Compare, by contrast, Paul's let-
ters.) In John 4 the author does not inform the reader(s) about a
meaning, but allows the meaning that emerges to be a matter of
what transpires among the actors in the text.

This standing back is taken a step further in the text itself
when the woman disengages herself from the topic of discussion
by putting forward yet another independent framework of actorial relationships which includes Jesus, but is set apart from
herself: "Our fathers worshipped on this mountain, and you
(plural, i.e., you Jews) say Jerusalem is the place where one must
worship" (v 20). In Jesus' reply he too disengages, but also includes the woman in a general way. The actorial setting is in any
case no longer that of Jesus and the woman: "...an hour comes
when you (plural) will worship the Father, neither on this mountain nor in Jerusalem" (v 21). The disengagement is complete
when in verses 23-24 the actors are true worshippers who worship the Father in spirit and truth. In that regard verse 22 once
more falls oddly out of the pattern. In it Jesus reengages in this
new actorial framework by claiming representation of the Jewish position. In so doing he also changes roles, from being a partner in conversation with the woman to someone who supremely
resolves the issue from the point of view, and in favor, of what
may appear to be the Jewish, but is in reality the Christian
position.

By their disengagement the woman and Jesus subject their
own discussion to this larger, but more fundamental actorial
framework, in which there is progression from the woman's
"our fathers" and "you (Jews)," to Jesus' true worshippers and
the Father. If this is recognized it also becomes clear that this
larger, but more fundamental, frame of reference sheds a certain light on the rest of the narrative, drawing it into its perspective, and tying all the statements together in a single syntax of
discourse. It does not take much reflection to recognize that in
as much as it is the statements in the text which create the network of interrelationships among the actors, the network of interrelationships in turn contributes to the syntactic binding of
the statements in the discourse. So, for example, at a relatively
simple level, the various statements of the woman and Jesus cannot be taken independently, but are related to each other as the

give and take between the two actors. The relationships between these statements are determined syntactically by their
occurrence in connection with, or in the mouth of, either of
these actors. Drawing this out more broadly, the disciples belong with Jesus — he talks to them with a different set of presup-
positions than those with which he addresses the woman — but
the disciples feel remote from the woman, not even daring to
penetrate into Jesus' discussion with her. The woman, on the
other hand, is bound by certain factors to the Samaritan villagers — being Samaritan and living in the same village. Jesus is a
stranger.

Once the woman disengages from the specific polarity between herself and Jesus by appealing to the Samaritan/Jewish
issue about the right place to worship, these more specific con-
figurations begin to dissolve. What is now at issue no longer separates them, but they face it together; it is no longer a question
of how they specifically would behave, but how the larger issue
between Samaritans and Jews is to be resolved, of which their
relationship is a very small part. In the final verses of our text,
when the villagers tell the woman that they no longer believe
on the basis of what she told them, but because they have seen
and know that Jesus is the savior of the world, not only is the
issue represented by the larger, more fundamental actorial
framework of Samaritans and Jews resolved, but all the other
more specific relationships are drawn into this resolution.

Only one, highly significant, structural tension remains.
There is a sense in which, with their statement, the villagers create a new framework of actorial polarity between themselves
and Jesus, on the one hand, and the woman, on the other. This
grouping stands in remarkable tension with Jesus' earlier sanction that the sower rejoices with the one who harvests. Jesus'
statement reengages in a remarkable way in the original — and
main — actorial framework of the narrative, that of himself and
the woman, but in such a way that he and the woman are at the
same time also engaged in what we have identified as the larger,
more fundamental actorial framework. With his sanction Jesus
engages the woman and himself in that larger framework, together contributing as sower and reaper to the resolution of the
issue represented by it. In that way the separation between the
actorial framework represented by Jesus and the woman, and
that of the opposition between Samaritans and Jews is obliter-
ated; the story of Jesus and the woman and the story of Jews and
Samaritans unfold as a single narrative.

We noted above that the narrative sequence of Jesus and the

disciples, which, at the level of the actual text, constitutes a superimposed story line compared with the main story line of
Jesus and the Samaritans, at the level of the narrative schemas,
is very much integral to the narrative as a whole. It is only the
change in actorial filling of roles, a feature of the discourse syntax of our text, which lets the disciples' sequence appear superimposed. In the first part of that sequence the disciples fill the
role which had been the woman's in the beginning of the narrative, providing Jesus with food or water and not understanding
the nature of the food or water about which he speaks. Furthermore, in the first part of the disciples' sequence, needs that had
been left unsatisfied in the beginning of the narrative, i.e., in the
discussion with the woman, are addressed.

There is of course also a change of actors from the woman to
the villagers in the final sequence, but in that case continuity
remains even at the discourse level because the woman herself
lets her role pass over to the villagers when she tells them that
Jesus may be the messiah.

In the second part of the disciples' sequence, the disciples fill
a completely different role, and so does Jesus. In his comment
about the harvest, Jesus does not act as a participant in the story,
but as someone who stands over it and comments on it, whereas
the disciples fill the role of spectators and are in that regard very
similar to the readers of the text.

The only actor who is essential to the story is Jesus. In his
case the actor is the role. This is most evident in the fact that his
identity is one of the major issues in the story. No other actor
can play his role. Even the fact that it is he and not the narrator
who interprets the story in the second part of the disciples' sequence makes a difference.

b. *The Spatial Setting*

With regard to the spatial setting it is above all significant
that the events take place in Samaria, and more specifically
close to the well of Jacob which plays an important part in both
Jewish and Samaritan history. Most significantly the area is also
qualified by the fact that the woman could place it in the context of "this mountain" as the place where "our fathers" worshipped, placing the events within a sacral realm. This may be a
feature in the text that is not sufficiently recognized. The area in
which the events transpire is a sacral realm for the Samaritans,
and Jesus is a Jew who entered into that realm, not because he
wanted to, but because he had to pass through it (cf. v 4). He
nevertheless becomes engaged by it, specifically as a result of his

encounter with the woman. When the woman says "our fathers worshipped on this mountain, and you say Jerusalem is where one must worship" (v 20), she draws attention to the fact that what had transpired up to that moment was within the area of the sacred. The narrative presents this as an insight which gradually grows, from the miraculous provision of drinking water by Jacob to the recognition that Jesus is a prophet, which prompts her comment about "this mountain". The spatial setting becomes progressively clarified, revealing also in this regard a close narrative-syntactic relationship between the various parts of the story up to this point. It is of course again the individual statements in the text which define and present this physical as well as socio-religious space, with the space in turn providing a framework which ties the various statements together in the syntax of the narrative.

With the woman's statement that "our fathers worshipped on this mountain, but you (Jews) say that Jerusalem is where one must worship" (v 20) she poses over and against the sacral realm of the Samaritans the opposing, but also intervening, religious space of the Jews, locating Jesus in the latter space. One might say that she interprets the socio-religious spatial situation, and particularly the way she and Jesus fit in it, trying to penetrate to its basis. Her interpretation further defines the Samaritan area socio-religiously: Jews and Samaritans do not associate, a Jewish man does not ask a Samaritan woman for a drink of water (v 9).

In his reply Jesus rejects the woman's interpretation; "neither on this mountain nor in Jerusalem" (v 21), but in spirit and truth (vv 23-24). It is acceptance of this space in which the opposition of Samaritan and Jew is dissolved which provides the resolution, when the villagers recognize Jesus as the savior, not distinctively of Samaritans or of Jews, but of the world. Note in this regard once more the contrary understanding in Jesus' answer in verse 22 in which he affirms the reality of the two spaces, affirming the superiority of the one over the other.

Within the general physical space of the narrative, Samaria, there is a significant specific differentiation, between the well where Jesus meets and engages the woman in conversation, and the village from which she comes, to which she returns, from where the villagers come to invite Jesus to stay with them, where he stays for two days, and where the resolution of the opposition between Jews and Samaritans is accomplished. This spatial differentiation provides a certain tension in the narrative, similar to, but not necessarily duplicating, the differentiation between the sower and the reaper. The well is the area of preparation, the village, that of the achievement of the resolution.

By contrast the similar spatial differentiation between the well where Jesus rests and the village to which the disciples go to buy food is of relative insignificance. Although the village may geographically be the same as that from which the woman came, it does not represent the same differentiation in this case; the disciples going to the village to buy food merely means that they are spatially away from where Jesus is.

In the narrative as a whole, thus, Samaria is the sacral space of the Samaritans in which the opposing socio-religious environments of Samaritans and Jews are resolved. Jesus, representing one of these, the Jewish environment, enters into that of the Samaritans, but in so doing he surrenders claim to the environment from which he comes, posing over and against the opposition between the two a more universal space where the true worshippers worship the Father in spirit and truth. In the concluding statement of the villagers they fundamentally affirm this universal space by recognizing Jesus as the savior of the world.

In Jesus' comment to the disciples in verse 38, Samaria is interpreted spatially, in a different way, as the area of fruitful Christian missionary activity. Also temporally it represents a different framework, presupposing that previous missionary work had already been done in the area and that the disciples, not Jesus, were now ready to reap the fruits of that labor. All of this further indicates that the comment is out of place in the general narrative framework.

c. *The Temporal Setting*

The temporal features of the text are less revealing. The time of the main story is delimited by Jesus' arrival at the well and the recognition by the villagers that he is the savior of the world. Within that time framework contemporaneous events are narrated: the disciples going to the village to buy food while Jesus is engaged in conversation with the woman; the events are geographically separated but temporally contemporaneous. Even when the disciples arrive at the well, they wait aside while Jesus is talking to the woman, which still leaves two temporal frameworks of activity although the geographic setting is now almost identical.

Between the woman's departure to tell the villagers about Jesus and the villagers' arrival to invite Jesus to stay with them there is a lapse of time with regard to Jesus. This time is at least partly filled by Jesus' conversation with the disciples, thus once more producing two contemporaneous temporal frameworks. What happens during the longest period of time is not narrated, merely stated, i.e., the period between Jesus going to the village and the villagers recognizing him as the savior of the world, according to verse 40, a period of two days.

Other time frames also enter into the picture with such self-evidence that the reader projects them without even thinking of it, like a native speaker producing grammatically perfect sentences without being aware of a grammar. Without such a projection of other temporal frameworks, whether intuitively or otherwise, the text would be altogether confusing in terms of its narrative syntax. When the woman speaks of Jacob providing the drinking water the reader automatically projects that incident into a time framework other than that of the events in which Jesus and the woman are involved. The same applies to her statement that "our fathers" worshipped on this mountain, whereas the Jews say that Jerusalem is where one must worship. In this case the time frameworks are not contemporaneous, although in the reference to the question of the place of worship the situation is somewhat complex; the worship of "our fathers" refers to a past time, whereas what "you (Jews)" say is, in a sense, atemporal. What is clear, however, is that all events, those that are contemporaneous as well as those that have a different temporal reference, are not included in the sequence of events of the main story line.

All of this becomes quite clear when one considers the difficulty which arises when the text does not provide for a different, future, temporal setting for the disciples reaping where they did not labor, but also not for the event to take place in the temporal framework of the narrative itself. It is told as if it were part of the events that are narrated, and yet it looks back on a time when others have labored. All a naive reading of the text can do with the statement is to take it as if it refers to a harvest which the disciples are about to reap in the Samaritan village, the past labor presumably referring to the witness of the woman, but the narrative provides for nothing of the kind. It is only Jesus who is invited and who stays in the village — "The Samaritans arrived with *him*, asking *him* to remain with them. And *he* remained there two days" (v 40). Nothing shows more clearly than this that temporal frames of reference are unavoidable in the reading of a text in order to arrange the narrated events in a meaningful way. Difficulties arise immediately when the text does not provide for the projection of a different temporal framework for events which do not fit into that of the narrative itself, such as the reference to the disciples reaping where they did not labor. One could well imagine the confusion that would have arisen if the text had not provided for a different temporal framework for Jacob's provision of drinking water than that of Jesus and the woman's discussion at the well.

The most significant temporal location of the text occurs when Jesus says, "But *an hour comes, and now is* when the true worshippers will worship the Father in spirit and truth" (v 23.) The *significance* of the statement is a matter that belongs in our discussion of the semantic component of the text. What concerns us here in the syntactic component is not the *meaning* itself, but *the way in which* that meaning comes to expression syntactically, i.e., the way the story is temporalized by Jesus' statement. The statement that the future is present in the events of the story sets the narrative within the temporal framework of Jewish eschatological expectations.

Conclusion

Our analysis of the syntactic component of John 4 has clarified the textual syntax at the three levels of its *surface narrative syntax*, its *syntactic deep structure*, and its *discursive syntax*. The analysis has shown that, contrary to an analysis of only the surface by traditional means, John 4 is a syntactically tightly cohesive text. There is much of what has been shown in the investigation so far that can be recognized by a sensitive intuitive reading of the text. In that regard the investigation, by showing how such a reading is possible syntactically, can be a means of controlling the reading, and especially contrary readings. (The question of the text's *meaning* will be investigated in the next section on "The Semantic Component.") The investigation has shown, for example, that the break which is frequently sensed between verses 15 and 16 when Jesus abruptly tells the woman, "Go, call your husband," is connected syntactically tightly with what precedes as the *preparation* phase for a program of *action* to satisfy the *needs* revealed in the previous discussion by the woman's *sanctions* in verses 11-12 and 15, in which she showed, respectively, that she did not recognize who Jesus was, nor did she understand what he meant by the water of life. By telling the woman to go and call her husband Jesus makes another attempt to complete the *preparation* of the program through which he will satisfy the needs mentioned, as well as others that are even more fundamental, engaging the woman in the program of revealing himself as the savior of the world to the Samaritan villagers. In so doing Jesus not only satisfies the above-mentioned needs, but also the woman's thirst for the water of life.

Our investigation of the syntactic deep structure revealed that up to the point when the woman departs for the village to witness about Jesus, leaving her jar behind, the various programs of action remained largely unconnected at this deeper level. From then on, however, the series of actions are closely linked, beginning with the woman's departure. This does not apply to the conversation with the disciples which is linked at a level closer to the surface as the interpretation of the series of linked actions.

The investigation of the text's discourse syntax showed how the conversation with the disciples is a way in which the author disengages himself from directly addressing the readers to interpret the meaning of the events by letting Jesus interpret them in conversation with the disciples. It also became clear how the author made effective use of spatialization and temporalization to bring out the meaning of the story.

Our investigation of the syntax of John 4 did not address the question of meaning as such, only the syntactic means by which the various parts of the text are linked to bring out that meaning. The next step in our study is to investigate what the meaning is that comes to expression in the text through its syntactic structure.

B. THE SEMANTIC COMPONENT

Introduction

In the analysis of the syntactic component of John 4 we made reference to subjects, objects and narrative programs. The inter-relationships between subjects and objects are characterized by the internal features of the narrative programs, i.e., statements of action governing statements of circumstance, or more specifically, an active subject performing an action which alters the relationship between a subject of circumstance and an object. On a textual scale which extends beyond individual narrative programs, the relationships between subjects and objects as well as the individual narrative programs are established by the four phases of the narrative schema — need, preparedness, perform-ance and sanction — at the surface level, and by the logical rela-tionships between circumstances at the deeper level of the semio-narrative syntax. Finally, syntactic integration takes place as a network of relationships between actors at different levels of engagement or disengagement, and by placement of the ac-tions in spatial and temporal settings.

In our analysis of the semantic component of John 4 it will be our task to investigate how meaning is generated in the text through this syntactic structure, beginning at the level of the discourse semantics with the concrete figures, such as Jesus, a Jewish man, and the Samaritan woman, and the issues separat-ing Jews and Samaritans; then moving on to the more abstract level of the values expressed by these figures: the security which adherence to either of the opposed groups of Jews and Samari-tans provides, or the physical nourishment represented by drinking water and the food which the disciples offer Jesus, as opposed to the value of the water of life, and of Jesus' "other food;" finally, to the opposition between good and bad, and be-tween life and death, at the deepest, most abstract, level of our text. That deepest level is not the *real* meaning of the text. The meaning of John 4 comes to expression in the totality of the text, which includes the deepest abstract level all the way to its sur-face manifestation in the concrete figures of the controversy be-tween Jews and Samaritans, and of this particular Jewish man and this Samaritan woman, the location where they meet, and their understanding that they are living in a time that is being fulfilled.

1. *The Discourse Structure*

a. *The Figures*

  i. *Water and food*

There is another way, in addition to the syntactic structure, in which the subjects, objects and narrative programs are bound together to constitute a structured whole, namely, by the components of meaning which they share and which link them together to produce the specific meaning of the text. For example, at a very elementary level, the terms "water" and "food" serve to collect different components of meaning to give expression to meanings, such as water, and to call to mind the figures (or images) of drinking water and water of life, and food, calling to mind the food which the disciples offered Jesus and Jesus' other food. In each case there are shared components of meaning, namely, what quenches thirst in the case of water and what satisfies hunger in the case of food, but other components that are distinctive. In the case of drinking water and the food offered by the disciples the terms call to mind images of, respectively, things liquid or solid, which have physical nourishment as their most relevant common component of meaning in our text. In the case of the water of life and Jesus' other food the images remain completely vague, but, for the reader at least, they call to mind spiritual nourishment as their most relevant common component of meaning. The story itself makes clear what it means to drink the living water and to be nourished by Jesus' other food. Thus, the distinctive components of meaning, physical and spiritual, which function to distinguish between the two types of water and the two types of food, at the same time serve to link, respectively, drinking water with the food offered by the disciples, and water of life with Jesus' other food.

On the other hand, water of life (literally "living water") has a component of meaning which links it with the spring water (also "living water") which Jacob provided miraculously for himself, his sons and their livestock. For the person who knows the legend — as the woman obviously does — Jesus' statement that the water of life which he gives "becomes a fountain of water springing forth to eternal life" (v 19) reminds vividly of the miracle of Jacob who lifted the cover of the well to let water spring forth to the surface, allowing everyone to drink. And yet Jesus' statement, coming after the woman's reference to Jacob's miracle, is intended specifically to bring to expression what distinguishes the water he offers from that of Jacob. The distinctiveness in meaning which separates Jacob's spring water from

Jesus' water of life cannot escape the reader. In fact, it is accentuated by the women, when, in her request that Jesus give her the water "so that I will not thirst nor come here to draw water" (v 15), she mixes decisive components of the one with those of the other in such a way that the water offered by Jesus appears as merely a continuously self-replenishing supply of drinking water. The component of meaning which distinguishes water of life from drinking water, and thus also from Jacob's spring water, escapes her.

Similarly the disciples do not recognize the distinctiveness of Jesus' other food when they think someone else brought him food similar to the kind they offered. That of course is what provides Jesus with the opportunity to clarify further the meaning of his other food by introducing the figure of "doing the will of the one who sent me, and completing his work" (v 34). That clarification should shed further light on the meaning of the water of life, due to the linking of its meaning with that of Jesus' other food. The way in which this can happen remains obscure at this stage of the narrative, but is made clear by means of the subsequent metaphor of the sower and reaper.

This network of relationships already serves to bring vividly to expression the related figures of water of life and Jesus' other food. The point of departure in each case is the ordinary meaning of the terms, water and food, against which water of life and Jesus' food are contrasted to bring out their meanings. Those meanings are enhanced by the series of figures that are called forth by the actions of, and the discussions between, the actors. In the case of water, Jesus asks the woman for a drink, but then tells her that if she knew who he was she would ask him to give her water of life. The woman poses against Jesus' offer the figure of Jacob's miraculous provision of water. When Jesus explains that the water which he offers, unlike Jacob's, is a continuously self-replenishing supply, she fails to recognize the difference between drinking water and the water offered by Jesus. In that way, however, the difference is allowed to stand out all the more clearly.

The series of figures in the case of food are simpler. The disciples offer Jesus food which he refuses because he has other food. The disciples do not recognize that "other" means another kind; they think it is the same kind brought by others. Jesus then explains that his food is to do the will of the one who sent him and to complete his work.

With the latter statement the clarification of the meaning of Jesus' food comes to a preliminary conclusion, and related to it, the meaning of water of life. Although, as has already been indicated, at this stage of the narrative it still remains obscure how Jesus' statement is related to water of life, except through its linkage with Jesus' other food. With Jesus' statement a new figure has been introduced which moves beyond the complex of figures that have to do with water and food to a figure which is itself in need of clarification, namely, "to do the will of the one who sent me." What does it mean to do the will of the one who sent him and to complete his work? That will be clarified finally by Jesus' stay with the Samaritan villagers and their recognition of him as the savior of the world. But in order that this might become clear a transition is provided in Jesus' explanation by means of the metaphor of the harvest. With that metaphor a new complex of figures appears.

ii.   *A sower and a reaper*

The metaphor itself is picturesque: the fields are ripe with the harvest, and the sower, although not a participant in the harvesting, rejoices with the reaper in its fruit. The meaning of this figure as a metaphor is dependent on other figures as well. It is connected on the one hand with the figure it interprets, Jesus doing the will of the one who sent him and completing his work, and through that with the entire network of figures concerning food and water. On the other hand, it is connected with that to which it points: what has already been announced and is about to happen, the villagers going out to meet Jesus. But even then the latter figure still does not clarify the metaphoric meaning of the harvest. It merely prepares the reader to recognize that meaning when it is presented, i.e., the subsequent events concerning the villagers. It is in any case clear that in some way or another the villagers' coming to meet Jesus has something to do with the fields being ready for the harvest: they are linked by the spatial figures of the disciples looking up to the fields ready for the harvest and the villagers on their way to meet Jesus.

In the second component of the metaphor of the harvest (the figure of the sower rejoicing with the reaper in the fruit of the harvest), the identity of the metaphoric sower is not immediately clear. However, the structural relationships of the narrative as a whole have suggested quite conclusively that the sower must be the woman. That conclusion goes very well with our present considerations. It resolves the uncertainty concerning the relationship between the water of life and Jesus' statement that his food is to do the will of the one who sent him. The water of life symbolizes the woman's mission to the inhabitants of her village; Jesus' other food, his preparation of her for that mission and his rounding it off when he goes to the village to "reap the harvest." When Jesus tells his disciples that his food is "that I do the will of the one who sent me, and that I complete his work," he distinguishes between work already completed — he is already nourished — and work still to be done. The water of life which Jesus had given to the woman is what enabled her to prepare for the completion of Jesus' own mission when he visits the people of her village. Thus, the water of life stands to Jesus' food as the sower stands to the reaper. Although the woman does not participate in the final events, it is her witness concerning Jesus which prepared for those events.

The figure presented by the metaphor of the harvest, picturesque as it is, can stand on its own. In the narrative, however, its function is to link, on the one hand, the complex of figures concerning water and food, culminating in Jesus' statement that his food is to do the will of the one who sent him, and, on the other, the series of figures describing the events that are about to take place, the villagers coming out to meet Jesus to invite him to stay with them, etc. In that way the series of figures concerning water and food prepare for an understanding of the significance of what is about to happen, and, in turn, the events that are about to happen round off the meaning to which that series of figures gave initial expression. In this way all of these figures are linked together in a single complex expression of meaning. These final events, however, conclude other series of figures as well. To these we now turn our attention.

iii.   *The identity of Jesus*

The figure of the villagers recognizing Jesus as the savior of the world concludes a long series of figures concerning his identity: the woman doubting whether he could provide the water he offered, challenging him whether he could be greater than Jacob who miraculously provided spring water; Jesus proving his miraculous ability by revealing to the woman his knowledge about her, to which she responds by recognizing him as a prophet; Jesus resolving the issue of the right place to worship with supreme authority, with the woman pointing out that it is Messiah who would announce everything, and Jesus claiming that he is Messiah; the woman witnessing to the villagers that the person she met is probably the messiah because he told her everything about her, which is then surpassed by the villagers' recognition that he is the savior of the world. The issue of Jesus' identity threads its way through the narrative by means of this series of figures, obviously reaching its objective in the confession of the villagers.

There is a significant difference between the series of figures concerning the identity of Jesus and the series concerning water and food. Both culminate in the confession of the villagers that Jesus is the savior of the world. In the recognition of Jesus as the savior of the world the meaning of the water of life and Jesus' other food finds concrete expression. However, in the series concerning water and food all the figures to the end remain in balance in such a way that the confession of Jesus as savior of the world is understandable only in terms of Jesus' instruction concerning the water of life and his other food. But in the series concerning the identity of Jesus, the recognition by the villagers completely supersedes everything that preceded, not invalidating it, but absorbing all of it at an incomparably higher level. The earlier figures are no longer necessary for an understanding of the villagers' recognition, as they explicitly state when they tell the woman that they no longer believe on the basis of her witness. In that regard it appears all the more significant that Jesus sanctions her activity in terms of the series concerning water, food and the harvest, by means of the metaphor of the sower rejoicing with the reaper in the fruit of the harvest. It will be important to note how this relates to the remaining series, that concerning the relationship between Jews and Samaritans.

iv. *Jews and Samaritans*

The series concerning the relationship between Jews and Samaritans is all encompassing, extending to the spatial setting within which the narrative unfolds, Samaria, presented at the very beginning as an alien environment through which Jesus had to pass (v 4). Within the framework of that setting a series of figures appear which give graphic expression to some of the characteristic features of the region, but finally transform it into an area of accepted hospitality, when Jesus stays in the village for two days, and the villagers recognize him, a Jew, as the savior of the world. The series of figures are in three sets. The first concerns Jesus' association with the Samaritan woman. He asks her for a drink of water, but she draws his attention to the fact that a Jewish man does not ask such a thing of a Samaritan woman, a convention which is then formulated in the more general terms of Jews and Samaritans not associating with each other. The second set concerns the — for Jews and Samaritans — divisive issue of the right place to worship, the woman mentioning to Jesus that their fathers said that this mountain was the right place to worship whereas the Jews say it is Jerusalem. The formulation is all the more divisive because "this mountain" is in the — for Jews — alien environment of the narrative, Samaria. As such, it could be intended as a challenge to Jesus, the Jew; he dissolves it by pointing out that true worshippers worship the father neither on this mountain nor in Jerusalem, but in spirit and truth. The final set of figures is of Jesus accepting the hospitality of the Samaritan villagers — they go out to meet him and invite him to stay with them, which he does for two days — and of the villagers' recognizing him as the savior of the world. Jesus' staying for two days contrasts sharply with his passing through Samaria because he "had to."

In the case of the series of figures concerning the relationship between Jews and Samaritans, thus, Jesus' staying with the villagers and their recognizing him as the savior of the world reverses the initial figure of Samaria as an alien environment; however, not in such a way that the final figure supersedes the initial one as in the case of the series concerning the identity of Jesus. The full meaning of the final figure comes to expression in its relationship of opposition to the initial one. That relationship of opposition also characterizes other sets of figures: Jesus conversing with the woman contrary to the convention that Jews and Samaritans do not associate with each other to which the woman draws his attention, and his resolution of the issue of the right place to worship dissolving the Jewish-Samaritan alternatives of this mountain or Jerusalem.

b. *The Themes and the Roles*

Each of these three series of figures brings to expression a different theme. The theme *nourishment*, physical and spiritual, is represented by the figures concerning water and food; *disclosure of the identity of Jesus* by the various titles attributed to him (greater than Jacob, prophet, messiah, savior of the world), and such figures as Jesus claiming to make available water of life, revealing his supernatural knowledge to the woman, solving the issue of the right place to worship, claiming to have "other" food, which is to do the will of the one who sent him; and finally, the theme, *antagonism between Jews and Samaritans*, by Jesus passing through Samaria because he had to, the woman asking Jesus how he, a Jew, could ask her, a Samaritan woman, for a drink of water, the issue of the right place to worship, Jesus' statement that the Samaritans do not know what they worship, but that the Jews do know, "because salvation is from the Jews," the Samaritan villagers' invitation to Jesus, and his staying with them for two days.

All three themes culminate in Jesus' staying in the Samaritan village and the villagers' recognizing him as the savior of the world. The recognition of Jesus by the villagers distinctly rounds off the series of images concerning the disclosure of his identity. At the same time it is the one series which loses significance because it is completely superseded by the villagers' final recognition. The clarity with which their recognition of Jesus ends the series of figures representing the disclosure of his identity tends to draw attention to this series as the main theme of the narrative. The problem which such a suggestion poses is that it not only fails to recognize the significance of the other two themes, nourishment and antagonism between Jews and Samaritans, but also leaves unexplained what it means for Jesus to be the savior of the world. It is precisely the other two themes which give expression to that meaning.

The theme, nourishment, specifically, spiritual nourishment (doing the will of God), expressed by the complex series of figures concerning water of life and Jesus' other food (interpreted by means of the metaphor of the harvest which connects it with the final events of the narrative, the woman witnessing that Jesus may be the messiah, and Jesus accepting the invitation of the villagers to stay with them) makes it clear that it is Jesus' activity throughout the narrative which reveals him as the savior of the world. That activity concerns specifically the antagonism between Jews and Samaritans, the theme of the third series of figures. For Jesus to do the will of the one who sent him and to complete his work, as part of the theme, nourishment, means here specifically to break down the barrier between Jews and Samaritans. In order to carry out that task he solicits the help of the Samaritan woman. And so the entire narrative can be recognized as an expression of Jesus' activity as savior of the world.

The initial statement that Jesus had to pass through Samaria now appears in a new light. It may be intentionally ambiguous, expressing two meanings. In the beginning of the narrative its meaning appears to be that, as a Jew, Jesus passed through Samaria only because he could not avoid it. In light of the conclusion of the narrative it may mean that he passed through Samaria because he had to do so in obedience to the divine will. The necessity was not due to external circumstances, but obedience to the one who sent him. It should be noted, however, that it is only after the divine will to break down the antagonism between Jews and Samaritans had been accomplished that it becomes possible to understand the statement in this new light. In terms of the development of the story the same statement may express two different meanings depending on the perspective out of which it is considered.

In addition to the linking of figures in series which give expression to distinct themes, there is also a linking of figures as they give expression to thematic roles. Such roles are not interchangeable, but the actors are. So, for example, the role of partner in conversation with Jesus in connection with water and then food is filled first by the woman and then the disciples. In that role the woman and the disciples separately contribute to Jesus' clarification of the meaning of water of life and Jesus' other food by occupying a position contrary to that of Jesus, manifesting an inability to understand either water or food in any other than the ordinary sense. In that role the woman and the disciples remain uninvolved in the actual events of the narrative. This remains true throughout the narrative for the disciples, but the woman becomes involved in another more active role, that of preparing the villagers for their role in the final sequence of the narrative, as Jesus had prepared her for hers.

In that role the woman probes the identity of Jesus and the antagonism between Jews and Samaritans to the point where her witness moves the villagers to invite Jesus to stay with them and where her insights into his identity can be superseded by their recognition that he is the savior of the world. Her insights, partial as they are, so to speak, sow the seeds which come to full fruition in the recognition of the villagers. Her actions in this role are no longer representative of ordinary water, because she practices what it means to drink water of life. Whereas she stands opposite Jesus in her previous role of discussion partner, she is now his associate in a relationship in which she stands to him as water of life stands to his other food. They are bound as sower and reaper are bound by related but distinct functions. In the development of the story she almost imperceptibly moves from distanced uninvolvement in the action to a role that is decisive, second only to that of Jesus.

The disciples fill a rather limited, but clearly defined, role as partners in conversation with Jesus at a point where the woman is no longer available, but more importantly because it requires an understanding of Jesus to which she does not, or does not yet, have access, even though they too are still in need of instruction. It is a role which can be filled only by disciples, whoever they are. The role can be defined as of those who are in need of further instruction, but who already have a certain understanding of Jesus' identity.

The role of the villagers is that of willing recipients of the revelation of himself by Jesus. They invite him to stay with them and recognize him as the savior of the world. It is a role which is filled by various other characters elsewhere in the gospel, notably by the first disciples in chapter 1. There, one after the other, they change over to the role of witnessing (1:37-51), a role which was filled originally and pre-eminently by John the Baptist (1:29-37, cf. 1:6-7).

Jesus' role is highly complex. It is he who engages actively in involving the woman in the action, although there are moments when it is she who takes the initiative; e.g., when she proposes the topic of the right place to worship. In that regard the initiative moves to her and finally to the villagers, even though Jesus' role all through remains the most decisive. It is significant, however, that his active role remains, on the one hand, almost exclusively limited to verbal engagement, as already mentioned, engaging the woman in the action, and, on the other, interpreting the nature of things, water of life, true worship, and his other food. His only nonverbal action is that he stays with the Samaritan villagers for two days.

These actions are part of Jesus' engagement in the story itself. Distinct from them, and thus constituting a distinctive role, is his explanation of certain events of the narrative itself in terms of the metaphor of the harvest. In contrast with the activity just mentioned, Jesus' explanation could equally well have been given by someone who was not involved in the events, for example, by the narrator.

The most decisive feature of Jesus' role is as giver of the water of life, as the one whose food it is to do the will of the one who sent him. To this activity all others are subservient. Each segment of his conversation with the woman concludes with the issue of his identity, as does his conversation with the disciples — "my food is to do the will etc." — and with the villagers. Nothing provides greater cohesion to the various parts of the story than this gradual disclosure of the identity of Jesus. It is also what provides cohesion between the story and the various other parts of the gospel, and thus to the gospel as a whole.

The network of relationships between the roles, not specifically the characters, creates a structure which contributes decisively to the meaning of the story. The role which provides cohesion to the whole is that of Jesus, specifically his role as giver of the water of life who completes the work of the one who sent

him. He fulfills that role most specifically in his preparation of
the woman for her role as the metaphoric sower, and as the one
who reveals himself to the villagers in such a way that they recognize him as the savior of the world in contrast with the woman's witness about him. Except for his staying with the
Samaritan villagers he fills his role concretely as one who
instructs.

The second most important role is that of the woman who, in
turn, prepares the villagers for their role of inviting Jesus to stay
with them as willing recipients of his self-revelation as the savior
of the world. In that way she contributes decisively to making
that revelation possible.

That is the essential activity in the narrative. Its substance is
provided by the interaction between Jesus in his role as instructor (as distinct from that of self-revealer, even though the latter
is carried out concretely through the role of instructor), and,
first the woman, then the disciples in their roles of persons who
need instruction. Never in the narrative does he explicitly reveal himself, except when he tells the woman that he is Messiah.
The role of self-revelation is carried out concretely through his
role as instructor. For the latter role he requires the counter-
role of those who receive the instruction; first the woman —
water of life is not drinking water, and true worship is neither
on this mountain nor in Jerusalem, but of the Father in spirit
and truth — and then the disciples — his food is not what they
have to offer, but to do the will of the one who sent him, and to
complete his work. The meaning of the story is to be found es-
sentially in Jesus' role of self-revelation as the savior of the
world, but *what* it means is disclosed in his conversations about
the water of life, true worship, and his other food.

These figures, themes and roles give concrete expression to
deeper-lying values which in turn represent the fundamental
outlook, the micro-universe, out of which the text is generated.
Our next task is to try to identify the values to which the
themes, roles and figures give expression, and then, as the final
phase of our analysis, to describe the micro-universe which they
represent.

2. *The Values Expressed by the Themes*

a. *Nourishment*

The drinking water which Jesus requested and which the
woman could have provided if she had wanted to, and the food
which the disciples offered Jesus, or thought someone else had

brought him, represent the value /sustenance/,[7] i.e., of the body, the relief of physical thirst and hunger. This is quite obvious in the narrative, although the figures, water and food, could also represent other values. So, for example, in our narrative the figure of Jacob providing water for himself, his sons and their livestock, although satisfying their thirst, represents a different value, namely, /(miraculous) power/. In all the other instances, food and water in our text, and the figures related to them, represent the basic value of /sustenance/ of the body. That is also what unites all the figures concerning water and food in our narrative.

The refusal of food, as Jesus does when the disciples offer it to him (vv 31-33), could give expression to the value /asceticism/, although that does not seem to be the point here. This is confirmed by the parallel to Jesus' refusal, expressed by the figure of the woman leaving her jar as she departed for the village (v 28). There is nothing to suggest that asceticism was involved. She obviously became so absorbed in something else that she forgot — for the time being at least — what she had come to the well for in the first place, similar to Jesus no longer pursuing the issue of a drink of water when he becomes absorbed in the conversation with the woman, prompted by her drawing his attention to the impropriety of him, a Jew, asking her, a Samaritan woman, for a drink of water.

The value /sustenance/, represented by the figures of drinking water and the food offered by the disciples, evidently appears in the story for the sake of posing over and against it the contrary value represented by the figures of water of life and Jesus' other food, identified by Jesus in his conversation with the disciples as "doing the will of the one who sent me, and completing his work" (v 34). We may formulate it as /obedience/. It is in the relationship between these opposed values that their meanings come to expression. That relationship as it comes to expression in the narrative can be presented on a logical square as follows:

---

[7] The slash signs with which terms are enclosed signify values. The terms that represent the values do not actually occur in the narrative; they represent abstractions from the figures and themes that give expression to them.

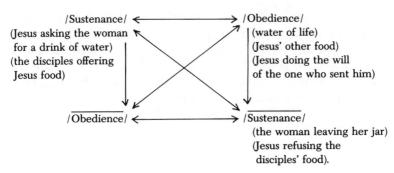

From this square it becomes clear that the rejection of /sustenance/ — represented on the square as /s̶u̶s̶t̶e̶n̶a̶n̶c̶e̶/ — does not represent a mere refusal of it, opposite to /sustenance/, but a value implied by the contrary of /sustenance/, namely, /obedience/. It is /obedience/ which calls for the /s̶u̶s̶t̶e̶n̶a̶n̶c̶e̶/. Only as the contrary of /obedience/ is the rejection of /sustenance/ called for. It is important to note that also logically both subcontraries, /o̶b̶e̶d̶i̶e̶n̶c̶e̶/ (i.e., disobedience) and /s̶u̶s̶t̶e̶n̶a̶n̶c̶e̶/ can be the case at the same time. It is possible to negate /sustenance/ and still not to affirm /obedience/. What that means according to the logic of the narrative is that the negation of /sustenance/, e.g., in the form of asceticism, does not necessarily imply /obedience/. The contradiction of /obedience/, i.e., /disobedience/, can still be the case even if one rejects /sustenance/.

On the other hand, /obedience/ does imply the contradiction, i.e., the rejection, of /sustenance/. It is not possible for both contraries, /sustenance/ and /obedience/ to be the case at the same time. What that means is that according to the narrative, /sustenance/ is negated as an implication of /obedience/. Similarly, Jesus asking the woman for a drink of water and the disciples offering him food implies /o̶b̶e̶d̶i̶e̶n̶c̶e̶/, not in some general sense, but specifically as an implication of /sustenance/, and that too understood specifically as the contrary of /obedience/. Before Jesus is presented with the call to /obedience/, i.e., before he is confronted by the woman's denial of his request for a drink of water, he unhesitantly asks the woman for a drink of water. Her reply, however, in which she calls his attention to the impropriety of him, a Jew, asking her, a Samaritan woman, for a drink of water, results in the need for a drink of water moving completely out of the perspective of the narrative as it develops further from that point on. The reason for this is apparently that the woman's reply presents Jesus with the call to /obedience/. Our further analysis will confirm that this is the case. When Jesus is confronted with the call to /obedience/, he can no longer be preoccupied with /sustenance/, as he tells the disciples in so many words, when they do not understand what he means when he refers to his other food (vv 31-34). One may thus establish a similar situation in connection with food. There is nothing to suggest that the disciples went to the village to buy food without Jesus' tacit approval, but by the time they return Jesus had already been presented with the call to /obedience/, which was contrary to the need for /sustenance/, and thus for the disciples' offer of food.

Jesus' doing the will of the one who sent him and completing his work represents the value /obedience/. This value is expressed concretely in the narrative by his activity of engaging in conversation with the woman and of staying with the villagers on their invitation; it is his other food. In his conversation with the disciples he explains to them that that activity of his is related to the activity of another person as the activity of the sower is related to that of the reaper, but in such a way that the former rejoices with the latter in the fruit of the harvest, an evident metaphor for the villagers' recognition of him as the savior of the world. Our previous analysis has left no doubt that the sower is a metaphor for the woman in her activity of witnessing to her fellow villagers concerning Jesus, the final outcome of which is their recognition of him as the savior of the world, represented metaphorically as the fruit of the harvest. Her activity expresses concretely in the narrative what it means to drink water of life; it is her /obedience/; that is why she abandons her jar when she leaves for the village, representing her abandonment of the desire for drinking water, the concern for /sustenance/, when she becomes engaged in the call for /obedience/.

We may now add these latter figures to the logical square presenting the values expressed in the narrative as we have analysed them thus far.

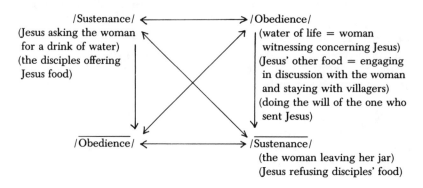

The series of figures which give expression to this system of values draw in the two other series of figures: Jesus' need for a drink of water moves out of the perspective of the narrative when the woman draws his attention to the impropriety of his asking her for a drink of water, a figure which contributes to the theme, opposition between Jews and Samaritans, and Jesus doing God's will finds its culmination in the villagers, recognizing him as the savior of the world, a figure which contributes to the theme, disclosure of Jesus' identity.

b. *The Disclosure of Jesus' Identity*

In the figures which give expression to the theme, disclosure of Jesus' identity, we encounter a situation in some respects similar to that concerning water and food; in both cases some of the figures call up values which have meaning in the narrative only in relationship to the counter-values to which they stand in opposition. In the case of the disclosure of Jesus' identity, all figures lead up to, and are surpassed by, the final one, the recognition of him as the savior of the world, in such a way that the earlier ones lose all further meaning. They have meaning, thus, only as they build up to this final recognition, and are exposed in their insufficiency by it. This is also stated with regard to the woman's recognition that Jesus may be the messiah: "It is no longer through what you said that we believe, for we ourselves have heard and we know that he is really the savior the world" (v 42). At the same time it is important to bear in mind that Jesus sanctions the woman's witness in relation to this final recognition by the villagers with the metaphor of the sower rejoicing with the reaper in the fruit of the harvest (v 36). This is in agreement with the distinction between the sower and the reaper. The villagers ironically confirm the distinction.

The values expressed by these figures are, on the one hand, Jesus conceived of in terms of /partisan salvation/ and, on the other, of /universal salvation/. The relationships between these values and the figures which give expression to them can be presented as follows on a logical square:

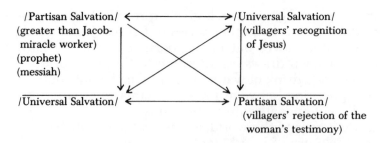

The implication of the recognition of Jesus in terms of /partisan salvation/, according to this logic, is that it is a negation of him as savior of the world, representing the value /universal salvation/. Nowhere in the text is a negative value explicitly attributed to /universal salvation/. It remains an implication of the attribution of positive value to national savior figures, representing the value /partisan salvation/. On the other hand, the negation of the value /partisan salvation/ is explicit in the villagers' rejection of the woman's testimony in which she presented Jesus as a national (i.e., Samaritan) savior.

A significant feature of the figures concerning the disclosure of Jesus' identity is that the Samaritan's recognition of him as the savior of the world is as such highly abstract, and in need of figures giving it concrete expression. As we will see, such an expression is probably given to it by the series of figures representing our third theme, the antagonism between Jews and Samaritans, i.e., those figures in the narrative which present the dissolution of that antagonism in the recognition that salvation is universal, i.e., in the Samaritan villagers' confession of Jesus as the savior of the world.

c.   *The Antagonism between Jews and Samaritans*

The series of figures concerning the antagonism between Jews and Samaritans are clearly also of two opposing kinds. On the one hand, there is the series which affirms this opposition: Jesus passing through Samaria because he had to, the parenthetic statement that Jews and Samaritans do not associate, the opposing positions of Jews and Samaritans concerning the right place to worship, and also Jesus' statement claiming that the Samaritans do not know what they worship, but that the Jews do, because "salvation is from the Jews." This antagonism is also confirmed by implication when the woman reminds Jesus that it is inappropriate for him as a Jew to ask her, a Samaritan woman, for a drink of water. This series of figures gives expression to a value which we can identify as /factional security/.

Opposed to it is another series of figures: Jesus asking the woman for a drink of water, his informing her that the time has come when true worshippers worship the Father in spirit and truth, and the Samaritans' inviting Jesus, a Jew, to stay with them, and Jesus accepting the invitation. It also comes to expression in Jesus' direct contradiction of the antagonism when he says that true worshippers will worship neither on this mountain nor in Jerusalem. What enhances these contrasting figures is that the action takes place in Samaria, through which Jesus passes because he had to, but where he finally accepts hospitality. The value to which these figures give expression may be formulated as /human solidarity/. The relationships between these values, and between the figures which represent them, can be presented as follows on a logical square.

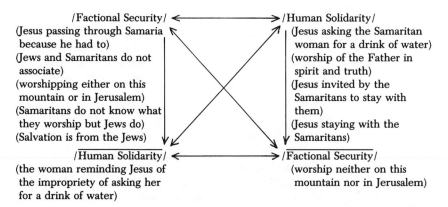

The tension which Jesus' statement in verse 22 represents in the narrative, "You do not know what you worship, but we worship what we know, because salvation is from the Jews," is confirmed by this network of relationships; it gives expression to the value, /factional security/, to which everything Jesus says and does is opposed, except for the ambiguous statement that he passed through Samaria because he had to.

d. *Conclusion*

Noteworthy is the close relationship between the opposed sets of values, /factional security/ versus /human solidarity/ and /partisan salvation/ versus /universal salvation/. In the single figure of the villagers' recognition of Jesus /as the savior of the world both /human solidarity/ and /universal salvation/ find positive expression. The closeness of the relationship between these two sets of values also becomes evident in the fact that it is possible to place all the figures expressing them under the one set /factional security/ versus /human solidarity/, revealing a remarkable unity of meaning.

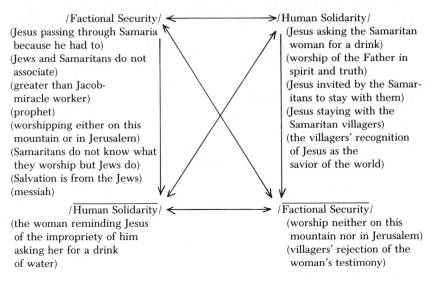

It is clear that the figures concerning Jesus' identity, expressing the opposed set of values /partisan salvation/ versus /universal salvation/ also give expression to the set /factional security/ versus /human solidarity/. All of these figures give expression to social values, religious values in the case of the figures giving expression to the /partisan salvation/ and /universal salvation/, and sociopolitical values in the case of the figures giving expression to /factional security/ and /human solidarity/. We may conclude then that the opposing sets give expression to a single set of opposed values at a deeper level.

That the integration of the figures concerning the identity of Jesus and the antagonism between Jews and Samaritans under a single set of opposed values, is not to be taken for granted is shown by the fact that the figures concerning nourishment cannot be similarly integrated. And yet, as we have seen, in what our text brings to expression there is close relationship between /obedience/ and /human solidarity/. When Jesus interprets what it means for him "to do the will of the one who sent me, and to complete his work," representing the value /obedience/, he points to figures that give expression to the value /human solidarity/, the villagers coming out to invite him to stay with them, including in his interpretation the woman's activity by means of the metaphor of the sower rejoicing with the reaper in the fruit of the harvest. The figures which give expression to the value /obedience/, namely, water of life and Jesus' other food, thus find concrete expression in those which express the value /human solidarity/, namely, Jesus engaging in discussion with the woman, the woman witnessing concerning Jesus, and Jesus staying with the villagers, as we have already shown above on the second square of the opposed values /sustenance/ and /obedience/.

The two sets of opposed values, /sustenance/ versus /obedience/ and /factional security/ versus /human solidarity/ with the coordinate set, /partisan salvation/ versus /universal salvation/, are generated from two distinct polarities in the micro-universe of John 4: the existential, which concerns issues of life and death, and the social, which concerns the way in which one relates to the world, which includes the relationship to other human beings. By giving attention to the way in which these two polarities are related to each in that micro-universe we should be able to come to an better understanding of the outlook out of which our text is generated.

3. *The Micro-universe of John 4*

In John 4, the value /obedience/ represents life, as the expression "water of life" makes adequately clear. But it is equally clear that the fundamental purpose of Jesus' activity is to give the opportunity of life (salvation) not only to the woman, but also to the villagers as the ultimate task set for him by God — his food is to do the will of the one who sent him and to complete the task — which is achieved when they recognize him as the savior of the world. The woman's activity is itself the partaking of life, drinking the water of life, and we may assume that Jesus' other food also sustains life for him. But it is a life that stands in opposition to the food that is intended for /sustenance/. Thus, in terms of the polarities we have already established between /obedience/ and /sustenance/ and everything that represents these opposed values, if /obedience/ represents life, /sustenance/ can only represent death. The figures which represent the opposed values /obedience/ and /sustenance/ thus give expression to the *existential* opposition between life and death which lies at the root of human existence.

In this existential polarity, the value /sustenance/, represented at a concrete level by an absorption by the concerns of the world which implies an evasion, a negation of life, represents an affirmation of death. Inversely, /obedience/, an affirmation of life lived in the face of death — one could say, in defiance

of it — implies a negation of death. This is stated in almost so
many words when Jesus tells the woman, "Everyone who drinks
of this water will thirst again; however, whoever drinks of the
water which I give will not thirst in eternity, but the water
which I give will become a well, springing up to eternal life" (vv
13-14). Thus we can place the oppositions representing the existential plane of human existence on a logical square as follows:

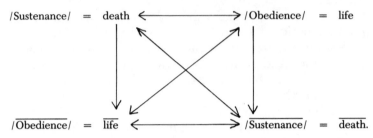

But our text also concerns another fundamental issue of
human existence, the *social* issue of the relationship to other
human beings. In our text this issue comes to expression in the
opposition between the security which we find in the familiar
group and openness to all human beings, which comes to expression in our text in the figures which represent the opposition between the sociopolitical values /factional security/ and
/human solidarity/, and the religious values /partisan salvation/
and /universal salvation/. It is an opposition between the alienation which human beings feel towards all but the familiar sociopolitical or religious group and a sense of integrity with all
human beings.

In the social polarity, the sociopolitical value /factional secur-
ity/ in our text, with its coordinate religious value /partisan sal-
vation/, represents social alienation concretely in terms of
membership in sociopolitical, religious groups opposed to each
other. Opposed to this in our text is the affirmation of a social
integration[8] with all of humanity, the breaking down of the bar-
riers between sociopolitical groups, and the understanding that

---

[8] The term "integration" has, of course, a very important social meaning in our
time. I use the term here in a broader sense than its concrete meaning in the current sociopolitical situation. This will become especially clear when I discuss the
way the opposition between social alienation and integration is handled in gnosticism where life is understood as equivalent with alienation from the world with all
of its social institutions, and integration in the world as equivalent to death. At the
same time, there should be no doubt that the contemporary meaning is included in
the micro-universe of our text as another way in which the opposition between
alienation and integration at the deepest, most abstract level of human existence
comes to concrete expression.

salvation is universal, representing the sociopolitical value /human solidarity/ with its coordinate religious value /universal salvation/. We can present this on a logical square as follows:

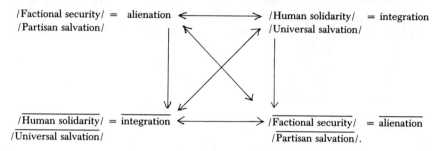

/Factional security/ = alienation ←————→ /Human solidarity/ = integration
/Partisan salvation/   /Universal salvation/

/Human solidarity/ = integration ←————→ /Factional security/ = alienation
/Universal salvation/   /Partisan salvation/.

Apart from the existential opposition between life and death and the social opposition between alienation and integration, there is a third, even more fundamental relationship to consider, the relationship which exists between these two sets of oppositions themselves. In our text that relationship is not understood as an opposition, but as we have seen, the value /obedience/ comes to concrete expression in actions which represent the value /human solidarity/, for example, Jesus' engaging in conversation with the woman and staying with the villagers on their invitation, as his other food, doing the will of the one who sent him and completing his work. According to our text, thus, the existential and the social values are coordinate, so that one can place all of them on a single square as follows:

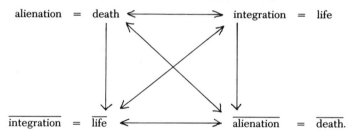

alienation = death ←————→ integration = life

integration = life ←————→ alienation = death.

With that, however, a crucial decision has already been made in our text at this level of its micro-universe. At an even deeper level of the text's micro-universe, a level which does not come to expression in it, the existential and social polarities are opposed to each other, as we will see when we consider other texts from the Fourth Evangelist's time.

What is involved in the opposition between the polarities, life/death and integration/alienation, can be illustrated best in Paul, who accepts both as relevant for human existence, but in radical opposition to each other.[9] It is not my intention to discuss his views in detail here. However, a brief consideration of the way the relationship between the issues of life and death and of alienation and integration comes to expression in his thought, and even more briefly in that of Matthew, can be helpful for an understanding of what is involved in John. In Paul's understanding, the human being exists in the tension between living in obedience to the Law and by faith, representing, respectively, the social and existential polarities. The most characteristic feature of his thought is that he rejects the attempt to escape from the tension between the two sets of polarities by denying one in favor of the other. In this way a new, single polarity representing the opposition between the existential and social micro-universes, between life/death and integration/alienation, becomes evident. It represents the micro-universe of the human being who is at the same time an individual and a social being. In the sense of Paul's thought, the relationship between these polarities in the micro-universe of the human being can be presented as shown below.

In the presentation of the Pauline and Matthaean micro-universes below, it should be noted that integration and alienation on the social plane are not Pauline or Matthaean concepts. The opposition for them lies at the even deeper, more universal level of good and evil, as distinguished by the Law, which do of course also manifest themselves in social opposition between alienation and integration. I use the terms integration and alienation here to bring out more clearly the similarity and contrast with John.

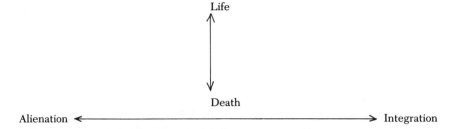

[9] For a discussion of the issue in Paul, see my "Polarities at the Roots of New Testament Thought," *Perspectives in Religious Studies. Essays in Honor of Frank Stagg* 11 (1984) 55-75 and "The Meaning of Christ in the New Testament: A Structuralist-Semantic Study," *Die Auslegung Gottes durch Jesus. Festgabe für Herbert Braun zu seinem 80. Geburtstag am 4. Mai 1983,* (ed. Luise and Willi Schottroff; Mainz: private publication, 1983) 17-56. Also published in a slightly revised form as "The Meaning of Christ in Paul's Writings. A Structuralist-Semiotic Study," *Biblical Theology Bulletin* 14 (1984) 131-144.

In Paul's thinking, resolution of the polarity of the individual, life/death, is provided by the gospel, whereas that of the social polarity, integration/alienation, is provided by the Law. That the Law represents the social polarity is shown by his statement that all the commandments of the Law are expressions of the single commandment to "love your *neighbor* as yourself" (Rom 13:9). In the relationship between the two polarities, what is achieved on the social axis by means of the Law (overcoming alienation by doing what the Law requires) is ignored by what is offered by the gospel through God's kindness (grace) on the existential axis of life and death; the free gift of God is completely independent of one's position on the horizontal axis between integration and alienation, between being a sinner (condemned by the Law), or righteous (obedient to the Law). "For the person who does not work (i.e., does not do what the Law requires), trusting (believing) rather in him who justifies the ungodly, his [/her] trust is taken as justification" (Rom 4:5).

It should be noted, however, that although the gospel does not make the gift of God dependent on human achievements in obedience to the Law, it does not invalidate such achievements. The human being, even though justified by faith alone according to Paul, continues to live on the horizontal plane of integration and alienation until the return of Christ. The gospel does not eliminate the distinction between good and evil as distinguished by the Law, and according to that distinction each will receive what is due on the horizontal plane of integration and alienation (cf. 1 Cor 3:11-15). The reward for what one achieves on that plane is in turn completely independent of what happens on the vertical axis of life and death. "For the person who works (does what the Law requires) the reward is not considered a gift, but is calculated in accordance with what is due" (Rom 4:4). Thus he could in the same sense also say: "Not those who hear the Law are just before God, but the doers of the Law will be justified" (Rom 2:13).

Paul, as we have seen, maintains the validity of both opposed polarities for humanity, life/death and integration/alienation, by disengaging them from each other. What happens on the one axis is irrelevant for, but not negated by, what happens on the other. This disengagement of the two polarities may be Paul's greatest achievement, even though it is what inevitably leads him to outright contradictions, such as the one just quoted: "Those who do what the Law requires will be justified (before God)" (Rom 2:13), and "No-one will be justified before him through works of the Law" (Rom 3:20, cf. Gal 2:16). The contradictions are resolved when one realizes that the two statements concern different aspects of human existence, belonging to the opposing polarities of life/death and integration/alienation which remain mutually unaffected by what happens on the other's axis.

It may be useful to present here two other, opposing ways of dealing with the tension between those two sets of polarities. Matthew offers a more one-sided solution. In a statement such as, "Not everyone who calls me, Lord, Lord, will enter into the kingdom of the heavens, but the person who does the will of my father who is in the heavens (i.e., what is prescribed by the Law)" (Mt. 7:21), he interprets the decisive factor in facing the ultimate not as faith in Christ, but obedience to the Law; the issue of life and death does not occur on the vertical, existential axis, but on the horizontal axis of social integration and aliena-tion. This is expounded in his Description of the Last Judgment in 25:31-46, according to which the final judgment will not be based on one's relationship to the Lord, but on one's behavior towards fellow human beings in need. In Matthew, obedience to the Law, doing what it requires, is not the means of securing one's justification, of establishing a claim before God. Doing what the Law requires brings to expression submission to God's justice. Matthew does not understand the Law in the sense of retributive justice, but of Torah, of a covenant which is estab-lished between God and his people, represented in the Parable of the Workers in the Vineyard (Mt 20:1-16) by the owner of the vineyard and the workers. They enter into a covenant in which the workers go to work in response to the owner's offer, "I will give you what would be just."

In Matthew the vertical polarity, life/death, has been ab-sorbed into the horizontal polarity, integration/alienation. The threat of death is overcome in the last judgement, not by faith (trust) in God's mercy (kindness) to the undeserving sinner, but by proof of one's engagement in the lot of one's fellow human beings as the expression of obedience to God's law; life has be-come identical with integration, death with alienation, on the horizontal, social plane of human existence. Existential anxiety is unrepresented in Matthew's micro-universe. He was evi-dently completely comfortable with doing what the Law re-quires. One could present his solution to the fundamental opposition between the polarities life/death and aliena-tion/integration as follows:

Death = ⟵————————————————————————————⟶ Life =
Alienation   Integration

Another, radically one-sided, solution to the opposition between the vertical and the horizontal polarities is offered by
gnosticism. When the tension between alienation and integration on the horizontal plane became intolerable, as happened in
the Hellenistic age, the validity of that polarity was denied; the
human being was taken to be an alien in the social, as opposed
to the existential, environment of the world, the realm of death.
Life — on the vertical plane of life and death — is gained by
negating the world and its demands of integration as the realm
of death. In the opposition between the vertical and the horizontal polarities, death and integration are taken to be identical.
Life means to recognize that one is an alien in the world. For
Paul, as we have seen, what happens on the social axis is imma-
terial for salvation by faith alone on the vertical axis of life and
death, and inversely, the achievement of integration with society by doing what the Law requires has nothing to do with an
act of God's kindness. In contrast, the typical gnostic view was
that life was identical with alienation, death with integration.
The two polarities are collapsed into a single, vertical one,
which can be presented as follows:

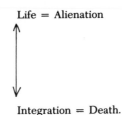

Life = Alienation

Integration = Death.

The Fourth Evangelist is not a gnostic, but the gospel contains many statements that give expression to a view that is similar to that of the gnostics, namely, that salvation can be achieved
only in opposition to this world. Examples are Jesus' promise to
the disciples that he goes to heaven (the house of his father) to
prepare a place for them and that he will return and take them
with him to be where he is (14:1-3), and his repeated statements
in the great prayer to the Father in chapter 17 that his followers
do not belong to this world, as little as he and the Father do (cf.
esp. vv 15-16). The problem of the tension between the vertical
polarity, life/death, and the horizontal polarity, integra-
tion/alienation, is dealt with in fundamentally similar ways in
gnosticism and in the Fourth Gospel. In both, life is understood

in opposition to engagement in the world. An important difference, however, is that, whereas liberation from involvement in the world comes about through knowledge (*gnosis*) in gnosticism, it takes place in a fellowship of love in the Fourth Gospel. How this is to be understood will become clear as we now follow the generative trajectory from the deepest level of its micro-universe to the surface level of the actual text.

Chapter 2

THE GENERATIVE TRAJECTORY OF JOHN 4: FROM THE ABSTRACT LEVEL TO THE CONCRETE TEXT

Introduction

In our analysis of John 4 we ended at the level of the micro-universe, not only of the text's author, but of the entire culture of which he was a part. With that the actual text was left temporarily behind. Syntactic and semantic abstraction is a useful means of determining the meaning of a text, but the abstractions themselves are not substitutes for the meaning; they are what the term signifies, abstractions. It is like analysing a difficult sentence in a foreign language by clarifying the meanings of its individual terms and its syntax, i.e., its components of meaning and the way they are structured to produce its meaning effect. After such an analysis it is necessary to return to the actual sentence to determine whether the analysis has provided the means of understanding it. In a similar way, to complete our investigation, and to fulfill its purpose, we need to reverse the analysis by following the generative trajectory of the text back from the deepest level the author's micro-universe to the level of the text itself. Similar to the analysis, we will follow the generative trajectories of the syntactic and semantic components separately, beginning in this case with the latter.

When I state now that the author of the Fourth Gospel made certain choices in dealing with the polarities in the micro-universe which he shared with his culture, this should not be taken as conscious choices, as little as the native speaker is aware of grammatical choices when she/he speaks or writes. The choices the author of a text makes (beyond the limits of her/his sentences) are determined by the framework of meaning out of which the text is generated. At the deepest semantic level those choices are determined by the given micro-universe of the culture which the author shares. The first level of choices concerns the values which the author attributes to the various components of that micro-universe. At a slightly higher level, i.e.,

closer to the surface level of the text, these values are transformed into themes, which at a still higher level come to expression concretely in the actual figures in terms of which the
narrative unfolds. Similar generative features of the text can be
stated with regard to the syntactic component, but to begin
with we will limit ourselves to the semantic component, following the generative trajectory of the text from its micro-universe
to its figures.

A.   FROM THE MICRO-UNIVERSE TO THE FIGURES

1. *The Micro-universe*

The author of our chapter dealt with the fundamental polarities in a way different from all three others we discussed above,
Paul, Matthew and the gnostics. In some ways he comes closer
to the gnostics, but compared with them he also reveals significant differences.

In our text, Jesus' refusal of the disciples' offer of food for the
sake of doing the will of the one who sent him appears to give
expression to a view very similar to that of the gnostics — denial
of the things of the world for the sake of heaven. Similarly, the
woman abandons her water jar for the sake of witnessing about
Jesus. These concerns are coordinated in Jesus' statement about
the sower rejoicing with the reaper in the fruit of the harvest (v
36); both represent the value /obedience/. Compared to the
gnostic view, however, our text has an important twist in this
affirmation of heaven against earth on the vertical polarity of life
and death. In John 4 the meaning of /obedience/ is interpreted
as an affirmation of the values /human solidarity/ and /universal
salvation/ on the horizontal plane of social integration versus
alienation, contrary to the values /factional security/ and /parti-
san salvation/.

In this regard one is almost reminded of Matthew. However,
in our chapter the vertical polarity is not absorbed into the horizontal as it is in Matthew; rather, the horizontal is absorbed into
the vertical. In the recognition of Jesus as the savior of the world
the values /universal salvation/ and /human solidarity/ are realized, but it is Jesus' responsibility before God, representing the
existential value /obedience/, which is fulfilled in that recognition. The values /human solidarity/ and /universal salvation/
are recognized on the vertical plane, i.e., before God, not on the
horizontal plane, before society. /Factional security/ and /parti-
san salvation/ are overcome, not by reconciliation with others,
but by entering into the community of those who recognize him

who was sent by God as the savior of the world, i.e., by being drawn out of the horizontal dimension of human strife into the vertical dimension of those who accept the call of a savior who represents the value /obedience (to God's will)/.

In Jesus' activity as savior of the world, the existential value /obedience/ is affirmed as a realization of the values /universal salvation/ and /human solidarity/. This agrees with another feature characteristic of the gospel: love as that which constitutes life and human solidarity, and hate which constitutes alienation and death. In the Fourth Gospel love always belongs with the divine: never is it said that God or Jesus hates. a. The Father loves Jesus (3:35; 10:17; 15:9; 17:24, 26); he also loves those who keep Jesus' commandments (14:23), i.e., Jesus' disciples (17:23); God's love for the world is motivated by his desire to save those who believe (3:16). b. Jesus loves the Father (14:31); also his disciples (13:1; 13:34; 14:23; 15:9; 17:23); he has particular love for certain individuals: Martha, Mary and Lazarus (11:5, cf. 11); and a certain disciple (13:23; 19:26; 21:7, 20; 21:20). c. Jesus tells his disciples that he gives them just one commandment, to love each other as he loved them; if they loved him they would keep his commandments (13:34f; 14:15, esp. vv 23-24, and 15:9-13). The love with which God loved Jesus should also be in his followers (17:26). d. Jesus' followers, specifically Peter, are called upon to love him (14:15, 21, 28; cf. 21:15-17). e. The Jews would love Jesus if God were their father (8:42), but they do not have the love of God in them (5:42).

Hate, the contrary of love, characterizes the world. The world loves darkness, because its works are evil. a. The world hates Jesus (7:7; 15:18, 23-25); also the Father (15:24); and Jesus' followers (15:18-19; 17:14; but note 7:7). One should not include in this category hate of one's own life in this world (12:25). b. Jesus does not come to judge, i.e., condemn, the world (3:17); it is by its own attitude of disbelief, its hate of the light, that the world judges itself (3:18-20, and especially 12:47-48).

Thus, one could say that a new community of love, standing over and against the world with its hate and strife, has been established by the revelation of God in Jesus. It shares with gnostic docetism a turning away from the world, an aloofness from it, aware of its own participation in the divine qualities revealed by Jesus. Decisively different from gnosticism, however, is the quality through which the community understands itself not to belong to the world. It is the exclusiveness of knowledge which separates the gnostics from the world; it is the graciousness of love which characterizes the gospel. More important for our purposes here is that, compared with a typical gnostic view, the polarity, alienation versus integration, is reversed. The Fourth Evangelist shares the gnostics' negative view of the world, but it is the world that is characterized by alienation. In that way the existential loneliness is overcome in a new society of those who belong to the new community that is characterized by the integrative power of love. The "Hymn of the Pearl" in the apocryphal *Acts of Thomas* may be an even more impressive example of the reversal of the alienation/integration polarity. Two-thirds of this fairytale-like story describes the caring love of everyone in the community of the prince's father's kingdom.

One can present the fundamental outlook of the Fourth Gospel and the "Hymn of the Pearl" as follows:

Love = Life

Hate = Death

Love and hate are not explicit in our chapter, although one can sense their presence even if it is only vaguely in the background. This is the micro-universe out of which John 4 is generated. At this fundamental level of the chapter's micro-universe a very important decision has thus already been made, not consciously, but in the sense of its generative grammar. It is a decision that is taken for granted in the fundamental outlook of the chapter. There is no further reflection on it. Compared with Paul and Matthew, our author shares the gnostics' negative view of the world, but compared with them, his understanding is that freedom from the binding to the world is achieved not through knowledge, but love. Love is the power by means of which the social values /partisan salvation/ and /factional security/, equivalent to the existential value /sustenance/, are surrendered in favor of the values /human solidarity/ and /universal salvation/ that are equivalent to the existential value /obedience/, that is, to the will of God, and not to the divisive demands of the world. What we need to do now is to see how that generation takes place, first by identifying the system of values generated out of this micro-universe.

2. *The System of Values*

In our previous discussion we already included considerations concerning the system of values for the sake of clarifying the micro-universe of our text. What we need to do now is to give attention to the system of values itself.

On the vertical plane, i.e., the only one recognized as relevant in John, the value /obedience/ represents life; the contrary value /sustenance/ represents death. Insofar as /obedience/ in our text is contrary to the worldly, human value /sustenance/ (cf., especially, vv 31-34), it represents a negation of the physical needs of society. /Sustenance/ represents an affirmation of these needs. The decisive generative move in our text is that the value /obedience/ has come to represent the means by which the divisiveness, i.e., alienation between Jews and Samaritans is overcome. By his obedience, Jesus realized the value /human solidarity/, culminating in the villagers' recognition of him as the savior of the world, which brings to expression the value /universal salvation/. In their invitation to Jesus that he stay with them, and the recognition of him as the savior of the world, the Samaritans removed themselves from the social plane of this world with its divisiveness, represented by the values /factional security/ and /partisan salvation/ — it is equivalent to death on the vertical plane. They did so by becoming participants in life, first by inviting Jesus to stay with them, thus realizing the value /human solidarity/, and then by recognizing him as the savior of the world, realizing the value /universal salvation/. Similarly, by dropping her jar, symbolizing her rejection of the value /sustenance/, in order to participate in doing God's will by telling the villagers about Jesus, and so realizing the value /obedience/, the woman also contributed to the realization of the values /human solidarity/ and /universal salvation/. Actually she already realized the value /human solidarity/ by her continued conversation with Jesus, a Jew, which represents an existential decision against the value /factional security/ of the society from which she came.

In the system of values underlying our text, thus, the existential value /obedience/ is affirmed as a decision for life, which represents, at the same time, negation of the worldly value /sustenance/, representing death and solidarity with the world. More decisive is that in our text the tension between /factional security/ and /partisan salvation/, on the one hand, and /human solidarity/ and /universal salvation/, on the other, is not resolved on the horizontal, social plane of activity in the world, but by removing Jews and Samaritans from their involvement in the world in which they are divided into opposed religious groups, and so making the social opposition between alienation and solidarity an issue of life and death. In this way, contrary to the fundamental gnostic solution which identifies life with alienation (from the world), and integration (in the world) as death, our author identifies alienation with death, and integration, concretely, the overcoming of the opposition between Jews and Samaritans, with life. The identification is similar to what we mentioned for Matthew. However, whereas Matthew understands the resolution of the opposition between alienation and solidarity to take place on the horizontal, social level, i.e., through activity in the world, which is for him at the same time the resolution of the opposition between life and death — to love the neighbor is not a work for which one can expect a reward in accordance with what is due, but an act of obedience, based on trust[10]—our author resolves the opposition between alienation and solidarity on the horizontal, social plane by interpreting it as an existential issue of life and death. Jews and Samaritans are reconciled, not as Jews and Samaritans, but as members of the new community of true worshippers who recognize Jesus as the savior of the world. The opposed socio-religious communities which belong to this world, and in which alienation is realized, are absorbed into a new community which does not belong to this world. In that way a negative value is attached to the horizontal social plane which represents alienation and death, with the community of true worshippers representing solidarity and life. With that, in the system of values underlying the chapter, the entire social plane has become identified with death, which is represented not only by the value /sustenance/ but, probably more importantly, the values /factional security/ and /partisan salvation/ as well. And so a transformation of values has been realized. By identifying the social values /universal salvation/ and /human solidarity/ with the ex-

---

[10] In the Parable of the Workers in the Vineyard (Mt 20:1-16), the laborers who had worked the whole day expected everyone to be paid in accordance with the amount of work they had done. Contrary to their expectations, however, the owner of the vineyard rewarded all the workers equally, disregarding the differences in the number of hours they had worked. A wage had been agreed upon only with the first workers (Mt 20:2). All the other groups trusted that the owner would be fair when he told them, "I will give you what would be just *(ho ean ē dikaion"* (v 4, cf. 5 and 7). The conflict is here between retributive justice and a justice based on the owner's kindness, represented, respectively, by the claim of those who worked the entire day, and the owner's justification of his action, "Am I not permitted to do what I want with what is mine. Or do you have an evil eye because I am generous?" (v 15).

istential value /obedience/, as representative of life, all the values involved become transformed. The existential value /obedience/ can no longer be taken in the sense of an isolation from the rest of humanity, but as something that takes place in solidarity with others. At the same time, the fundamentally social values, /human solidarity/ and /universal salvation/ are no longer understood as social, but as existential. Similarly, the negative existential value, /sustenance/, is taken to be equivalent to the social values /factional security/ and /partisan salvation/.

The understanding in our chapter that life in an existential sense is equivalent to solidarity in the social sense, and all that follows from it, can then be presented logically as in the diagram below.

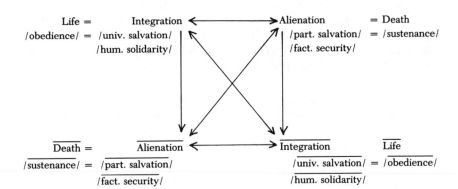

This square presents the logic behind the system of values of John 4. As already indicated, the values have to be understood in relation to each other. So, for example, /sustenance/ is not evaluated negatively by itself, but in relationship to /obedience/, i.e., as it comes to stand in opposition to /obedience/. At the surface level of our text this is clear when Jesus unhesitantly asks the woman for a drink of water, /sustenance/, but then abandons all concern for the drink when her response demands of him an engagement in a discussion with her concerning matters of life and death, ending in her witnessing about him to the villagers, and so contributing decisively to his task of doing the will of the one who sent him, /obedience/. Our analysis has shown that for him to do the will of the one who sent him (v 34) refers to his activity in relation to the woman, and to complete that work in the activity he was about to engage in with regard to the Samaritan villagers. In this way /sustenance/ is negated in relationship to, and in favor of, /obedience/. This is even more explicit in relation to the disciples. Jesus had evidently agreed, at least tacitly, with their departure to buy food, /sustenance/, but when they offer the food to him he rejects it because, in the meantime, he had been confronted with the task of doing God's will, /obedience/, as he himself explains (v 34).

Similarly, negation of the value /factional security/ has meaning only in opposition to /human solidarity/. The qualification "factional" already has a negative connotation in itself which is defined by its opposition to solidarity with all of humanity, expressed by the value /human solidarity/. /Human solidarity/ thus implies the negation of /factional security/, and in the same way /factional security/ implies the negation of /human solidarity/. Similarly, /partisan salvation/ and /universal salvation/ should be understood in opposition to each other. Affirmation of the one implies negation of the other.

Our chapter of course does more than present the system of oppositions between the values. As we have already noted more than once, it affirms certain values, and negates others. This can be presented on a semiotic square as follows:

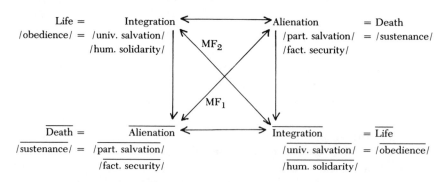

We know already that in our text the Fourth Evangelist affirms that participation in life, associated with the value /obedience/, is achieved through realization of the values /universal salvation/ and /human solidarity/. The way this is brought about according to the text is by negating the value /sustenance/, representing death, and the values /partisan salvation/ and /factional security/, representing social alienation. We refer to this move in the deep structure of the text as a macro-function, MF_1. As indicated on the square, these negations are implied, i.e., presupposed, by the affirmation of the value /obedience/, representing life, and the values /universal salvation/ and /human solidarity/, representing life and alienation from the world, but social integration at the deeper level of the text's micro-universe. This action is represented by MF_2 on the square. Affirmation of life and social integration and the values /obedience/, /universal salvation/ and /human solidarity/, implies, i.e., presupposes, that death and social alienation, and the values /sustenance/, /partisan salvation/ and /factional security/ are negated. The inverse is not true. Negation of death and social alienation, and the values representing them, does not imply affirmation of life and social integration, and the values representing them.

The text typically first presents the values that are to be negated — /sustenance/, /factional security/ and /partisan salvation/, and the negation of the opposed values, /obedience/, /human solidarity/ and /universal salvation/. (There is no figure in the text which represents the actual negation of /obedience/. It remains an implication of the affirmation of the opposed value /sustenance/.) The fundamental purpose is then to move from the affirmation of the former values to their negation, and to the affirmation of the latter, including /obedience/. The move from the presentation to the negation of the former values is represented as MF_1 on the semiotic square, and the move from the negation to the affirmation of the latter as MF_2. The system of values represented by these moves constitutes the meaning of the story at its deepest level, the macro-structure of the text. It is what Teun van Dijk referred to in the following, highly significant, statement: ". . . semantic macro-structures are necessary to explain in sufficiently simple terms how it is possible that throughout a text the selection of lexical items and the underlying formation of semantic presentations is heavily restricted by some global restraint."[11] The rest is merely a question of how this is realized concretely in the text, which does not mean that its meaning is limited to this deepest level.

Our next step is to note how this system of values is thematized and then presented concretely in the figures and images of the text.

3. *Thematization*

From the fact that in our text's system of values there is a move from the presentation of the values /sustenance/, /factional security/ and partisan salvation/ to their negation, and the affirmation of the contrary values /obedience/, /human solidarity/ and /universal salvation/, it follows that the themes also represent that move. Thus the theme *nourishment* moves from

[11] Teun A. van Dijk, *Some Aspects of Text Grammars*, (The Hague/Paris: Mouton, 1972) 160.

the presentation of the natural human needs of water and food to their negation in favor of the spiritual needs of the water of life and Jesus' other food, representing the move from /sustenance/ to /obedience/. Similarly, the theme *antagonism between Jews and Samaritans* represents a move from the affirmation of /factional security/ to its negation, and the affirmation of the contrary value /human solidarity/, and *disclosure of Jesus' identity*, the move from the affirmation of /partisan salvation/ to its negation and the affirmation of the contrary value /universal salvation/.

This move from the one set of values to the other, opposed set in the system of values is effected by means of the various roles of the characters in the story. We can now distinguish more clearly than in the analytical part of our inquiry three basic roles: a. presentation of the values /sustenance/ (drinking water and the disciples' food), /factional security/ (the opposition between Jews and Samaritans), and /partisan salvation/ (the opposition between worship on either "this" mountain or in Jerusalem), and negation of the contrary values (for example, in the woman's reminding Jesus of the impropriety of his asking her for a drink of water), b. the move from the one set of values to the other, and c. negation of the given set of values, and affirmation of the contrary set, /obedience/ (doing the will of the one who sent Jesus by the woman and himself), /human solidarity/ (the Samaritans' invitation that Jesus stay with them, and his acceptance of the invitation), and /universal salvation/ (the true worshippers worshipping the Father in spirit and truth, and the Samaritans' acceptance of Jesus as the savior of the world). All the other roles, for example, Jesus' conversation partners, etc., are subservient to these three. The main role is clearly that of effecting the move from the one set of values to the other.

We will discuss the characters who fill these roles more specifically later. At this stage it is worth noting that none of these roles is bound to a single character. So, for example, it is Jesus himself who, to begin with, presents the value /sustenance/ by asking the woman for a drink of water; actually it is already hinted at by the image of him sitting on the side of the well, weary from the journey. It is also his role initially to present the value /factional security/ through the figure of having to pass through Samaria because he *had to*. Nevertheless, his is the main role of effecting the move from the one set of values to the other, a role which he fulfills successfully with the essential collaboration of the woman. It is noteworthy that, on the one hand, the disciples never move beyond the role of presenting the value /sustenance/, and, on the other, that the villagers are found only in the role of negating the values /factional security/ and /partisan salvation/, and affirming the opposed values /human solidarity/ and /universal salvation/.

As the previous paragraph suggests, these themes and roles find concrete expression in the figures and images of the story.

4. *Figures and Images*

The basic images by means of which the theme *nourishment* is brought to expression are water and food. The value /sustenance/ is represented by drinking water and the disciples' food and /obedience/ by water of life and Jesus' "other" food. Water of life and Jesus' other food are interpreted by Jesus as doing the will of the one who sent him and completing his work. These images are made effective by a series of figures (or a figurative course).

Jesus' asking the woman for a drink of water presents the value /sustenance/. This value is not negated in the text by an explicit rejection of the drink of water by Jesus and not by the woman's refusal of the request, which is motivated by the convention of non-association of Jews and Samaritans, representing the value /factional security/. However, the further development of the story leaves no doubt that Jesus does negate /sustenance/ as presented originally by his request for a drink. In his statement in verse 34 he distinguishes between doing the will of the one who sent him and completing his work. Doing the will of the one who sent him obviously refers to that in which he had already been involved, namely, his engagement in discussion with the woman, ending with her leaving her water jar behind as she departed to witness concerning him in her village. The negation of the value /sustenance/ is made explicit by his refusal of the disciples' offer of food with the justification that he has other food of which they do not know. One may assume that in declining the disciples' food, Jesus also declines drinking water. In this regard the woman's action of leaving her water jar behind is more explicit as a negation of /sustenance/ in terms of the image of drinking water. Her negation is reinforced by the affirmation of /obedience/ by witnessing concerning Jesus. Her actions evidently mean an acceptance of the water of life offered by Jesus, an image which is paralleled by that of his "other" food, the two together representing the value /obedience/.

The action of the disciples, offering food to Jesus, represents an affirmation of /sustenance/. Within the framework of our text's system of values it implies the negation of /obedience/, but they obviously never realize that.

The negation of the value /sustenance/ by two figures that occur in close proximity to each other in the text (vv 28 and 32), the woman leaving her water jar behind and Jesus declining the food offered by the disciples, marks a decisive transition in the movement from the one set of values to the other. These two figures are followed immediately by an affirmation of the value /obedience/, expressed by the woman witnessing concerning Jesus, by Jesus' interpretation of his own activity in terms of the image of his other food, clarified further as doing the will of the one who sent him, and staying with the villagers for two days as the completion of his work.

The theme *disclosure of Jesus' identity* comes to expression basically by means of the titles ascribed to him, a greater miracle worker than Jacob, a prophet, the messiah and the savior of the world. The first three represent the value /partisan salvation/, and the fourth, the value /universal savior/. Actually the title messiah is ambiguous; the woman understands it in a partisan, i.e., Samaritan, sense, whereas Jesus evidently intends it in a sense which concerns everyone, as the context of his prior conversation concerning true worship reveals. These images once again become effective in a series of figures.

The value /partisan salvation/ is presented by the woman challenging Jesus that he is not greater than "our father Jacob," i.e., a greater miracle worker. Jesus meets this challenge by demonstrating his extraordinary knowledge about the woman, which is promptly sanctioned by her when she identifies him as a prophet and when she suggests that he may be the messiah because he told her everything about herself. The negation of this value occurs only at the end of the text when the villagers reject the woman's witness in favor of their deeper insight into Jesus' identity, namely, that he is the savior of the world. The negation of the woman's testimony, and so of the value /partisan salvation/, is followed immediately by an affirmation of the value /universal salvation/ by attributing to Jesus the dignity of the savior of the world.

The negation of /partisan salvation/ and the affirmation of /universal salvation/ is brought to expression even more concretely by means of the figures representing the theme *antagonism between Jews and Samaritans*. Under this theme the value /factional security/ is presented by means of the figures of Jesus passing through Samaria because he *had to*, the clarifying remark that Jews and Samaritans do not associate, the controversy concerning the right place to worship, and Jesus' statement that the Samaritans do not know what they worship, but the Jews do, because salvation is from the Jews.

Affirmation of /human solidarity/, when Jesus asks the woman for a drink of water, precedes the presentation of /factional security/. The woman reminding Jesus of the impropriety of him, a Jew, asking her, a Samaritan woman, for a drink of water, introduces the negation of /human solidarity/, and affirmation of /factional security/ which the divisive convention represents. At the same time her statement asserts that Jesus, by his openness to her, had already negated the convention, and thus the value /factional security/. With her statement she indicates that his affirmation of /human solidarity/ by his openness to her implies the negation of /factional security/, represented by the divisive convention.

It is worthy of note that it is the same action with which Jesus presents one of the values to be negated, /sustenance/, by asking the woman for a drink of water, with which he also affirms the value /human solidarity/. It is the decisive importance of this latter value which motivates him under the circumstances to deny the value /sustenance/ and to engage in the affirmation of /obedience/ by his further discussion with the woman in obedience to the will of the one who sent him, representing the affirmation of /human solidarity/.

The woman, by her participation in the conversation with Jesus, also contributes to the negation of the divisive convention which represents /factional security/, and the affirmation of /human solidarity/. It is important to note that in doing so she too makes an existential decision against worldly solidarity, representing /death/. Her decision culminates in the dropping of her water jar and witnessing concerning Jesus, representing the value /obedience/.

In the discussion of the right place to worship the woman once more presents the value /factional security/ by drawing attention to the divisive views of Jews and Samaritans on the matter. Jesus explicitly negates /factional security/ by insisting that the time has come when worship would be neither on "this mountain," nor in Jerusalem, and then affirms the opposing value /human solidarity/ by proposing that true worshippers will worship the Father in spirit and truth, i.e., without factional distinctions. Then, remarkably, he himself reaffirms /factional security/ by maintaining that the Samaritans do not know what they worship but Jews do, because salvation is from the Jews. It is noteworthy that this affirmation of /partisan security/ is never reversed in the text, but is in a sense confirmed by the subsequent reference to the disciples harvesting where they did not sow (v 38), a metaphoric reference to the Samaritans as the missionary field, benefiting from, and thus finding themselves on the receiving end of the privileged activity of the disciples. The point of view of these two passages runs counter to everything we have learned so far about the macro-structure of the text. That is another reason for considering them secondary.

In the story itself it is neither Jesus nor the disciples, but the Samaritan villagers, prepared by the woman's witness, who take the initiative in affirming /human solidarity/. By coming to Jesus they negate /factional security/, represented by the convention of non-association between Jews and Samaritans, and by inviting him, a Jew, to stay with them, they affirm /human solidarity/ concretely between Jews and Samaritans. Jesus confirms their set of values by accepting the invitation, and staying with them for two days.

The recognition of Jesus as the savior of the world draws all three themes together. With their confession the villagers seal the solidarity of Jews and Samaritans; they affirm the value /human solidarity/ by recognizing Jesus, a Jew, as their savior. In their recognition of him as the savior of the *world* they also affirm the value /universal salvation/, and as the crowning of Jesus' activity of doing the will of the one who sent him, and completing his work, their confession sanctions affirmation of the value /obedience/. They exclude the woman from this sanction, but, as we know, Jesus included her with his metaphor of the sower who is not identical with the reaper, but rejoices with the reaper in the fruit of the harvest. The entire story can thus be presented on a single semiotic square, representing the concretization of the macro-structure of our text in the figures of the story. It will be noted that compared with our previous presentation of the semiotic square above (without the figures) death and alienation now comes on the upper left corner of the square, with integration and life on the upper right corner. The reversal has no significance, except that it is more convenient to read the square, now with the figures, in our accustomed way from left to right.

By means of the square we can read the story paradigmatically, beginning on the upper left side with the figures representing death and alienation, and the values /sustenance/, /partisan salvation/ and /factional security/, downwards in the columns to the bottom left side, representing the implied negation of life and integration, and the values /obedience/, /universal salvation/ and /human solidarity/. From this set of values we follow the movement from the top left to the bottom right along the arrow representing macro-function 1 to the figures representing the negation of alienation and death, and the values which give expression to them. Finally we follow from the bottom left to the top right along the arrow representing macro-function 2 to the figures representing the affirmation of integration and life, and the values /universal salvation/, /human solidarity/ and /obedience/.

What may be the most important thing to note is that Jesus' "engaging in discussion with the woman," and "staying with the Samaritan villagers" occurs under "life" and the value /obedience/, as well as under "integration" and the value /human solidarity/. That once more underlines the integrity — in the deep structure of our text — of life and integration, and of the existential value /obedience/ and the social value /human solidarity/.

THE ENTIRE SEMANTIC COMPONENT OF JOHN 4 ON A SINGLE SQUARE

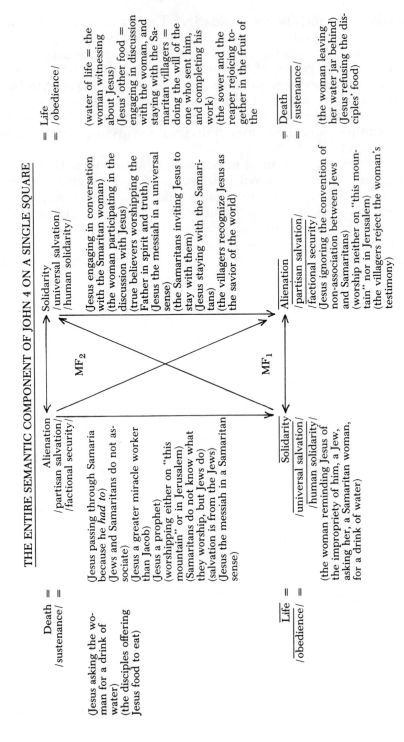

B. FROM THE FUNDAMENTAL SYNTAX TO THE
SURFACE LEVEL OF THE TEXT

Introduction

Having now followed the generative trajectory of the text's semantic component from the abstract level of its micro-universe to the level of the figures in which its meaning comes to concrete expression, we now need to do the same with the syntactic component. We will begin at a level where there are merely subjects of circumstance in conjunction with or disjunction from objects — at that level the objects are the values /sustenance/, /obedience/, etc. — and active subjects performing functions of disjoining or conjoining the subjects of circumstance with the objects. As we move up to the surface level of the text's discourse syntax the roles of these subjects will be taken over by characters, and the value-objects by the concrete objects in the process of actorialization. In that way the communication of meaning in the text will take on the form of a story, which also means that it becomes located in a spatial and a temporal framework. Our task will be to note the structure of relationships between subjects and objects, and how these abstract entities are concretized in actual persons, such as Jesus and the woman, and real things, such as drinking water, the water of life, etc.; how relationships are changed by the actions of subjects, e.g., Jesus' revealing knowledge to the woman about her husbands, or the woman's leaving Jesus to witness about him to the villagers, and how the text is placed in a specific place and time. Our task will be to see whether the abstract syntactic structure which we have identified for the text is recognizable in its concrete form.

It may be worth reminding ourselves here again that we are describing a synchronic, grammatical-generative process, not a diachronic procedure which took place, consciously or subconsciously, in the mind of the author as he produced the text. Our task is to describe how the text brings its meaning to expression, not how the author went about producing the text. Only where the interpretation of the text's generative grammar itself demands it have we considered, and will again if necessary consider, features of its actual production, for example, the tension produced in the semantic and syntactic structure of the text by Jesus' statements in verses 22 and 38.

1. Opposed Sets of Values

The fundamental generative-syntactic step in our text is to

place subjects in circumstances of conjunction with or disjunction from the value-objects of the system of values. From that system we can identify the following objects with their formal designations in parentheses: /obedience/ (O_{1c}), /sustenance/, which in the text's system of values is the negation of /obedience/ ($\bar{O}_{1c}$), /human solidarity/ ($O_{3'}$), /factional security/, the negation of /human solidarity/ ($\bar{O}_{3'}$), /universal salvation/ (O_{15}), and /partisan salvation/, the negation of /universal salvation/ ($\bar{O}_{15}$).

a. *Sustenance versus obedience*

We can place an unspecified subject in circumstances of conjunction with, or disjunction from, these value-objects, and place them on logical squares in order to determine whether our identification of the value-objects and their relationships to a subject are logically correct.

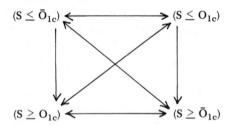

$$(S \leq \bar{O}_{1c}) \longleftrightarrow (S \leq O_{1c})$$

$$(S \geq O_{1c}) \longleftrightarrow (S \geq \bar{O}_{1c})$$

(S = a subject; O_{1c} = /obedience/; $\bar{O}_{1c}$ = /sustenance/)

The way to test our identifications is to ask whether, according to the logic of our text, each of the contraries implies its subcontrary. Does conjunction with the value-object /sustenance/, $\bar{O}_{1c}$, imply disjunction from the value-object /obedience/, O_{1c}, whereas the inverse does not? In order to test whether this applies to our text we have to replace the generic subject, S, with subjects from our text, S_1, the woman, and S_2, Jesus, and the value-objects /sustenance/ and /obedience/, (O_{1c} and $\bar{O}_{1c}$), with their representations in the text, O_1 and O_{1b}, drinking water and the water of life, or O_{10} and O_{10b}, the disciples' food and Jesus' other food. This gives us the following square, taking the woman and Jesus as the examples:

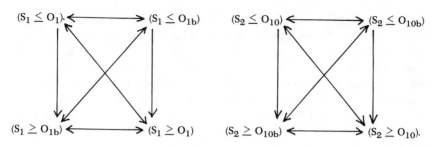

$(S_1 = $ the woman; $O_1 = $ drinking water; $O_{1b} = $ the water of life; $S_2 = $ Jesus; $O_{10} = $ food; $O_{10b} = $ Jesus' other food)

Conjunction with drinking water according to our text does imply disjunction from water of life (when Jesus engages in the discussion about the water of life, the concern for drinking water is abandoned; when the woman goes to witness about Jesus to the villagers she leaves her jar behind, and Jesus declines the disciples' food in favor of his other food), but disjunction from water of life or Jesus' other food does not necessarily mean conjunction with drinking water or the disciples' food (for example, in the beginning of the story the woman lacked drinking water, which was why she came to the well, as well as the water of life). Thus, both contraries are not true at the same time, but both sub-contraries are.

The same relationships apply to Jesus and the two kinds of food.

b. *Factional security versus human solidarity*

The square in the case of /factional security/ versus /human solidarity/ looks like this:

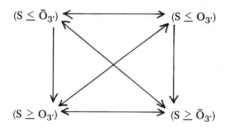

$(S = $ a subject; $O_{3'} = $ /human solidarity/; $\bar{O}_{3'} = $ /factional security/)

Here too a test of the relationships between the circumstances of conjunction and disjunction are in agreement with the logical square. It is worth exploring one of the series of figures that belongs on this square by substituting concrete objects representing the values /factional security/ and /human solidarity/ for these value-objects. The concrete objects themselves will not be presented on the squares; they will be considered only in their functions as representations of the value-objects. The woman's statement that Samaritans say that the right place to worship is on "this" mountain, whereas Jews say the right place is Jerusalem, places Jews and Samaritans in conjunction with the principle of non-association of Jews and Samaritans, representing the value /factional security/, $(S_{3'} \le \bar{O}_{3'})$. When Jesus says an hour is coming when Jews and Samaritans will worship neither on this mountain nor in Jerusalem, this conjunction is negated; i.e., Jews and Samaritans become disjoined from the negation of their association with one another $(S_{3'} \ge \bar{O}_{3'})$. When he then adds that the true worshippers will worship the Father in spirit, the statement gives expression to the common worship of all believers, including Jews and Samaritans. By that Jews and Samaritans become conjoined with their association with one another $(S_{3'} \le O_{3'})$. We can place these three circumstances on the logical square as follows:

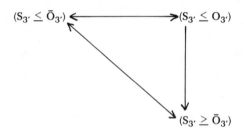

$(S_{3'}$ = Jews and Samaritans; $O_{3'}$ = /human solidarity/; $\bar{O}_{3'}$ = /factional security/)

There is no way in which the Jews and Samaritans can worship together without negating, i.e., disjoining themselves from, the principle of their dissociation from one another; $(S_{3'} \le O_{3'})$ implies $(S_{3'} \ge \bar{O}_{3'})$. However, they can negate the principle of dissociation without necessarily associating with each other; $(S_{3'} \ge \bar{O}_{3'})$ does not imply $(S_{3'} \le O_{3'})$.

On the other hand, there is no way in which they can adhere to the principle of dissociation while associating with each other. Adherence to the principle of dissociation $(S_{3'} \le \bar{O}_{3'})$ implies that they also do not associate with each other $(S_{3'} \ge O_{3'})$. Thus we can complete the square as follows:

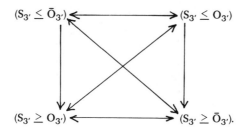

$(S_{3'} = \text{Jews and Samaritans}; O_{3'} = /\text{human solidarity}/; \bar{O}_{3'} = /\text{factional security}/)$

Note that disjunction from association of Jews and Samaritans, i.e., lack of their association with one another, does not imply affirmation of the principle of dissociation. Lack of association between Jews and Samaritans could be for other reasons than adherence to the principle of dissociation.

In a similar way other circumstances not represented by figures in the text can be derived by implication from those that are represented. Jesus' passing through Samaria because he had to represents adherence to the principle of dissociation ($S_2 \leq \bar{O}_{3'}$), because it implies that he does not associate with Samaritans ($S_2 \geq O_{3'}$), and that Jews and Samaritans do not associate on principle ($S_{3'} \leq \bar{O}_{3'}$) implies that they also do not do so in fact, ($S_{3'} \geq O_{3'}$), because if they were to do so ($S_{3'} \leq O_{3'}$), they would automatically contradict the principle ($S_{3'} \geq \bar{O}_{3'}$), which is a contradiction of ($S_{3'} \leq \bar{O}_{3'}$).

Finally, the Samaritans' entering into association with Jesus, a Jew, by inviting him to stay with them ($S_{12} \leq O_{3'}$) implies their negation of the principle of dissociation ($S_{12} \geq \bar{O}_{3'}$). Furthermore, associating with Jews ($S_{12} \leq O_{3'}$) contradicts not associating ($S_{12} \geq O_{3'}$) and negating the principle of dissociation ($S_{12} \geq \bar{O}_{3'}$) contradicts its affirmation ($S_{12} \leq \bar{O}_{3'}$).

Thus we can recognize every one of the following subjects, S_1, S_2, $S_{3'}$, and S_{12}, in a circumstance of conjunction or disjunction with each of the two objects, $\bar{O}_3$, and $O_{3'}$, on the four corners of the logical square as presented above, even though all do not come to expression in figures in the text; logically they are part of the argument of the text.

c. *Partisan salvation versus universal salvation*

The square representing the values /partisan salvation/ versus /universal salvation/ is as follows:

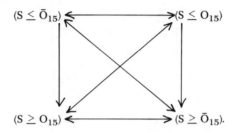

$(S = $ a subject; $O_{15} = $ /universal salvation/; $\bar{O}_{15} = $ /partisan salvation/$)$

In this case only S_1, $S_{3'}$, and S_{12} are involved. Here again, the woman's nationalistic conceptions of Jesus' identity, which expresses a partisan conception of salvation $(S_1 \leq \bar{O}_{15})$, imply the lack of a universal conception of it $(S_1 \geq O_{15})$; similarly, the Jews' and Samaritans' partisan conception of salvation $(S_{3'} \leq \bar{O}_{15})$, expressed in their contradictory claims about the right place to worship, implies their lack of a universal conception of salvation $(S_3 \geq O_{15})$. And so also the villagers' partisan conception $(S_{12} \leq \bar{O}_{15})$, expressed in their acceptance of the woman's testimony, implies their lack of a universal conception $(S_{12} \geq O_{15})$.

Logically the woman's conjunction with a partisan conception of salvation $(S_1 \leq \bar{O}_{15})$, would be contradicted by her negation of it $(S_1 \geq \bar{O}_{15})$ and similarly, her lack of a universal conception $(S_1 \geq O_{15})$ would be contradicted by the acceptance of such a conception $(S_1 \leq O_{15})$. However, the text does not have figures for such transformations, and they cannot be inferred or assumed.

d. *Transformations from one set of values to another*

Our text, of course, does not merely present these possible conjunctions and disjunctions in principle; it shows how one set of conjunctions and disjunctions are transformed into the contradictory set. We can present these transformations on semiotic squares, first in terms of an unidentified subject. The transformations in connection with the values /sustenance/ versus /obedience/ would appear as follows:

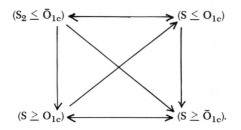

$(S = \text{a subject}; O_{1c} = /\text{obedience}/; \bar{O}_{1c} = /\text{sustenance}/)$

The transformations in connection with the values /factional security/ versus /human solidarity/ would be as follows:

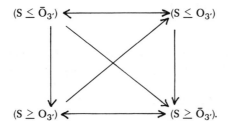

$(S = \text{a subject}; O_{3'} = /\text{human solidarity}/; \bar{O}_{3'} = /\text{factional security}/)$

And the transformations in connection with the values /partisan salvation/ versus /universal salvation/:

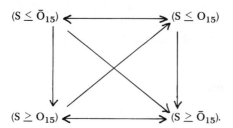

$(S = \text{a subject}; O_{15} = /\text{universal salvation}/; \bar{O}_{15} = /\text{partisan salvation})$

One can summarize the syntax of these squares by saying that they all express the move from the circumstances of conjunction and disjunction which represent the values /sustenance/, /factional security/ and /partisan salvation/ to those which represent the values /obedience/, /human solidarity/ and /universal salvation/. At the surface level of the text these subjects and objects take on concrete forms. That will concern us when we come to the discourse level of the syntactic component, in the processes of actorialization, temporalization and spatialization.

2. *Subjects and Objects representing the Values*

There are however other more specific syntactic structures which we need to clarify at this stage, i.e., the relationships between the actual subjects of the text and the value-objects, their circumstances of conjunction and disjunction, and in turn the relationships between these when a circumstance is transformed into its contradictory, and finally, between the transformations themselves. With regard to the relationships between the transformations themselves, we must note that, where one circumstance implies another, the transformation which brings about the latter has to take place before the one which brings about the former.

We already gave some attention to these matters above when we tested the correctness of our proposed more general circumstances of conjunction and disjunction by replacing the unspecified subject with concrete subjects from the surface level of the text, and the value-objects with the concrete objects which represent them. We need to give more specific attention to these now, limiting ourselves to the relationships of the actual subjects to the value-objects. In doing so it should be remembered that at this level we are concerned only with the syntactic relationships between subjects and objects, etc. Even though we will discuss this in terms of actual subjects and the value-objects we are concerned with them only as subjects and objects, and the relationships between them, not with their specific, concrete forms.

a. *The savior of the world*

In our analysis of the narrative syntax in Part One of this study, we presented the final action in the story as the Samaritan villagers conjoining themselves with the recognition of Jesus as the savior of the world and disjoining themselves at the same time from belief in Jesus in the sense of the woman's testimony. We represented it as follows:

$$F_{19}[S_{12} => (O_{7c} \leq S_{12} \geq O_{14a'}) -> (O_{7c} \geq S_{12} \leq O_{14a'})]$$

in which S_{12} represents the villagers, O_{7c} belief in Jesus in the sense of the woman's testimony, and $O_{14a'}$ recognition of Jesus as the savior of the world. It now becomes clear that in our analysis our attention was focused on what was happening to the Samaritan villagers: their rejection of belief in Jesus in the sense of the woman's testimony and their affirmation of him as savior of the world.

As we now look at the same event, no longer from the point of view of the text's surface structure, but from that of its system of values, it becomes clear that when the villagers attribute to Jesus the title savior of the world, recognizing him as a universal savior, they affirm salvation for everyone, i.e., they conjoin themselves with the image of salvation in that sense, representing the value /universal salvation/ (O_{15}). At the same time the villagers reject their previous understanding of Jesus as the messiah, i.e., in the woman's partisan sense of salvation limited to a we-group which negates salvation for everyone, representing the value /partisan salvation/ ($\bar{O}_{15}$). We may then present the villagers' performance in this sense as follows:

$$F_{19c'}[S_{12} => (\bar{O}_{15} \leq S_{12} \geq O_{15}) -> (O_{15} \leq S_{12} \geq \bar{O}_{15})].$$

Affirmation of Jesus as messiah in the woman's partisan sense and thus of salvation limited to a we-group ($S_{12} \leq \bar{O}_{15}$) implies disjunction from the conception of salvation for everyone ($S_{12} \geq O_{15}$), even though this is not explicitly stated about the villagers. It does not have to mean an explicit negation of the conception, but merely the absence of such an idea. Similarly, conjunction with the conception of salvation for everyone ($S_{12} \leq O_{15}$) implies negation of salvation limited to a we-group ($S_{12} \geq \bar{O}_{15}$). This negation is explicit in the text when the villagers reject the woman's testimony of Jesus in favor of the understanding of Jesus as savior of the world. At the same time it is possible to negate both understandings of salvation, ($S_{12} \geq O_{15}$) as well as ($S_{12} \geq \bar{O}_{15}$); for example, a person may reject all forms of salvation.

We can clarify this by placing the circumstances on a logical square.

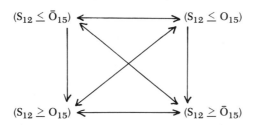

$(S = \text{a subject}; O_{3'} = /\text{human solidarity}/; \bar{O}_{3'} = /\text{factional security}/)$

In the combined functions which follow, thus, it should be borne in mind that lines of implication always run from left to right. Thus, in the case of the previous function above, $F_{19c'}$, from ($S_{12} \leq \bar{O}_{15}$) to ($S_{12} \geq O_{15}$) and from ($S_{12} \leq O_{15}$) to $S_{12} \geq \bar{O}_{15}$), but not from right to left.

From the point of view of the semantic deep structure of the text, i.e., of its system of values, the story is doing more than narrate what happened to the Samaritan villagers; it brings to expression the affirmation of certain values, and the negation of others.

That the image of Jesus as the savior of the world represents the value /universal salvation/, and the image of him in the woman's sense, /partisan salvation/, does not come to expression at any level of the text's syntax. That relationship remains a purely semantic feature. What remains equally obscure syntactically is that by recognizing Jesus, a Jew, as the savior of the world and by sealing the rejection of the convention of non-association of Samaritans and Jews, which they did when they invited Jesus to stay with them, the Samaritans, as we shall see, also affirm the value /human solidarity/ and negate /factional security/.

That these meanings are not evident syntactically poses no problem; it merely indicates that there is more than one perspective from which to approach a text. From the point of view of its syntactic structure, the flow of the narrative, we become aware of the characters, what they do and what happens to them; from the point of view of its semantic structure, its system of values, we become aware how what the characters do and what happens to them give expression to meaning. This is also true for an intuitive understanding of the text. In our ordinary reading of a narrative text we are aware that there is meaning in what characters do in a story and in what happens to them. Thus we approach such a text intuitively from both perspectives; we follow the actions and experiences of the characters, and we try to discern the meanings expressed in those actions and experiences.

b. *Water and food*

It is not our intention here to discuss every aspect of the text's fundamental syntax. What we need to do is to investigate the syntax of the figures we have identified in the text. It will be noted that frequently these figures, to begin with, merely present a circumstance in which a subject finds itself. That circumstance is then changed by an action which we formulate syntactically as a function.

So, when Jesus asks the woman for a drink of water, his request establishes a conjunction between himself and water, representing /sustenance/ ($\bar{O}_{1c}$). Thus he affirms for himself the value of drinking water as /sustenance/. We present this circumstance as follows:

$$F_{1a'}[S_2 => (S_2 \leq \bar{O}_{1c})].$$

There is no prior circumstance of disjunction that is changed by Jesus' performance. His request merely establishes that he, as a subject, finds himself in a circumstance of conjunction with an object, drinking water, representing the value /sustenance/. It should be noted that, from the point of view of the system of values of our text, this conjunction does not have to mean that Jesus is actually in possession of drinking water. It merely establishes that with his request he affirms drinking water as a value, /sustenance/, for himself.

There is no explicit indication in the text that Jesus reverses this affirmation. However, the fact that he does not pursue the request further as the conversation proceeds implies a dissociation from the request. Furthermore, when he declines the disciples' offer of food, drinking water is evidently included. The woman, on the other hand, gives explicit expression to a disjunction from the value of drinking water as /sustenance/ when she drops her water jar; her disjunction from drinking water ($S_1 \geq O_1$) represents concretely disjunction from the value /sustenance/ ($S_1 \geq \bar{O}_{1c}$). Her prior conjunction is established by the very fact that she came to the well to draw water ($S_1 \leq O_1$). This act represents her conjunction with the value /sustenance/ ($S_1 \leq \bar{O}_{1c}$). We can present her action as the following function:

$$F_{10'}[S_1 => (S_1 \leq \bar{O}_{1c}) \text{ —} > (S_1 \geq \bar{O}_{1c})].$$

When the disciples offer food to Jesus, they conjoin him with food; this act represents the value /sustenance/. Here too there is no prior disjunction. We present the disciples, action syntactically as follows:

$$F_{13'}[S_8 => (S_2 \leq \bar{O}_{1c})].$$

Jesus negates this circumstance of conjunction by declining the disciples' offer, which we can present as follows:

$$F_{13b'}[S_2 => (S_2 \leq \bar{O}_{1c}) \text{ -} > (S_2 \geq \bar{O}_{1c})].$$

In this presentation we have noted how the value /sustenance/, affirmed in the figures of Jesus asking the woman for a drink of water and the disciples offering Jesus food to eat, is changed into a negation of that value by means of the figures of the woman leaving her water jar behind and Jesus declining the disciples' offer of food. See the upper left hand and lower right hand of the diagram on page 120.

We have noted earlier that there are no figures expressing the negation of /obedience/ and that in the system of values underlying our text, the negation of /obedience/ remains an implication of the affirmation of /sustenance/. In its system of values, however, the text does bring to expression the affirmation of /obedience/, the contrary of /sustenance/. The figures expressing /obedience/ are on the upper right side of the diagram on page 120.

When the woman, leaving her water jar behind, goes to the village to witness concerning Jesus, she appropriates water of life, which gives expression to the value /obedience/ ($S_1 \leq O_{1c}$). That she previously lacked water of life as an affirmation of /obedience/ ($S_1 \geq O_{1c}$) is presupposed by her action and is expressed concretely by Jesus' statement to her that, if she knew who it was to whom she was speaking, she would ask him to give her water of life (v 10). We can present her action as follows:

$$F_{16'}[S_1 => (S_1 \geq O_{1c}) -> (S_1 \leq O_{1c})].$$

One could say the woman was involved in an exchange of drinking water, representing /sustenance/, for water of life, representing /obedience/. We can present this as a combination of F_{10} and $F_{16'}$:

$$F_{16'}[S_1 => (\bar{O}_{1c} \leq S_1 \geq O_{1c}) -> (O_{1c} \leq S_1 \geq \bar{O}_{1c})].$$

Similarly, Jesus, by engaging in discussion with the woman and staying with the villagers (doing the will of the one who sent him and completing his work), partakes of his other food, which represents the value /obedience/. Syntactically, by his action he is conjoined with his other food ($S_2 \leq O_{10b}$), which represents his conjunction with the value /obedience/ ($S_2 \leq O_{1c}$). In his case too we have to assume that he was previously disjoined from his other food and thus also from /obedience/. It is implied by his request for, i.e., conjunction with, drinking water. His request for drinking water ($S_2 \leq O_1$), representing his conjunction with /sustenance/ ($S_2 \leq \bar{O}_{1c}$), implies a disjunction from his other food ($S_2 \geq \bar{O}_{10b}$), representing his disjunction from the value /obedience/ ($S_2 \geq O_{1c}$). We can present his action as follows:

$$F_{14a'}[S_2 => (S_2 \geq O_{1c}) -> (S_2 \leq O_{1c})].$$

An exchange of objects is involved; i.e., food as /nourishment/ for his other food, representing /obedience/. We can clarify this exchange syntactically by combining functions $F_{13b'}$ and $F_{14'}$ in a single complex function:

$$F_{14a''}[S_2 => (\bar{O}_{1c} \leq S_2 \geq O_{1c}) -> (O_{1c} \leq S_2 \geq \bar{O}_{1c})].$$

c. *Jews and Samaritans*

In the same way we can note how the affirmations and negations of other values can be formulated syntactically as circumstances of conjunction and disjunction between subjects and objects and as reversals of such circumstances. When it is stated that Jesus passed through Samaria "because he had to," our text presents him as avoiding association between Jews and Samaritans, which gives expression to the value /factional security/. Syntactically, Jesus as the subject is conjoined with the avoidance of association between Jews and Samaritans as the object. This conjunction represents the value /factional security/ ($S_2 \leq \bar{O}_{3'}$). His avoidance of association implies that he does not associate with Samaritans. This avoidance represents his disjunction from /human solidarity/ ($S_2 \geq O_{3'}$). We can write this relationship as ($\bar{O}_{3'} \leq S_2 \geq O_{3'}$). Note that ($S_2 \geq O_{3'}$) does not imply ($S_2 \leq \bar{O}_{3'}$). Not associating with Samaritans does not imply an affirmation of the convention of dissociation of Jews and Samaritans. There could be other reasons for not associating with Samaritans.

The woman, by reminding Jesus of the impropriety of him, a Jew, asking her, a Samaritan woman, for a drink of water (v 9), indicates her intention to avoid associating with a Jewish man. Syntactically she too is disjoined from /human solidarity/, which is represented in our text by the association of Jews and Samaritans. We present this as the circumstance ($S_1 \geq O_{3'}$). The parenthetic remark in the same verse, which clarifies why she makes the statement, identifies her statement as an implication of her affirmation of the convention of the avoidance of association of Jews and Samaritans. The remark places her in a circumstance of conjunction with /factional security/, represented by the convention of dissociation between Jews and Samaritans ($S_1 \leq \bar{O}_{3'}$).

According to our text her disjunction from /human solidarity/, represented by association of Jews and Samaritans, is an implication of her conjunction with /factional security/, represented by the convention of non-association ($O_{3'} \leq S_1 \geq O_{3'}$). Here too the inverse does not apply. The woman's disjunction from association does not imply her conjunction with the convention; there could be other circumstances which prevent her from associating with Jews, such as, the absence of Jews in her environment, but according to our text that is not the case here. Thus disjunction from /human solidarity/ also does not imply conjunction with /factional security/, represented by these more concrete objects.

The parenthetic remark, of course, does not apply only to the woman, but to Jews and Samaritans in general who do not associate on principle. Non-association on principle represents the value /factional security/, which we write as ($S_{3'} \leq \bar{O}_{3'}$). That Jews and Samaritans avoid association comes to expression also in the disagreement concerning the right place to worship.

Jesus' statement that the Samaritans do not know what they worship, but the Jews do, once more presents him in conjunction with the negation of association of Jews and Samaritans, and thus with /factional security/ $(S_2 \leq \bar{O}_{3'})$.

But then, when Jesus asks the woman for a drink of water and engages in discussion with her, he affirms by his action association of Jews and Samaritans and thus /human solidarity/ $(S_2 \leq O_{3'})$. His action can be written as a performance in which he reverses his circumstance of disjunction to one of conjunction with the value /human solidarity/:

$$F_{2b'}[S_2 => (S_2 \geq O_{3'}) \to (S_2 \leq O_{3'})].$$

As the woman reminds him, the implication of his action is that he disregards, i.e., negates, the convention of non-association of Jews and Samaritans. His action represents a negation of the value /factional security/. His association with the Samaritan woman is an inevitable violation of the convention and thus a rejection of /factional security/; $(S_2 \leq O_{3'})$ implies $(S_2 \geq \bar{O}_{3'})$. By his action his conjunction with /factional security/ is changed into a disjunction from it:

$$F_{2a'}[S_2 => (S_2 \leq \bar{O}_3) \to (S_2 \geq \bar{O}_{3'})].$$

Actually all of this is a single action which we can present by combining $F_{2a'}$ and $F_{2b'}$ in a single performance:

$$F_{2c'}[S_2 => (\bar{O}_{3'} \leq S_2 \geq O_{3'}) \to (O_{3'} \leq S_2 \geq \bar{O}_{3'})].$$

Jesus' statement, that an hour is coming when Samaritans and Jews will worship the Father neither on this mountain nor in Jerusalem, also disjoins Jews and Samaritans from the convention of their non-association with one another and thus from /factional security/. We write this disjunction as $(S_{3'} \geq \bar{O}_{3'})$. By worshipping neither on this mountain nor in Jerusalem they negate their conjunction with /factional security/, expressed in the disagreement concerning the right place to worship. We can write this reversal in their circumstances as follows:

$$F_{7a''}[S_{3'} => (S_{3'} \leq \bar{O}_{3'}) \to (S_{3'} \geq \bar{O}_{3'})].$$

When Jesus then adds that the true believers, which include Jews and Samaritans, will worship the Father in spirit and truth, Jews and Samaritans are joined together with each other in worship. This conjunction represents the value /human solidarity/, which we can write as $(S_{3'} \leq O_{3'})$. That act of worship can thus be written, with regard to Jews and Samaritans, as the following function:

$$F_{7b''}[S_1 => (S_{3'} \geq O_{3'}) \to (S_{3'} \leq O_{3'})],$$

the disjunction $(S_{3'} \geq O_{3'})$ being an implication of $(S_{3'} \leq \bar{O}_{3'})$, Jews and Samaritans refusing common worship, and so negating

/human solidarity/. These two performances can once more be combined into a single one as follows:

$$F_{7c''}[S_{3'} => (\bar{O}_{3'} \le S_{3'} \ge O_{3'}) -> (O_{3'} \le S_{3'} \ge \bar{O}_{3'})].$$

The woman, by participating in the discussion with Jesus, also accepts association of Jews and Samaritans. Her action represents an affirmation of the value /human solidarity/ $(S_1 \le O_{3'})$ and thus reverses her previous disjunction, $(S_1 \ge O_{3'})$. Her performance can be written as:

$$F_{2b''}[S_1 => (S_1 \ge O_{3'}) -> (S_1 \le O_{3'})].$$

The implication of her participation in a discussion with a Jew is that she too, by her action, negates the convention of non-association of Jews and Samaritans and thus the value /factional security/. That performance is written as:

$$F_{2a''}[S_1 => (S_1 \le \bar{O}_3) -> (S_1 \ge \bar{O}_{3'})].$$

These two performances can also be combined in a single one:

$$F_{2c''}[S_1 => (\bar{O}_{3'} \le S_1 \ge O_{3'}) -> (O_{3'} \le S_1 \ge \bar{O}_{3'})].$$

When the Samaritans invite Jesus to stay with them, they too affirm association of Jews and Samaritans and so /human solidarity/. We write this affirmation syntactically as $(S_{12} \le O_{3'})$. We have no statement of their having negated /human solidarity/, although we may assume that that had been the case $(S_{12} \ge O_{3'})$. Thus we can write their act of engagement in association with Jesus, a Jew, as follows:

$$F_{18b'}[S_{12} => (S_{12} \ge O_{3'}) -> (S_{12} \le O_{3'})].$$

One can also assume that their association implies a negation of dissociation, and thus of /factional security/. We write this negation as $(S_{12} \ge \bar{O}_{3'})$. One can assume further that they too previously affirmed the convention of non-association and thus /factional security/ $(S_{12} \le \bar{O}_{3'})$. This reversal in their attitude can be written as:

$$F_{18a'}[S_{12} => (S_{12} \le \bar{O}_{3'}) -> (S_{12} \ge \bar{O}_{3'})].$$

Once more, bearing in mind that some of this is not explicit in the text, we can combine the two performances into one:

$$F_{18c'}[S_{12} => (\bar{O}_{3'} \le S_{12} \ge O_{3'}) -> (O_{3'} \ge S_{12} \le \bar{O}_{3'})].$$

Jesus' acceptance of their invitation is syntactically again a conjunction of him with the association of Jews and Samaritans and thus with /human solidarity/. Now it is, however, not a performance, but merely a reaffirmation of an already existing circumstance, namely $(S_2 \le O_{3'})$.

We have noted a number of circumstances that are not explicitly given in the text, but can be assumed or derived by implication from others. This is not unusual in language. So, for example, the direct object of a sentence is given explicitly by means of the accusative case in some languages, whereas in others it is arrived at by inference, e.g., by its placement in a sentence. Transformational grammar can show how what is made explicit in one language is left to inference in another. Something similar happens in discourse. These circumstances that are not explicitly expressed, but can be assumed or derived by implication, are important for an understanding of the text; they contribute in important ways to the meaning expressed in it, as we shall see below.

d. *Savior figures*

Finally, with regard to the set of values /partisan salvation/ versus /universal salvation/, the woman's discussion in terms of national savior figures, challenging Jesus that he is not greater than "our father Jacob," and attributing to him the dignity of first a prophet and then the messiah, reveals her to be thinking of salvation in terms of a we-group, which negates salvation for everyone. This negation represents the value /partisan salvation/ ($\bar{O}_{15}$). Syntactically her statements present her in conjunction with the image of salvation limited to a we-group, and thus /partisan salvation/ ($S_1 \leq \bar{O}_{15}$), which implies her disjunction from salvation for everyone, or /universal salvation/ ($S_1 \geq O_{15}$).

As we have already noted, the woman's statement that "our fathers" said that one should worship on this mountain, whereas the Jews say Jerusalem is the right place to worship, conjoins Jews and Samaritans with the image of their dissociation from one another and thus with /factional security/ ($S_{3'} \leq \bar{O}_{3'}$). That statement at the same time conjoins also the Jews and Samaritans with the image of salvation limited to a we-group and thus with /partisan salvation/ ($S_{3'} \leq \bar{O}_{15}$).

Jesus' statement that the hour is coming when worship will be neither in Jerusalem nor on this mountain disjoins all believers, including Jews and Samaritans, from that limited conception of salvation and thus from /partisan salvation/. We can write the involvement of Jews and Samaritans in this negation of /partisan salvation/ as ($S_{3'} \geq \bar{O}_{15}$) and the reversal of their circumstance as:

$$F_{7a'}[S_{3'} => (S_{3'} \leq \bar{O}_{15}) \rightarrow (S_{3'} \geq \bar{O}_{15})].$$

Worshipping neither on this mountain nor in Jerusalem is an implication of worship of the Father in spirit and truth, which expresses the value /universal salvation/. We can write the participation of Jews and Samaritans in such worship as ($S_{3'} \leq O_{15}$), and the transformation of their previous avoidance of such worship ($S_{3'} \geq O_{15}$) into participation in it as:

$$F_{7b'}[S_{3'} => (S_{3'} \geq O_{15}) \rightarrow (S_{3'} \leq O_{15})].$$

We can once more combine the two performances into one:

$$F_{7c'}[S_{3'} => (\bar{O}_{15} \leq S_{3'} \geq O_{15}) -> (O_{15} \leq S_{3'} \geq \bar{O}_{15})].$$

Conjunction with the limited conception of salvation, which represents the value /partisan salvation/ ($S_{3'} \leq \bar{O}_{15}$), implies disjunction from the conception of salvation for everyone, which represents the value /universal salvation/ ($S_{3'} \geq O_{15}$).

As we know, Jesus' statement applies to worshippers in general, S_6. We can write the performance in this more general sense as

$$F_{7d'}[S_6 => (\bar{O}_{15} \leq S_6 \geq O_{15}) -> (O_{15} \leq S_6 \geq \bar{O}_{15})].$$

Jesus' claim to be the messiah (v 26), in the context of the rest of his conversation, is to be understood in a universal sense. In this case we can establish only his conjunction with salvation in that sense without a performance which altered it from a circumstance of disjunction. We write Jesus' conjunction with universal salvation as ($S_2 \leq O_{15}$).

Finally, as we have already noted, the Samaritan villagers' rejection of the woman's conception of salvation in a limited sense and their affirmation of Jesus as the savior of the world, appropriating for themselves the image of salvation for everyone, can be written in terms of the system of values to which it gives expression as

$$F_{19c'}[S_{12} => (\bar{O}_{15} \leq S_{12} \geq O_{15}) -> (O_{15} \leq S_{12} \geq \bar{O}_{15})].$$

Actually this is the combination of two distinguishable performances, their rejection of the woman's partisan conception of the messiah and thus of /partisan salvation/:

$$F_{19a'}[S_{12} => (S_{12} \leq \bar{O}_{15}) -> (S_{12} \geq \bar{O}_{15})]$$

and their recognition of Jesus as universal savior, which represents the value /universal salvation/:

$$F_{19b'}[S_{12} => (S_{12} \geq O_{15}) -> (S_{12} \leq O_{15})].$$

As we have already noted, with those two performances combined, they place a seal on their rejection of the convention of non-association of Jews and Samaritans and so of /partisan salvation/. With the same act they engage in the association with Jews, affirming the value /universal salvation/, by inviting Jesus to stay with them in a performance which we presented above as $F_{18c'}$.

These transformations can be plotted on semiotic squares. In that way we can note which circumstances are implied by which and thus which transformations by which, along the vertical axis of implication. In the case of the transformation expressing the values /sustenance/ versus /obedience/, we have the following square:

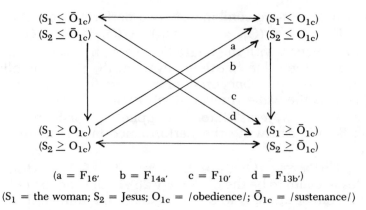

$$(a = F_{16'} \quad b = F_{14a'} \quad c = F_{10'} \quad d = F_{13b'})$$

$(S_1$ = the woman; S_2 = Jesus; O_{1c} = /obedience/; $\bar{O}_{1c}$ = /sustenance/)

The transformations expressing the values /factional security/ versus /human solidarity/ result in the following square:

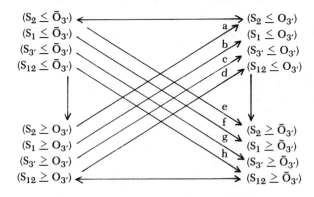

$(a = F_{2b'} \ b = F_{2b''} \ c = F_{7b''} \ d = F_{18b'} \ e = F_{2a'} \ f = F_{2a''} \ g = F_{7a''} \ h = F_{18a'})$

$(S_1$ = the woman; S_2 = Jesus; $S_{3'}$ = Jews and Samaritans; S_{12} = the villagers;
$O_{3'}$ = /human solidarity/; $\bar{O}_{3'}$ = /fictional security/)

The transformations expressing the values /partisan salvation/ versus /universal salvation/ appear as follows on the semiotic square:

$$(S_{3'} \le \bar{O}_{15}) \longleftrightarrow (S_{3'} \le O_{15})$$
$$(S_{12} \le \bar{O}_{15}) \qquad\qquad (S_{12} \le O_{15})$$
$$(S_{3'} \ge O_{15}) \qquad\qquad (S_{3'} \ge \bar{O}_{15})$$
$$(S_{12} \ge O_{15}) \longleftrightarrow (S_{12} \ge \bar{O}_{15})$$

$$(a = F_{16'} \quad b = F_{14a'} \quad c = F_{10'} \quad d = F_{13b'})$$

$(S_{3'}$ = Jews and Samaritans; S_{12} = the villagers;
O_{15} = /universal salvation/; $\bar{O}_{15}$ = /partisan salvation/)

What we find as we move to the discourse level of our text is that the subjects become actual characters and the value-objects are represented by concrete objects in a process of actorialization. In that way the characters come into relationship with the objects by real actions in space and time, in processes of spatialization and temporalization. In this way the meaning of the text is brought to expression as a story.

However, before we discuss that step in the generative trajectory of our text, there is one further syntactic relationship we need to clarify at the surface level of the semio-narrative syntax, i.e., the relationship between the transformations concerning the values /sustenance/ and /obedience/ and those concerning the other two sets of opposed values, /factional security/ versus /human solidarity/ and /partisan salvation/ versus /universal salvation/.

3. The Relationships between the Fundamental Syntactic Structures

One can establish to begin with that those transformations which change the circumstances of Jesus and the woman from representing the value /sustenance/ to representing /obedience/ all function as preparation for the transformation from circumstances representing the values /factional security/ and /partisan salvation/ to those representing the values /human solidarity/ and /universal salvation/. Thus one can consider the square representing the transformations from the circumstances representing the value /sustenance/ to the circumstances representing the value /obedience/ as the preparation phase for the squares representing the transformations from the circumstances representing the values /factional security/ and /partisan salvation/ to the circumstances which represent the values /human solidarity/ and /universal salvation/.

By doing the will of the one who sent him and completing his work, i.e., actualizing the value /obedience/, Jesus brings about the transformation of the various subjects from circumstances representing the values /factional security/ and /partisan salvation/ to those representing the values /human solidarity/ and /universal salvation/. In this the woman acts as his helper when she goes back to the village to witness concerning him. /Obedience/ is the power through which it becomes possible to actualize the values of /human solidarity/ and /universal salvation/. We may present this relationship as follows:

A (need)	B (preparedness)	C (performance)	D (sanction)
	/obedience/	/human solidarity/	
		/universal salvation/	

One should at least ask whether /human solidarity/ does not function as preparation for /universal salvation/, whether true believers can worship the Father in spirit and truth without being prepared for it by prior reconciliation with each other, somewhat in the sense of Mt 5:23-24: "If you take your offering to the altar, and there remember that your brother has something against you, leave your offering at the altar and go, first reconcile yourself with your brother, and then come and make your offering." That relationship, however, does not appear to be expressed in our text.

There do not seem to be other syntactic relationships between the performances expressing affirmation of the values /human solidarity/ and /universal salvation/, except that they are parallel realizations which contradict the values /factional security/ and /partisan salvation/, and that they are prepared for by the transformations expressing /obedience/. Semantically, it will be remembered, the values /factional security/ and /partisan salvation/ are very close to being equivalent, as are the values /human solidarity/ and /universal salvation/.

We can clarify the relationship between performances expressing the value /obedience/ and those expressing the value /human solidarity/ by referring to one concrete, but difficult, example: Jesus' asking the woman for a drink of water and what follows from that. We stated earlier that it is as an affirmation of the value /sustenance/ that he asked the woman for a drink, an action by means of which he, at the same time, negated the value /factional security/ and affirmed the value /human solidarity/. Thus it would seem that it was his affirmation of the value /sustenance/, and not /obedience/, which prepared him for affirmation of the value /human solidarity/.

However, when the woman points out to him that by his action he is negating the value /factional security/, Jesus no longer pursues his request for a drink of water, and in his conversation with the disciples it becomes clear that he had abandoned the quest for /sustenance/ in favor of /obedience/. It appears thus that, even though in the first instance it is Jesus' concern for /sustenance/ which functions as preparation for his action of affirming /human solidarity/, the moment it becomes clear that the affirmation of /human solidarity/ is what is involved, the concern for /sustenance/ itself is transformed into /obedience/.

One may thus have the impression that it is the transformation of circumstances giving expression to the value /factional security/ into those which give expression to /human solidarity/ which prepares for the transformation of a circumstance which gives expression to the value /sustenance/ into one that gives expression to /obedience/, and not the other way around. That is nevertheless not the case. What happens in the text is that when the transformation with regard to the values /factional security/ and /human solidarity/ takes place it becomes clear that the appropriate preparedness for that transformation is not a circumstance giving expression to the value /sustenance/, but one that gives expression to /obedience/. At the surface level of the text Jesus recognizes that in order to carry out the action transforming circumstances representing the value /factional security/ into those that represent /human solidarity/, the required preparedness is /obedience/ and not the need for /sustenance/. To put it in simpler terms, it becomes clear that the achievement of /human solidarity/ is not a function of need for /sustenance/, but of /obedience/.

It is important to note that nowhere in the text are the two subjects who prepare for the change in circumstances from those representing the values /factional security/ and /partisan salvation/ to those representing /human solidarity/ and /universal salvation/, Jesus (for the woman), and the woman (in turn for the villagers), the acting subjects. The transformations are always acts by the subjects themselves who undergo the changes of circumstances, prepared for their acts by the persuasion of the subjects of circumstances representing the value /obedience/. A chain of persuasion is involved; the woman is persuaded by Jesus, and Jesus is persuaded by the one who sent him. In each case an appeal to the will is made. None of the acting subjects are placed under obligation.

4.   The Meaning of John 4 as a Story

With that we come to the surface level of the text, the actual story of John 4. At this level the subjects of the semio-narrative structures are actual characters, the value-objects are represented by concrete objects, and the meaning of our text, as a story, comes to expression in time and space.

In an immediate sense, the temporal setting appears to be straightforward. It is presented as having been in the time of Jesus, i.e., in the first century C.E., which means that the events and the relationships between the characters have to be understood historically in terms of that time. Internal to the story there is overlapping time; that of Jesus conversing with the woman while the disciples are off in the village buying food, and that of Jesus conversing with the disciples while the woman is off in the village telling the villagers about him, and the villagers are coming to him to invite him to stay with them. Another temporal setting is introduced by Jesus in verse 38 when he tells the disciples that he is sending them to reap where they did not labor. The time-frame is changed into that of some future activity of the disciples, preceded by prior activity of other unidentified workers.

When we consider the statement in verse 21, "an hour is coming when neither on this mountain, nor in Jerusalem . . ," a decisively important temporal feature of the text becomes evident. The events which transpire in the story are placed in "the hour which is coming and now is," anticipating that statement in 5:25. This temporalizing of the text is crucial to the expression of its meaning.

The spatialization of the events is also highly significant. The story transpires in Samaria, through which Jesus, a Jew, passes because he has to. With that the tension between Jews and Samaritans, representing the value /factional security/ and in a derived sense /partisan salvation/, is immediately established. It is an ideal setting in which the issues of the conflicting values, /factional security/ versus /human solidarity/ and /partisan salvation/ versus /universal salvation/, can be addressed.

What provides this setting with all the greater potentiality of expressing meaning is the actorialization of the subjects and objects: S_2, Jesus, a Jewish man, passing through Samaria because he had to, encountering S_1, a Samaritan woman whom he engages in discussion, and finally receiving hospitality from S_{12}, an entire Samaritan village. Furthermore, there is the actorialization of $S_{3'}$, Jews and Samaritans, who have no association with each other, and contradict each other on the crucial question of the right place to worship. All of this brings to powerful expression the conflict in values between /factional security/ and /partisan salvation/, on the one hand, and /human solidarity/ and /universal salvation/, on the other. The events of the story effect a resolution of the conflict in the vindication of /human solidarity/ and /universal salvation/ over the divisive values, /factional security/ and /partisan salvation/.

Other significant features of the main characters are that S_1 is a Samaritan *woman*, which enhances the impropriety of a Jewish man associating with her, and that S_2 is someone sent by God (v 34). Jesus is no mere Jew in the story. His actions are done in obedience to the one who sent him. In this way the events of the story are placed within the framework of divine authority. That this is so is recognized by the villagers; in their recognition of Jesus as the savior of the world they sanction the implicit claim that the events that transpired are more than fortunate incidents in human affairs. The reconciliation of Jews and Samaritans brings to expression the salvation of all the world in an act of /obedience/. What transpired in this act of /obedience/ was, to put it in the words of Jesus, doing the will of the one who sent him and completing his work.

All the other actors in the story, subjects as well as objects, are to be understood within the framework of the events that transpire among the main characters. Jacob, water of life, spring water, thirst, water jar, food, miraculous activity, worshippers, messiah, fields, harvesting, serve to present the events of the story as a piece of human history, in which the values /human solidarity/ and /universal salvation/ are realized concretely in actions which, in turn, realize the value /obedience/.

There is an exception to the dependent meaning of these other actors. In the context of the story, its temporal and spatial setting, and of the tension between the representative characters, Jews and Samaritans, the objects "this mountain" and Jerusalem have great potentiality of meaning. The polarity between these two objects as the contradictory "right" places to worship, which represent concretely and symbolically the division between Jews and Samaritans, brings to vivid expression, not only the values /factional security/ and /partisan salvation/, but also /sustenance/, as /self-preservation/, and the negation of /obedience/. Thus when Jesus announces the hour which is coming, and now is, when the true worshippers will worship the Father in spirit and truth, the entire conflict of values in our text is resolved. In that single statement all the text's positive values are affirmed: /obedience/, "for the Father seeks such to worship him," is the basis of the affirmation of /human solidarity/ and of /universal salvation/ in the common worship of God. Jesus' announcement is sanctioned with powerful succinctness in the conclusion of the story when the Samaritan villagers, in an act of obedience, recognize as the savior of all the world the Jew whom they, in an expression of human solidarity, contrary to convention, had invited to stay with them. With that the fullness of time has become a reality for the first time in the gospel, but that is something that takes us beyond the limits of this investigation.

PART TWO

INTERPRETATION OF THE MEANING OF JOHN 4

Introduction

In what follows I try to interpret how meaning is brought to expression in John 4; in linguistic terms, how John 4 means. In traditional terms, it is not a *commentary on* John 4, but an *exegesis of* the text. So, for example, it will not be my purpose to present all that can be said about the statement that Jews and Samaritans *ou synchrōntai*. For that the reader may consult the more than sufficient number of commentaries that are available on John. Historical-critical information will not be ignored in this interpretation; it forms the background against which it is carried out.

My attempt to bring out the meaning of the passage was made in the context of as much relevant historical-critical information as I could gather from the large number of commentaries on the Fourth Gospel and individual investigations of John 4,[1] primarily in articles. I included more theologically oriented

[1] In the case of commentaries I found that I had to be selective, limiting myself to some 35 of the most promising. The need for the enormous number that is available is incomprehensible, the redundancy more than one would expect. I now consider consulting 35 for a responsible interpretation of John excessive. Time can be better spent. The only reason why one would want to consult that number, and more, is the ambition to write a commentary that supersedes all others. How one could still have the courage to do that after consulting a few of the best is incomprehensible. If one subtracts the dogmatics from M.-J. Lagrange, *Évangile selon saint Jean* (EBib; Paris: Gabalda, 1923; 8th ed., 1948) one can find in it more than eighty percent of what needs to be known historical-critically about John. What is needed is a contemporary *interpretation*, an *exegesis*, of the Fourth Gospel, similar to Bultmann's for his time, what some would call a theological interpretation. The only recent one which explicitly makes that claim is superficial beyond belief, which is a mystery of the publishing world. Deserving special mention among the German commentaries is Ernst Haenchen, *Das Johannesevangelium: Ein Kommentar* (aus den nachgelassenen Manuskripten herausgegeben von Ulrich Buse; Göttingen: Vandenhoeck & Ruprecht, 1980); ET: *John 1. A Commentary on the Gospel of John Chapters 1-6.* (trans. and ed. Robert W. Funk; Philadelphia: Fortress, 1980). Worth mentioning for the English reader because of its sober judg-

studies, such as Rudolf Bultmann's commentary,[2] as well as studies like Birger Olsson's text-linguistic analysis,[3] Gail O'Day's investigation of irony in John,[4] Walter Rebell's didactic

ments on the crucial issues is Barnabas Lindars, *The Gospel of John* (NCB; Greenwood, S.C: Attic, 1972; reprinted 1977).

I took note of every individual investigation on John 4 made during the past 25 years on which I could lay my hands. With some important exceptions of which I was able to make good use, what appears in journal articles is a useless wasteland, much of it sheer fantasy and far-fetched attempts to say at all costs something new. Worth mentioning here is L. Schottroff, "Johannes 4:5-15 und die Konsequenzen des johanneischen Dualismus," *ZNW* 60 (1969) 199-214, not that I agree with it, but it addresses the question of the meaning of the passage in a fundamental way.

[2] Rudolf Bultmann, *Das Evangelium des Johannes* (KEKNT; 10th ed.; Göttingen: Vandenhoeck & Ruprecht, 1941; reprinted, 1959); ET: *The Gospel of John: A Commentary* (trans. and ed. G.R. Beasley-Murray, R.W.N. Hoare, and J.K. Riches; Philadelphia: Westminster, 1971).

[3] Birger Olsson, *Structure and Meaning in the Fourth Gospel: A Text-Linguistic Analysis of John 2:1-11 and 4:1-42* (Lund: CWK Gleerup, 1974).

[4] Gail Radcliffe O'Day, "Irony and the Johannine Theology of Revelation: An Investigation of John 4" (Ph.D. Dissertation, Emory University, 1983), revised and published as *Revelation in the Fourth Gospel* (Philadelphia: Fortress, 1986). The actual quotations are from "Irony," with cross-references to *Revelation*.

Important for O'Day is not only irony in the text, but also the way in which the reader is involved in the story. "First, it is important to notice one of the ways in which John involves the reader in the text. He draws the reader from one narrative focus to another, as for example in the transition scene of vv. 27-30, when the story moves from the well to the village and back to the well, so that the reader is not given the opportunity to rest comfortably in one place, but is kept slightly off balance. One cannot simply observe this narrative, but must move with it.

"Similarly, . . . John carefully juxtaposes and balances one scene with another, (e.g., vv. 7 and 8, vv. 27 and 28, the placement of imperatives in the dialogues). A comparison of one set of characters with another is unavoidable. If we recall what was said in chapter two about co-textual irony (irony that arises from a contradiction, disparity, etc. between the text and its literary context), we can obtain an early indication of one of John's narrative techniques" ("Irony," 137; *Revelation*, 54-55). The following remark gives an indication of what she means, "John's use of irony to create and recreate the dynamics of revelation is most obvious in the scenes in which individuals or groups encounter Jesus. The characters, and by extension the reader, are drawn into dialogue with Jesus and asked to sort through the incongruities and move through one level of meaning to another. The large number of dialogues, discourses, and encounter scenes in the gospel point to the importance that John places on the communication process. The fourth gospel is not just a report of Jesus as revealer, but allows the reader to experience the revelation for himself or herself" ("Irony," 121). Also, "The dialogues of Jn 4 provide the reader with the opportunity to become involved in the verbal interplay between the characters, but also allows him or her the distance and freedom to observe what is being enacted" ("Irony," 122; *Revelation*, 48).

At the end of her study she concludes, "John does not *present* the story of Jn 4 to the reader, but instead narrates it in such a way that the reader *participates* in the narrative and the revelatory experience communicated by it. . . . John's principal means of engaging the reader is through his use of irony in Jn 4:4-42. . . . The

knowledge-sociological study,[5] and my own semiotic investiga-

reader is . . . made aware that the narrative is not one-dimensional, but multi-dimensional, with two contrasting narrative levels often occurring simultaneously. Another important ironic technique is John's frequent use of repetition. We have noted other ironic techniques — the ironic contrast between what is anticipated and what is said (vv. 17 and 18), ironic questions based on misunderstanding or false assumptions and perceptions (vv. 12, 33), and the more general pattern of question and indirect response (vv. 9 and 10, vv. 12 and 13-14)" ("Irony," 211-12; *Revelation*, 89-90). "Irony does not *force* the reader to decide, but *allows* the reader to become engaged. In irony the elements of demand and distance are held in a taut, highly charged balance" ("Irony," 213; *Revelation*, 91).

[5] Walter Rebell, "Gemeinde als Gegenwart: Ein didaktischer und wissenssoziologischer Zugang zum Johannes-Evangelium mit einer Auslegung der Kapitel 3 und 4" (Habilitationsschrift Universität-Gesamthochschule-Siegen, 1985). Quoting a statement of S. Kracauer (*Geschichte - Vor den letzten Dingen*. [Frankfurt/M: Suhrkamp, 1973] 242), "Akkuratesse im Approximativen vermag statische Elaborate an Präzision zu übertreffen," he interprets the Fourth Gospel as follows: "Logisch ausgefeilte Passagen, wie sie etwa im Corpus Paulinum zu finden sind, sucht man im Joh-Ev vergeblich. Mühsam und langatmig ist oft der Gedankenverlauf, besonders in den Reden und Dialogen. Dieser Gedankenverlauf bringt verschiedene Aspekte eines Themas, dem er sich kreisend nähert, zum Aufleuchten, läßt aber auch vieles ungesagt oder deutet es bloß an" (1). He quotes R. Guardini, *Jesus Christus. Sein Bild in den Schriften des Neuen Testaments. Zweiter Teil: Das Christusbild der Johanneischen Schriften.* (Würzburg: Werkbund-Verlag, 1940), "Bei Johannes . . . wird der Lesende immer wieder — fast möchte man sagen, grundsätzlich — aufgehalten. Er kommt aus dem einen Satz nicht einfachhin in den anderen hinüber. Er wundert sich, wieso gerade dieses an dieser Stelle gesagt werde. Der Gedanke scheint mit dem voraufgehenden und folgenden nicht richtig zusammenzuhängen" (2. 106). In that sense he concludes, "Und gerade auf diese Weise scheint das Evangelium seine Botschaft vermitteln zu wollen und zu können" (ibid.).

Quoting positively a thesis of I. Baldermann (*Die Bibel - Buch des Lernens: Grundzüge biblischer Didaktik* [Göttingen: Vandenhoeck & Ruprecht, 1980] 218-235), he argues "daß dieses besondere joh Sprachmuster eine didaktische Funktion hat. Es bereitet dem Leser zunächst Schwierigkeiten: 'Wo er rasch dem Ziel der Darstellung näherkommen möchte, hält ihn der Evangelist bei jedem einzelnen Schritt fest, auch Wiederholungen und scheinbar unwichtige Einzelheiten nicht vermeidend.' Angesichts einer solchen Gedankenführung besteht die Gefahr, daß der Leser ermüdet, daß er gar den Text arrogant und verschlossen findet und sich abwendet. Ist jedoch die Faszination, die vom Text ausgeht, stärker als der Anstoß, den der Leser an ihm nimmt, wendet dieser sich also nicht ab, wird er vom Text einen Weg geführt, und es eröffnen sich ihm überraschende Einsichten. Dieses im Text liegende Potential, das den Leser einen Weg führen kann, macht nach Baldermann den Text 'didaktisch' " (4).

Rebell then formulates the issue in terms of the sociology of knowledge, "Wenn wir gesagt haben, daß der Text den Leser einen Weg führen kann, gilt es nun, ergänzend zu fragen: wohin geht dieser Weg? — Die Antwort, die hier gegeben wird, ist kurz gesagt diese: das Joh-Ev führt den Leser in eine Welt sui generis ein, in die — um es wissenssoziologisch auszudrücken — symbolische Sinnwelt der joh Gemeinde" ("Gemeinde als Gegenwart," 4-5). Furthermore, "Am Anfang steht die Überlegung, daß Menschen stets in einer 'gedeuteten Welt' und nicht etwa in der empirisch vorfindlichen Leben" (6). These considerations are further elabo-

tion above.[6] However, my interpretation is not an engagement with that literature. It is an attempt to understand the story of Jesus and the Samaritan woman informed as far as possible by all relevant material, not an engagement with the secondary literature. For that reason I do not enter into controversies about the interpretation of details, except where such an interpretation affects, or is helpful, for the meaning of the text. In writing the first draft I had only the text of John 4 in front of me. After its completion I went back through my notes and marked copies of the secondary literature to make sure I did not miss anything of significance. Even then I avoided shifting the focus from the text of John 4 to what is said about it in the secondary literature.

In violation of the rule of thumb, "if it is worth saying it should be in the text, not the footnotes," the secondary literature is placed almost exclusively in the footnotes. The interpretation thus takes place at two distinct levels: a reading of John 4 in the main text, and a presentation of the secondary literature, and occasional engagement with it, in the footnotes. Furthermore, the secondary literature is not presented in dialogue with my interpretation, but with the text of John 4: the footnotes are intended to shed light on the text of John 4, not on my interpre-

---

rated in terms of such areas of inquiry as Ernst Cassirer's "Symbollehre" (15), and Ludwig Wittgenstein's philosophy of language (28-29).

The discussion of the symbolic world of the Fourth Gospel is in turn expanded in terms of its didactic function, "Diese phänomenologische Analyse der joh symbolischen Sinnwelt muß nun ergänzt werden durch didaktische Überlegungen. Das Joh-Ev stellt in seiner Textwelt keinesfalls eine Wirklichkeit dar, die fraglos Gültigkeit hatte, sondern es lud seine Gemeinde ein, eben dieser seiner Wirklichkeit zuzustimmen, in sie hineinzufinden und dabei Veränderungsprozesse, ohne die eine Teilnahme an der neuen Wirklichkeit nicht möglich ist, zu durchlaufen; das Evangelium wollte also etwas vermitteln und damit didaktisch tätig sein. . . . Seine psychagogische Kraft entfaltet das Joh-Ev nicht durch Argumente, sondern indem es in seine Textwelt hinein verstrickt, indem es eine Sogwirkung ausübt, und zwar auch und gerade über die irrationalen Metaphern und Gedankenzusammenhänge, die also offenbar einen festen Platz im Aufbau des Evangeliums haben und nicht in jedem Fall literarkritisch aufgelöst werden müssen" (8).

At the end of his investigation, he concludes, "Zu nichts anderem dient die feinsinnige dramaturgisch orientierte Didaktik der Perikope, als dazu, den Leser zu einer Umstrukturierung von Wirklichkeit zu führen, die einem Übergang in eine neue Welt gleichkommt. . . . Der Text Joh 4,1-42 umschließt eine Reihe von Einzelzügen, die z.T. gegenläufig sind, und sammelt sie auf eine Mitte hin, oder besser gesagt; ein guter Teil dieser Integrationstätigkeit wird dem Leser selbt abverlangt, *er* ist es, der den Text kohärent machen muß . . ." (188-89).

[6] I consider that investigation, like any grammatical investigation, as mere scaffolding in our endeavor to understand a text; it is not part of the meaning of the text, but an abstraction.

tation of it. It is for that reason that only rarely do I engage in discussion with the secondary literature. My intention is that the readers should have the information on the basis of which they can make up their own minds. The purpose of the references to the secondary literature is to open up the interpretation, not to close it off in the sense of my own interpretation. Having had to go through the manuscript a number of times editorially, I found it possible to move from interpretation to footnotes without difficulty, in the awareness that the relationship is dialectical. The footnotes are not intended merely to reinforce the interpretation, but to open up as wide a range of vision on the text as possible.

In a final reading of the interpretation, I introduced remarks at crucial points indicating how the semiotic analysis informed my reading of the text. Even in those cases I did not refer back to the analysis as I was interpreting the text. It is only in hindsight that I give recognition to the ways in which the analysis informed my reading. A second set of footnotes identifies relevant sections in Part One by page numbers. The interpretation is not intended to be a vindication of the analysis, certainly not an attempt to be right over and against other interpretations. The procedure is that, having investigated the grammar of the text in Part One — its syntax as well as semantics — similarly to what one would do with a difficult text in a foreign language, we now return to our text to see if we can read it, supplementing the analysis with a consideration of information from the secondary literature in the footnotes.

In comments on studies similar to this, it has been pointed out to me that it is possible to recognize conclusions to which I came on the basis of my analysis without the analysis. I consider that a compliment, and a confirmation of the analysis. If my analysis were to suggest something about the text which cannot be recognized by a sensitive reader *without* the analysis, irrespective of whether or not such a reader had the benefit of an analysis, I would consider the analysis to have introduced alien material into the text. A person who depends on a grammar to unravel the meaning of a text in a foreign language will not understand the text until she or he has come to the point where she or he can read the text without the grammar. It is in that sense that I refer back to the semiotic study: it is merely an admission at certain points in my reading of John 4 that I benefited from a grammar before I tried to read the text this time around.

With regard to historical-critical issues: it is important to know what our author may have meant when he wrote that

Jews and Samaritans *ou synchrōntai*. The discussion of the possible meanings can be very informative in itself. So, for example, the suggestion by David Daube[7] that Jews and Samaritans do not use utensils in common may provide interesting contemporary flavor, and so also the many other possibilities that have been proposed. Exactly what the author had in mind is no longer determinable. Such knowledge would, however, add no more than an interesting detail. Whatever interpretation one accepts for the expression, as far as the meaning of the text is

[7] David Daube, "Jesus and the Samaritan Woman: The Meaning of *syngraomai*," *JBL* 69 (1950) 137-47. The conception had already been mentioned by Adolf Schlatter, *Das Evangelium nach Johannes* (Schlatters Erläuterungen zum Neuen Testament; Stuttgart: Calwer, 1908; 3rd ed., 1947) 3. 65. According to Daube, "The dative *heterō*, that is, if we translate 'to use together', would be connected, not with the main body of the verb, *chraomai*, but with the prefix *syn*: 'to use together one with the other', not 'to use one another' " (143). He admits, however, that he "has found no clear case where the dative after *synchraomai* depends on the *syn*," but nevertheless maintains, "The possibility of this construction must have existed" (144). D.R. Hall ("The meaning of *sygchraomai* in John 4:9," *ExpTim* 83 [1971] 56), however, quoting a number of *syn* compound verbs in the New Testament, points out, "In the case of all these verbs, the noun in the dative is governed by the whole verb. The prefix *syn* does not govern an object of its own (whether expressed or implied), but intensifies the simple verb." He concludes, "The Rabbinic ruling quoted by Dr. Daube is, of course, still significant as an illustration of the general attitude of Jews and Samaritans. But the important thing for John was not that Jesus was willing to break a ritual prohibition, but that by his friendliness he broke down the barrier of hatred and suspicion dividing Jew and Samaritan" (57).

See also the comment of Lindars, "It is a technical term, stemming from a decree of the Sanhedrin of A.D. 65/6, from which the harsh quotation about Samaritan women ['the daughters of the Samaritans are deemed unclean as menstruants from their cradle' — *Niddah* 4:1] is derived. It cannot, then, have been operative in the time of Jesus, though it could well have been known to John" (*The Gospel of John*, 181).

T.E. Pollard ("Jesus and the Samaritan Woman," *ExpTim* 92 [1981] 148) points out that Augustine already gave an interpretation similar to Daube, "In *Tractate XV*, ch. 4. para. 11, after quoting Jn 4:8-9 according to the Vulgate Latin, Augustine says, 'You see that they were aliens: indeed, the Jews would not use their vessels. And as the woman brought with her a vessel with which to draw water, it made her wonder that a Jew sought drink of her — a thing which the Jews were not accustomed to do.' " He considers it reasonable to conclude "that Augustine, writing about AD 410-420, either himself invented this interpretation which Daube has proposed over 1500 years later or simply drew on a traditional interpretation with which he was familiar and which he took for granted." What could make Augustine's interpretation all the more significant is that the Vulgate text, which has *coutuntur*, does not suggest it. Alexander Souter (*A Glossary of Later Latin to 600 A.D.* [Oxford: Clarendon Press, 1949] 82), gives as the meaning of *coutor*, "(= *synchrōmai*), consort with (SS, et VG. Ioh. 4. 9); presume upon (IGNAT. ad Magn. 3.1)." Only the latter is relevant here since the former is derived from the Greek of our text.

concerned, it is clear that Jesus violated an important custom which regulated association of Jews and Samaritans.

With regard to the meaning of the text, the Buddhist parallel alluded to by Bultmann[8] may be more revealing than the precise local custom of Jews and Samaritans. This is not to say that both incidents, this and the Buddhist one, including the variety of interpretations, are not interesting in themselves, and illuminating of the sociological settings of the stories. In the Buddhist story, when the young girl of the Candala caste protested that she would defile him, Ananda replied that he did not ask her about her caste or her family, but for a drink of water if she could give it to him. What is common to our story and that of Ananda[9] is probably more important for the meaning of our text than illuminating it with local color through historical-critical reconstruction. The feature common to both incidents is that a man asks a drink of water of a woman with whom he is, by the weight of custom, not supposed to associate. The drink of water may not be important in and of itself; the important feature is the fact of association, as the explanatory remark in our text makes clear, Jews and Samaritans *ou synchrontai*. That same meaning, association where custom forbids,[10] could also be brought to expression in other ways, e.g., by asking for something to eat, or through Jews eating with gentiles, which apparently led to such a sharp confrontation between Paul and Peter in Antioch (Gal 2:11-21).

The meaning of the story is not to give information about the relationships between Jews and Samaritans, interesting as that may be in itself, especially for social-historical and sociological

---

[8] Bultmann, *Das Evangelium des Johannes*, 131; *The Gospel of John*, 179.

[9] Cf. Schottroff, "Die implizierte Anwort Jesu (auf die Frage der Frau) müßte lauten: weil ich, *obwohl* ich ein Jude bin, nicht danach frage, ob Du eine Samaritanerin bist . . . ." Her own understanding of the first part of the encounter with the woman, which she takes as an independent legend with its own emphasis, different from that of the evangelist, comes to expression when she continues, "weil ich nicht wie andere Juden die Samaritaner meide oder gar hasse" ("Johanneischen Dualismus," 203). According to her, "die Legende ist Ausdruck einer innerjüdischen Argumentation. Mit der Pointe V. 9 sind ja implizit die Juden angeredet als die Überlegenen, die die Schranke gegen die Samaritaner errichten. Die Geschichte ist zweifellos von jüdischer Seite her gedacht . . . . Bei den Juden soll sich etwas ändern durch Jesu ungewöhnliches Verhalten als Jude. Die Legende ist polemisch, sie kritisiert etwas, das die anderen Juden nicht so machen wie der Jesus dieser Geschichte" (204-5).

[10] Note Lindars, "The most that can be said is that the Indian parallel provides a clue about the kind of incident that the story seems to presuppose, and accounts for the setting as far as verse 9. All the rest of the story grows out of the argument of the discourse" (*The Gospel of John*, 175).

studies of New Testament times, which can frequently be helpful in clarifying the meaning of a text. The comment makes
clear that the concrete incident of the request for water is not
told for its own sake, but serves to bring to expression another
meaning: Jesus violates the custom that Jews and Samaritans *ou
synchrontai*. Daube's suggestion gives the incident even more
local color as far as our story is concerned — Jesus would have
had to use the woman's jar from which to drink, but that is not
the meaning which the author intends. The meaning of that incident could just as well have been expressed by means of the
story of Ananda and the Candala girl; both are transformations,
expressions in concrete form, of the same meaning, the restric-
tions laid on the association between people by local custom.

It should be borne in mind, however, that the common
meaning of the two incidents — a man violates the custom
which prohibits him from having association with a woman by
asking her for a drink of water — is also not the point of our
story. It too merely contributes to the meaning of our text. In
the case of the story of Ananda, if one takes it as quoted by
Bultmann to illustrate his point, one may well have the impression that the incident itself brings to expression the meaning of
the story, but in its larger context it too may merely have contributed to a more fundamental meaning. In our story that is
clearly the case.

The difference between commenting on the text and interpreting its meaning — not that the two cannot be interrelated
in a single work — can be illustrated further by reference to the
fact of the drink of water. In the case of Ananda water as such
remains insignificant, but in our story it becomes the occasion
for carrying the discussion further. Nevertheless, as the parallel
of the disciples' offer of food makes clear, water itself is not what
is important, but water as physical nourishment similar to food,
in contrast with the water Jesus offers and the food which he
eats. Thus the same image, water, contributes to the bringing to
expression of two distinguishable meanings in our text. One is
the concrete meaning of Jesus' violation of a custom which regu-
lates the relationships between Jews and Samaritans. The other
comes to expression through the ambiguity of the term water,
the difference between the this-worldly concerns of the woman
and the disciples, on the one hand, and those of Jesus, on the
other. This transcendence of meaning in the incidents with the
woman and the disciples makes it clear that the story concerns
more than Jesus' violating the custom that Jews and Samaritans
ou synchrōntai.

In this interpretation of the meaning of John 4, images, such as water or food, and figures, such as Jesus asking the woman for a drink of water or the disciples offering him food, will be taken as bearers of meaning, and not as exhausting their meanings in themselves.*[1] This is not to disparage the significance of the images and figures themselves, but to focus attention on them as bearers of meaning.

The interpretation will be basically literary-critical,[11] but not in a technical sense. By "literary" I mean that it will follow the flow of the story, but "critically," i.e., not ignoring that the reader already knows the story. I do not consider these contradictory. One may read the story naively, literarily, but the alternative to that does not have to be unliterarily, i.e., a reading which no longer notes that some things which become clear in the course of the story are not known in the beginning. To illustrate — without claiming here that this is necessarily the correct interpretation of this particular feature of the story: when it is said in verse 4 that Jesus "had to" (*edei*) pass through Samaria,

---

[11] A literary approach to the interpretation was already made by Hans Windisch, "Der Johanneische Erzählungsstil," *EYXAPISTHPION: Studien zur Religion und Literatur des Alten und Neuen Testaments, Hermann Gunkel zum 60. Geburtstags, den 23 Mai 1922, dargebracht von seinem Schülern und Freunden* (Göttingen: Vandenhoeck & Ruprecht, 1923) 174-213. Cf. especially his concluding remarks, "Die Untersuchung des Stils . . . will durch Analyse der Stilformen die unmittelbare Wirkung, die es auf den Leser ausübt, beschreiben; sie will, unter Absehen von allen historischen Fragen und von all den zahlreichen kleinen und großen Unstimmigkeiten, die künstlerischen Werte, die Gefühlswerte, auf denen die Wirkung seiner Erzählungen vor allem beruht hervorholen. Wenn die historische Kritik, in ihrer Anwendung auf Johannes, oft eine erklärende Wirkung hat, so daß der Leser entweder das Interesse an der Kritik oder das Interesse an dem Evangelium einbüßt, so ist die stilistische Untersuchung geeignet, unbillige Urteile über die Kritik zu dämpfen und dem Leser des Evangeliums wieder etwas von der Stimmung zurückzugeben, die es verlangt, wenn es als ein Menschheitsbuch, als ein Buch der Weltliteratur und als ein Buch, das eine Botschaft Gottes an die Menschen bringt, gewürdigt werden soll" (213). He showed by means of the story of Jesus and the Samaritan woman, "wie leicht sich die johanneische Erzählung in die bei uns übliche dramatische Form umgießen läßt" (178), by presenting it in dramatic form (178-79).

The approach to a literary interpretation was also made by Lothar Schmid ("Die Komposition der Samaria-Szene Joh 4.1-49," *ZNW* 28 [1929] 148-158), "Zum Schluß sei noch ausdrücklich darauf hingewiesen, wie eng natürlich die von uns behandelte Frage der Kompositionskunst des johanneischen Schriftstellers mit der historischen Fragestellung zusammenhängt. Je mehr wir in den johanneischen Erzählungen die bewußte schriftstellerische Gestaltung erkennen, desto vorsichtiger werden wir naturgemäß" damit sein, diese Erzählungen, mindestens als Ganzes, für historisch zu halten" (157).

---

*[1] 104-107, 117-21

the meaning is evidently ambiguous; does the author refer to the fact that the shortest route from Judea to Galilee passed through Samaria,[12] or is *edei* meant, as it frequently does, in the sense of divine necessity? In due course it becomes clear that the entire story was heavily under the influence of the latter[*2] — note Jesus' statement, "my food is to do the will of him who sent me, and to complete his work" — but it is important for the flow of the narrative to note that this is not clear in verse 4.[13]

The following example reveals the advantage of the critical reader, who might appreciate what the naive, first-time reader may miss. If it is correct to assume, as I propose in this study, that Jesus sanctioned the woman's activity among her fellow villagers with the statement that, although it is one person who sows and another who reaps (v 37), "the reaper and the sower rejoice together" (v 36),[*3] the critical reader would recognize the consummate irony with which the story ends when the villagers say to the woman, "we no longer believe because of what you said, because we have heard and we know that he is truly the savior of the world" (v 42). It is a point the first-time reader will probably miss. The woman rejoices in what the villagers say in criticism of her, because their coming to the full realization of their faith in Jesus is precisely the harvest for which she sowed. In order to recognize this irony the reader has to be prepared for it by a critical reflection on other parts of the story, such as, in this case, Jesus' statements in verses 36-37. I do not deny that there may be genial readers who can see all of this in a first reading, but with regard to this story they have not made themselves known.

1. *The Surrounding Text*

The story of Jesus and the Samaritan woman is a self-contained unit, which either the evangelist, or a redactor, placed in the present context. Verses 1-3 form a transition from what precedes to what follows after the Samaritan incident in verses 43ff. As far as the flow of the gospel narrative is concerned our story

---

[12] According to Josephus it was normal for Galileans on their way to feasts in the Holy City to pass through Samaria, but not without incidents (*Ant.*, 20.6.1 § 118).

[13] Cf. Olsson, "Jn 4:1-4 may be read as follows: Our Lord (*ho kyrios*) in his omniscience sees the situation (*egnō*), he leaves (*aphēken*) Judea of his own volition and must (*edei*) then, in accordance with God's salvation plan, pass through Samaria" (*Structure and Meaning*, 145). The solution may be too neat, too simple.

[*2] 113, 124, 186-87
[*3] 45-46, 80-81, 114, 116, 120

is a kind of interlude, bracketed by verse 4, "he had to pass through Samaria," and verse 43, "after two days he went from there to Galilee." Verse 44, "Jesus himself witnessed that a prophet has no honor in his own country," is not immediately comprehensible before verse 45, "when he arrived in Galilee the Galileans welcomed him, having seen all he did in Jerusalem at the feast." It may be the way in which the evangelist, or a redactor, integrated our story into the larger whole of the gospel, in the sense of Jesus, a Jew (cf. 22), having left Judea under pressure (if that is how verse 1 is to be understood), finding hospitality among the Samaritans.[14] "His own country" may thus not refer to Galilee, as one might expect, but gives expression to the meaning "his own people."[15] If that is the case, the verse would express another kind of irony: the Samaritans *do not know* what they worship, but "we" Jews do know, "for salvation is from the Jews" (v 22). Yet Jesus knew that a prophet was not honored in his own country, i.e., among his own people, the Jews, but he had just been honored by the Samaritans who "have heard and *know* that he is the savior of the world" (v 42).

For our story the precise reasons why Jesus left Jerusalem for Galilee are unimportant. He does not leave Jerusalem for Samaria, but on his way to Galilee an important, if unexpected, interlude takes place in Samaria, important enough to delay him two days from completing his journey. Two days may not be a very long time, but to stay over for that period when one only passed through because one had to (verse 4) is a certain expression of not being in a hurry.[16]

2. *Jesus Makes Incredible Claims (4:4-15)*

As already indicated above, that Jesus had to (*edei*) pass

---

[14] Cf. O'Day, "The function of this setting and these traditions will become clear as we observe the interplay between Jesus and the Samaritans, but it is not too early to note that this Samaritan context sets the entire text in an ironic framework — 4:42 will underscore the point that Jesus has success among the Samaritans but not among his own people" ("Irony," 141; *Revelation*, 56).

[15] Cf. Olsson, "To see Judea and Jerusalem as Jesus' *patris* also agrees with the Gospel as a whole" (*Structure and Meaning*, 144). It is, however, a questionable interpretation when he continues, "When God's son came into the world he came primarily to *Judea, Jerusalem* and the *Temple*, his Father's house, 2:16." Judea is alien territory for Jesus, Galilee a refuge (cf., e.g., 4:1-3; 7:2-10).

[16] So Hermann Strathmann (*Das Evangelium nach Johannes* [NTD 2; Göttingen: Vandenhoeck & Ruprecht, 1963] 89), "Den Jerusalemern konnte Jesus sich nicht anvertrauen (2,24). Den Samaritern schenkt er zwei Tage." Cf. also Zahn (*Das Evangelium des Johannes* [Kommentar zum Neuen Testament; Leipzig: A. Deichert'sche Verlagsbuchhandlung, 1912] 263), "Jesus bleibt nicht nur diesen Nachmittag und die folgende Nacht, sondern zwei volle Tage in Sychar."

through Samaria on his way to Galilee is ambiguous.[*4] It could simply mean that on the usual route from Judea to Galilee he had to pass through Samaria, but the intention could also have been that he was subject to the divine will. At this stage the former meaning is the most obvious, but in due course it will become clear that the entire narrative is subject to divine necessity.

The author next gives geographic information which places the story in a setting that is important for what is to transpire.[17] The geographic information has no significance in itself. Its significance is that it spatializes the narrative,[*5] placing it in a setting which affects almost everything that is about to transpire, which happens immediately upon Jesus asking the woman for a drink of water. The significance of this spatialization is highlighted when one considers the inverted spatialization in that other Samaritan story, the Parable of the Good Samaritan (Lk 10:25-37), in which a Samaritan shows hospitality beyond the boundaries of his own region in the alien setting of Judea, where the local religious leaders failed to do so.

Jesus arrives at Jacob's well, close to the land which Jacob gave to his son Joseph. The well lies close to a village which the author identifies as Sichem.[18] The location is rich in patriarchal

---

[17] Cf. Schottroff, "Die Szene spielt nicht an einem beliebigen Ort, der nur aus geographischen oder historischem Interesse so genau (V. 5. 6a) beschrieben wird, sondern an einem für das Geschehen bedeutsamen Ort: im Zentrum der Samaritaner, in Sichtweite ihres Kultortes Garizim und . . . an einem Brunnen, der ein samaritanisches Heiligtum war" ("Johanneischen Dualismus," 199). According to her, however, the locality can be significant only for the legend of Jesus the Jew asking a Samaritan woman for a drink, on which the first part of the narrative is based. She considers the issue of the relationship between Jews and Samaritans to be completely outside the realm of interest of the evangelist whose concerns are contrary to such worldly issues.

[18] Identification of the village is uncertain. Sichar is mentioned neither in the Hebrew Scriptures nor in rabbinic literature. The ruins of Sichem lie close to the site of Jacob's well, but Askar, which lies a little farther off, is also mentioned as a possibility. Neither is certain. According to Theodor Zahn, ". . . der Umstand, daß die Lage des Orts nach dem von Jakob dem Joseph geschenkten Grundstück oder Landgut bestimmt wird und nicht umgekehrt, zeigen, daß es sich um eine auch nach der Vorstellung des Erzählers unberühmte und trotz der Benennung als *polis* unbedeutende Ortschaft handelt cf. 11,54" (*Das Evangelium des Johannes*, 231). The reason may however have had more to do with the other, religiously more important features of the setting. For a discussion, cf. Raymond E. Brown, *The Gospel according to John* (AB; Garden City: Doubleday, 1966) 1.169; also M.-J. Lagrange, *L'Évangile de Jésus-Christ* (Études bibliques; Paris: Gabalda, 1948) 103

[*4] 113
[*5] 96-98

history. The reader immediately has a clear indication that it is no ordinary place, and in due course will discover its central significance, when the woman tells Jesus "our fathers worshipped on this mountain, but you (Jews) say that Jerusalem is the place to worship" (v 20).

The specific significance of the well for the story becomes clear when the woman asks Jesus whether he thinks he is greater than "our father Jacob who gave us the well, and himself drank from it, and his sons and their livestock" (v 12).[19] There is no reference to such an incident in the Hebrew Scriptures, but the Palestinian Targum of Gen 28:10 mentions five signs performed by Jacob, the fifth being: "after our father Jacob had lifted the stone from the mouth of the well, the well rose to its surface and overflowed and was overflowing twenty years: all the days that our father dwelt in Haran."[20] This may be the incident that is brought to mind here.

The village itself is not significant for the story. Its importance is that it is located close to the well and the mountain, and subsequently that it is the Samaritan locality in which Jesus is received, thus, as with the woman, the fact that it is Samaritan.

Jesus is presented as tired from the journey and sitting down in that condition.[21] The author may intentionally have

(with a picture of the site facing 102); and *Évangile selon saint Jean*, 103-104. Other discussions of the site with excellent pictures and illustrations are, R.J. Bull, "An Archaeological Context for Understanding John 4:20," *Biblical Archaeology* 38 (1975) 54-59 and H.-M. Schenke, "Jacobsbrunnen-Josephsgrab-Sychar. Topographische Untersuchungen und Erwägungen in der Perspektive von Joh. 4,5,6," *ZDPV* 84 (1968) 159-184, who reports extensively on visits to the site, with involved discussions of the text.

[19] Cf. Hermann Strathmann, "Es scheint eine leise Ironie des Evangelisten mitzuklingen, wenn er die Frau rühmen läßt, daß sogar das Vieh des Patriarchen aus diesem Brunnen getrunken haben" (*Das Evangelium nach Johannes*, 85). See also Rudolf Schnackenburg, "Vielleicht soll das Nächste [he means the woman's question] spöttisch klingen; aber obwohl die Frage eine verneinende Antwort erfordert, kann im Unterton auch eine Ahnung von der Größe Jesus mitschwingen" (*Das Johannesevangelium* [HTKNT 4; Freiburg: Herder, 1965] 1.464; ET: *The Gospel According to St. John; Volume One, Introduction and Commentary on Chapters 1-4* [trans. Kevin Smyth; New York: Herder and Herder, 1968] 1.429). Furthermore, Lindars, "The question is sarcastic, but ironically it is perfectly true. Moreover, by mentioning the cattle (and Jacob had vast flocks and herds [Gen. 31-3]), the woman hints that it must be a very copious supply of water" (*The Gospel of John*, 182). Similarly Olsson, ". . . Jesus' companion speaks, indirectly and unwittingly, the truth about Jesus: he is greater than Jacob, the father of the Samaritans" (*Structure and Meaning*, 180).

[20] Quoted following José Ramón Díaz, "Palestinian Targum and New Testament," *NovT* 6 (1963) 77.

[21] "*houtōs*: either 'in this tired condition', or, more probably, 'at once', 'without

presented Jesus as a tired traveller when the woman encounters him, in contrast with the recognition of him as the powerful "savior of the world" to which the story moves step by step.[22] There is a marked progression from the tired traveller sitting at the well[*6] who does not even have something with which to draw water to the mocking "greater than our father Jacob" (v 12), to the woman recognizing him as a prophet (v 19), her wondering whether he is not the messiah (v 29), and finally the villagers recognizing him as the savior of the world (v 42).[23] The

more ado' "; so C. K. Barrett, *The Gospel according to St. John: An Introduction with Commentary and Notes on the Greek Text* (2nd ed.; Philadelphia: Westminster, 1978) 231. Note the excellent description of Haenchen, "*outōs*: nach Ammonius (Catene, ed. Cramer S. 216, 21) besagt soviel wie *hōs etyche*: Jesus setzt sich einfach auf den Boden" (*Das Johannesevangelium*, 239; *A Commentary on the Gospel of John*, 219). Somewhat naively Zahn, "Daß Jesus sich am Jakobsbrunnen, etwa auf der steinernen Einfassung desselben oder auf einer dort angebrachten Sitzbank, niedersetzt, anstatt mit den Jüngern den kurzen Weg bis Sychar oder den etwas weiteren bis nach Sichem (Neapolis) zu machen, wird dadurch erklärt, daß er von der Wanderung ermüdet war (6); er war es also mehr als seine Begleiter . . ." (*Das Evangelium des Johannes*, 234).

[22] Barrett emphasizes the fundamental significance of this contrast for the story: "As frequently in John (see on 3.3), the thought turns upon a misunderstanding of the person of Jesus. He is in appearance a thirsty and helpless traveller; in fact he is the Son of God who gives living water" (*The Gospel according to St. John*, 233).

[23] Cf. Schmid, "Die Stufen, in denen sich die allmähliche Erkenntnis der Frau vollzieht, sind die: Zuerst ist Jesus für sie *Jude*, allerdings ein außergewöhnlicher, da er eine Samariterin um Wasser bittet; dann merkt sie auf Grund seiner Reden vom *hydōr zōn*, daß er offenbar *größer* sein will als Jakob, was sie schließlich auf die Vorstellung führt, er sei ein *Wundermann*; das Wissen Jesu um ihr Vorleben aber läßt sie in ihm einen *Propheten* erkennen; und endlich erfährt sie von ihm geradeaus, daß er der *Messias* sei. Die Klimax der Erkenntnis ist damit aber noch nicht zu Ende. Die höchste Stufe ist der Frau nicht erreichbar, sie wird aber erstiegen von den Samaritern, die in Jesus den *sōtēr tou kosmou* sehen. Die Stufen sind also: 1) Jude, 2) größer als Jakob im Sinne eines Wundermannes, 3) Prophet, 4) Messias, 5) Heiland der Welt. Daß die Samariter in diese Klimax einbezogen werden, ist ein Beweis für den engen und unzerreißbaren Zusammenhang zwischen dem Gespräch (7-26) und der Szene mit den Samaritern (39-42), der ja auch daraus ersichtlich ist, daß beide Szenen durch die VV. 28-30 ausdrücklich miteinander verbunden sind" ("Komposition der Samaria-Szene," 152-53). Similarly, Haenchen, "Die Erkenntnis der Samariter, daß Jesus der Weltheiland ist, beschließt unüberbietbar die Aussagen über Jesu Bedeutung: ein Jude — mehr als Jacob — ein Prophet — der Messias — der Retter der Welt" (*Das Johannesevangelium*, 248; *A Commentary on the Gospel of John*, 226). Furthermore, Schnackenburg recognizes that there are three main themes in this section, "das 'lebendige Wasser', das Jesus and er allein spendet (VV 10-14); die 'Anbetung in Geist und Wahrheit' (VV 20-24); 'Sämannsarbeit und Erntefreude' (VV 35-38)" (*Das Johannesevangelium*, 457, cf. 456; *The Gospel According to St. John*, 421, cf. 456). He points out, however, "Diese *in gewisser Weise selbständigen Themen* dürfen aber nicht den Blick

reader, of course, knows this all along, and in that regard engages in the story as a knowledgeable spectator. The reader does not need to discover that Jesus is truly the savior of the world. Thus this revelation cannot be the purpose of the story. Its meaning must lie elsewhere. The gradual disclosure of the identity of Jesus is not what is meant by the story, but its meaning is brought to expression *by means of* that disclosure."[7]

It should be noted that up to this point Jesus is the only character in the story. He leaves Judea for Galilee (v 3) and arrives tired at the well (vv 4-5). Subsequently, he alone is invited and stays with the villagers for two days (vv 39). The disciples are never part of the story. When they appear on the scene they merely serve to give Jesus opportunity to comment on the story (vv 31-38)."[8] The comment that they left to buy food (v 8) does not explain how it is that they are not present when the woman arrives. On the contrary, the comment prepares for their return to prevent it from taking place as if out of the blue; their departure to buy food is the way of introducing them into the story so that they could appear subsequently when they are needed.[24] They never figure in the story itself, not even after their return. By introducing them at the appropriate point the author is able to have Jesus momentarily disengage from the story and comment on it without leaving the scene. Actually we are at a second level of disengagement. First the author disengages by not addressing his readers directly, but by telling a story, i.e., assuming the role of a narrator. Here, at a second level of disengage-

---

dafür trüben, daß der Evangelist als Hauptthema stets die Selbstoffenbarung Jesus for Augen hat" (457, emphasis added; *The Gospel According to St. John,* 421).

[24] Cf. Lindars, "The idea of obtaining food also introduces a secondary motif similar to the primary motif of the living water, which will be taken up by John in verses 31-8. We can conjecture that when John first gave this discourse as a homily it did not contain verses 8 and 27, 31-8, which he has only introduced in the process of dovetailing the homily into the book" (*The Gospel of John,* 180). Cf. O'Day, "Instead of viewing vv. 8 and 27 as clumsy seams which reflect the evangelist's attempts to attach one story to another, these verses should be viewed as signs of this author's careful craftsmanship as he intentionally interweaves two complementary dialogues into a complex narrative with one beginning, middle and end" ("Irony," 125; *Revelation,* 50). Also, "Although at first sight v. 8 may seem to interrupt the flow of Jesus' dialogue with the Samaritan woman, its effect on the total narrative is not intrusive at all. Rather, this verse focuses the reader's attention on the fact that although there are two distinct sets of characters who have a relationship with Jesus — the Samaritan woman and the disciples (who function in this narrative as one undifferentiated body), the actions of these two groups are never completely independent of one another" ("Irony," 132-33; *Revelation,* 52).

"[7] 167-69, 177-81
"[8] 4, 95

ment, he has a character in the story come to speech to comment on it, in contrast with verse 9 where the author/redactor reengages by coming to speech himself, "Jews and Samaritans do not associate."*[9] In that regard what Jesus tells the disciples should be recognized as of considerable significance for the meaning of the story from the point of view of the author.[25] It gives his interpretation of its meaning; at least an important aspect of it.

That it is the sixth hour (v 6), i.e., noon, underscores Jesus' tiredness, but has caused many a question, and undue speculation, about the appropriateness of the woman fetching water at that time of day.[26] It is a detail ignored by the author. Jesus sits at the well, and a woman arrives to draw water, a scene frequently repeated in ancient near eastern folklore.[27] Jesus asks

---

[25] So Wilhelm Heitmüller, "Zum Verständnis der folgenden Ausführungen müssen wir uns noch mehr als sonst gegenwärtig halten, daß nur der Form nach Jesus, in Wirklichkeit der Evangelist redet" (*Die Johannes-Schriften* [Göttingen: Vandenhoeck & Ruprecht, 1918] 79).

Note especially Rebell, "Nur selten wird in der Auslegung erkannt oder berücksichtigt, wie sehr das Gespräch zwischen Jesus und der Samariterin (VV. 7-26) und das anschließende Gespräch zwischen Jesus und seinen Jüngern (VV. 27-38) aufeinander bezogen sind, daß das eine jeweils konstitutiv für das andere ist und beide zu einem Ganzen verknüpft sind; die Samariterin-Perikope besteht also nicht aus *einem* Gespräch, sondern aus *zwei* Gesprächen. Das Gespräch mit der Samariterin findet während der Abwesenheit der Jünger statt und ist gerahmt vom Fortgang der Jünger (V. 8) und deren Rückkehr (V. 27). Dabei wird in V. 8 durch die Erwähnung von "*trophē*" bereits auf ein Thema des späteren Gesprächs mit den Jüngern angespielt (vgl. VV. 31-34), das erste Gespräch wird also von dem zweiten thematisch umgriffen" ("Gemeinde als Gegenwart," 171).

[26] So Zahn, "Daß die Frau, wie V. 15 zeigt, wenn nicht täglich, so doch manchmal den beträchtlichen Weg von Sychar zum Jakobsbrunnen zu machen pflegte, um dort Trinkwasser zu holen, wird in irgendwelchem Volksglauben begründet gewesen sein, welcher an dem durch die Tradition geheiligten Brunnen haftete; denn in Sychar selbst wie in der ganzen Niederung umher fehlt es berhaupt nicht an gutem Quellwasser" (*Das Evangelium des Johannes*, 236). More to the point is O'Day, "The evangelist is not concerned that she has come to draw water at a rather unusual hour — the temporal reference is made in relation to Jesus' arrival at the well, not hers" ("Irony," 142; *Revelation*, 58).

[27] Note the striking parallel about Moses in Josephus (*Ant.* 2.11.1 = § 257), "Sitting down on a well, he rested from labor and weariness, at noon, not far from the village." The events which follow do not resemble our story. Olsson notes the following parallels, "Jn 4, Gen 29 and Ex 2:15ff have a great deal in common, even if we confine ourselves to the Bible texts: a man in flight comes to a well, where he stops/settles; it is high noon; women come to the well, dialogue with the stranger, the women go home and tell the news, the stranger is invited to stay and he sojourns for a while" (*Structure and Meaning*, 172).

Paul D. Duke suggests the following structure for this kind of story: "A first-

---

*[9] 92-96

her for a drink of water,[28] as reasonable a request as can be expected under the circumstances described.[29] It is the last detail of the story that remains within the framework of normal expectations.[30]

Jesus' request immediately brings out what is at issue about his being in Samaria.*[10] The author does not rely on knowledge

century reader steeped in the stories of the Hebrew faith would recognize the ironic situation of John 4 more quickly than do modern readers. The situation is precisely that of some Old Testament stories in which a man meets a woman at a well (Gen 24:10-61;29:1-20; Exod 2:15b-21). The common theme of these stories is betrothal. The common structure is striking: (1) a man is traveling in a foreign land; (2) he goes to a well; (3) he meets there a maiden; (4) water is given; (5) the woman hurriedly runs home to tell; (6) the man is invited to stay; (7) a betrothal is concluded. There are naturally variations upon this pattern consistent with major themes of plot and characterization, but these variations are meaningful precisely because the structure itself was so set in the consciousness of the people" (*Irony in the Fourth Gospel* [Atlanta: John Knox, 1985] 101). He takes over the designation of these as "type-scenes" from Robert Alter, *The Art of Biblical Narrative* (New York: Basic Books, 1981).

We have already noted above the story of Ananda and the Candala girl, which, of course, is not a betrothal story.

[28] Cf. O'Day, "As is typical in Johannine dialogues, Jesus is the initiator of the conversation. He is not the one asked, as is normally the case in the Synoptic dialogues, but is the one who does the asking" ("Irony," 142-43; *Revelation*, 58).

Note Rebell, "Verglichen mit dem Gespräch zwischen Jesus und Nikodemus ist das Gespräch zwischen Jesus und die Samariterin anschaulicher und ausführlicher. Die Samariterin kommt häufiger zu Wort als Nikodemus (Nikodemus dreimal, die Samariterin sechsmal). Viel stärker als in der Nikodemus-Szene liegt ein wirklicher Gespräch vor" ("Gemeinde als Gegenwart," 173). This is even more so in comparison with the subsequent discussion with the disciples (vv 31-38). Also significant is his remark, ". . . die Samariterin ist nicht in gleicher Weise in ihrem eigenen Vorstellungskreis gefangen wie Nikodemus in dem seinen. In V. 15 bittet sie um das Wasser, das Jesus geben kann, und greift damit das Angebot Jesu von V. 10 auf. Damit zeigt sie — auch wenn sie das, was es zu empfangen gilt, mißversteht — immerhin eine gewisse Bereitschaft, sich neu zu orientieren" (ibid.).

[29] With regard to the literary connection between the two parts of Jesus' conversation with the woman, cf. O'Day, "Each of these subsections begins with a request/command by Jesus (indicated by the imperative) — v.7 - *dos moi pein*; v. 16 - *hypage phōnēson ton andra*" ("Irony," 134; *Revelation*, 53).

It is correct that the ultimate purpose of Jesus' request for a drink in the story is in what follows. That, however, does not justify taking it "daß die Bitte um Wasser nicht ernst gemeint ist" (Strathmann, *Das Evangelium nach Johannes*, 84).

[30] See Zahn, ". . . das Wort *dos moi pein* (ist) nichts anderes als die natürliche Äußerung des Verlangens Jesu, seinen Durst zu löschen cf 19, 28. Daß er trotzdem weder zum Trinken noch zum Essen kommt, findet V. 31-34 seine Erklärung. Nicht Jesus ist es, . . . sondern die Äußerung der Verwunderung des Weibes über diese Bitte des Juden an sie, die Samariterin (9a), gibt die Verhandlung zwischen beiden alsbald eine Wendung auf das religiöse Gebiet" (*Das Evangelium des Johannes*, 236).

---

*[10] 16-17, 123-24

that can be presupposed of his readers to make them aware of this. Thus, he (or an editor) reengages, coming to speech himself to inform the readers about a feature he considers necessary for a proper understanding of the story. The woman's reply makes clear to every reader that what Jesus did contravened accepted practice between Jews and Samaritans, specifically that a Jewish man did not ask a Samaritan woman for a drink of water.[31] The remark that Jews and Samaritans *ou synchrōntai* merely places the woman's remark in a more general setting,[*11] which is what ultimately concerns the author, as the question of the right place to worship makes clear.[32] That it concerns a Jewish man and a Samaritan woman focuses on the issue at a particularly sensitive point. The actorialization, a Jewish man and a Samaritan woman, heightens the significance which had been prepared for by the spatialization,[*12] Jesus, a Jew, passing through Samaria and sitting down at Jacob's well, with all the spatial and actorial features that follow.

At this stage of the story it is only an incident between a Jewish man and a Samaritan woman. However, there are several levels in the narrative. Jesus who is the incognito savior of the world is engaged with a woman for whom he is a mere Jew who has asked her for a drink of water. So it will remain in the entire first part of the story, until the woman almost mockingly says to him, why don't you give me this water so that I will not have to come and draw from the well again. The woman can have no conception of what Jesus is talking about. He promises to give her living water when he does not even have something with

---

[31] Cf. J.H. Bernard, (*A Critical and Exegetical Commentary on the Gospel according to St. John* [New York: Charles Scribner's Sons, 1929] 1.137), "The Samaritan woman affects surprise — for her words are ironical — that a Jew should ask *her* for water." Also, "the woman makes her little jibe — half-jest, half-earnest — recalling to Jesus the old feud between Jews and Samaritans" (ibid.). Bernard assumes that the woman did actually give Jesus water to drink, recalling that "the precept of kindness was universal: 'If thine enemy be thirsty, give him water to drink' (Prov. 25:21)" (ibid.).

Too sharp is Friedrich Büchsel (*Das Evangelium nach Johannes* [NTD 4; Göttingen: Vandenhoeck & Ruprecht, 1934] 63), "Die Frau lehnt ab; unfreundlich, überlegen, scharf weist sie Jesus auf den Gegensatz hin, der Juden und Samaritern trennt."

[32] See O'Day, "By enlarging upon what the Samaritan woman has already made clear, the evangelist appears to direct the reader's attention to the issue of Jewish/Samaritan relations and the breach of conduct which is taking place in the scene" ("Irony," 145; *Revelation*, 59).

[*11] 56-59, 110-11
[*12] 96-98

which to draw.[33] That the woman with her jar is also incapable
of drawing water is never mentioned in the story; the author
himself may not be aware that one cannot draw water from a
well with a jar (v 28),[34] but then she may, according to the author, have had the proper equipment with which to draw water,
even if it is not specifically mentioned. That it is living water

[33] Cf. Zahn, "Andrerseits zeigt die ehrerbietige Anrede mit *kyrie* V. 11. daß sie
nicht zu offenbarem Hohn gestimmt ist . . . . Sie mag zwischen der Meinung, daß
sie es mit einem eitlen Prahler zu tun habe, und die Empfindung, daß seinem Wort
doch ein tieferer, ihr noch verborgener Sinn zu grunde liege, geschwankt haben"
(*Das Evangelium des Johannes*, 239).

Bultmann writes, "Dieser Sprachgebrauch, der vom 'lebenden Wasser', vom
'Brot des Lebens', vom 'wahren Licht', vom 'wahren Weinstock' redet, stammt aus
der Sphäre des gnostischen Dualismus. Denn hier ist die Anschauung entwickelt,
daß allem Irdischen — sei es Nahrung oder Kleid, Geburt oder Hochzeit, Leben
oder Tod — als dem Vorläufigen, Vergänglichen, Unechten das Himmlische als das
Echte, Ewige, Endgültige korrespondierend gegenübersteht. Solche Entsprechung
bedeutet nicht nur die Abwertung des Irdischen, sondern folgt aus der Grundan-
schauung des gnostichen Dualismus, daß die Intention des Menschen, wenn die
sich auf diese irdischen Dinge richtet, sich selbst mißversteht, da sie im Grunde gar
nicht diese will, sondern ihre himmlischen Entsprechungen; sie will im Grunde ja
das *Leben*" (*Das Evangelium des Johannes*, 133; *The Gospel of John*, 182).

Referring to a remark by Schnackenburg, "Nun spricht Jesus ein geheimnisvol-
les Wort, das sofort das Gepräch auf eine höhere Ebene erhebt" (*Das Johannesevangelium*, 462; *The Gospel According to St. John*, 426), Schottroff remarks,
"Damit ist von Schnackenburg nicht nur zutreffend der Bruch zwischen V. 9 and
V. 10 beschrieben, sondern auch zugleich mit Johannes gegen die Tendenz der
alten Jakobsbrunnenerzhlung Stellung bezogen. Denn gerade das meint Johannes
ja auch, daß es sich die Spannungen zwischen Juden und Samaritanern in den innerweltlichen Niederungen abspielen und darum für die Glaubenden irrelevant
sind" ("Johanneischen Dualismus," 209). It is not clear whether the final phrase
agrees with the intention of Schnackenburg. Schottroff is on more secure ground in
appealing to Bultmann's interpretation. "Prononcierter noch als Schnackenburg is
die Beschreibung des Bruches zwischen V. 9 und V. 10 bei R. Bultmann. Die
Frage: Juden und Samaritaner werde [quoting Bultmann] überraschenderweise
sofort fallen gelassen (V. 10ff.), und an ihre Stelle tritt die charakteristische joh.
'Dualismus': irdische oder göttliche Gabe — vor welcher Frage das Problem: Juden
und Samaritaner gleichgültig wird" (ibid.; cf. Bultmann, *Das Evangelium des Johannes*, 131; *The Gospel of John*, 179).

Similar is the understanding of C.H. Dodd (*The Interpretation of the Fourth
Gospel* [Cambridge: University Press, 1960] 314), "Whether it is the temple in Jerusalem or the temple on Gerizim, whether pure traditional Judaism or the 'adulter-
ated' version offered by the Samaritan cults, all such ways of religion belong to *ta
katō*; they are in the sphere of *sarx*. In contrast Christ inaugurates worship *en pneumati*, or, in terms more familiar to Hellenistic readers, worship *en alētheia*, that is,
on the plane of full reality."

[34] According to Lagrange, the well "est un des plus profonds, sinon le plus profond
de Palestine. Depuis que les Grecs l'ont nettoyé des débris qui l'avaient comblé en
parti, il mesure 32 mètres de profondeur" (*Évangile selon saint Jean*, 106). For a
description, see also Schnackenburg, *Das Johannesevangelium*, 460; *The Gospel
According to St. John*, 242.

which Jesus offers her, i.e., spring water rather than water collected in a cistern, is what brings to mind Jacob's miracle which produced running water from the well.[*13]

Jesus' problem is, to begin with at least, that he is incapable of getting through to the woman. All the way to the end of the first part of the story he remains for her a tired Jewish traveller who makes such remarkable claims that she could not take him seriously. The reader is of course aware how wrong she is, and yet it is through her that the reader, if at all, learns that the talk about living water and food of which the disciples do not know does have meaning, that this is not merely a tale about a messenger from heaven who encounters a woman at a well, but a story of how religious strife can be overcome in a new community of worshippers that transcends the differences between the Jewish and Samaritan religious communities, when the villagers recognize Jesus as, not specifically their savior, but the savior of the world.[*14]

To begin with, the woman is sober minded, level-headed. What is it about this Jew who asks her for a drink of water? Notwithstanding the readers' knowledge that Jesus is right, and the woman ignorant, in the "real world" Jesus represents sheer fantasy. He talks about her asking him to give her a drink when it is obvious that he does not have the means of drawing water. In a different setting her mocking of him would have been altogether appropriate. To recognize that does not draw away from the earnestness of the story, but enhances it. It is precisely by talking sense that she misses what is going on. She is not a foolish woman, but one who knows how things function in the "real world." What she does not recognize is that by talking sense, in mocking Jesus, she speaks the truth contrary to the way she understands it. It is important to note that although she answered Jesus' request for a drink by reminding him of the inappropriateness of such a request, she herself too evidently had no problem engaging in conversation with him, thus also violating the custom.

When Jesus tells her that if she asked him he would give her water of life, the specific meaning of his offer within the story is

---

[*13] 104-105
[*14] 185-88

still unclear.[35] The gift of eternal life? Salvation? Water is an im-

[35] See O'Day's remark, "The expression's structural relation to *hē dōrean tou theou* signals the reader (if not the woman) that Jesus does not have simple running water in mind, but the precise referent of *hydōr zōn* remains open. The woman will not be able to interpret *hydōr zōn* correctly until she can recognize the identity of the person with whom she speaks" ("Irony," 148-49; *Revelation*, 60). By not disclosing his identity to the woman, Jesus creates the distance which engages her and the reader, ". . . Jesus does not explicitly supply the woman with the knowledge that she needs to make this next move in the dialogue. Instead of telling the Samaritan woman who he is, he leaves her with a question. Is is a question, however, which says more than a declarative statement could. Through his conditional statement, Jesus asks the woman to reassess her perception of the present situation. . . . This verse draws attention to the fact that the conversation between Jesus and the Samaritan woman is being conducted on two levels simultaneously — one level as perceived by the woman and one as perceived by Jesus. These levels provide the basis of the irony of the dialogue, for they are at odds with one another. The clue given here by Jesus to his true identity is an invitation both to the woman and to the reader to grasp both levels of the conversation and their inherent contradictions to move through the woman's level to Jesus" ("Irony," 149-50; *Revelation*, 60-61).

Strathmann thinks it is clear: "Der Trinkende ist der an Christus Glaubende, der in diesem Glauben das ewige Leben haben wird" (*Das Evangelium nach Johannes*, 85). So also Schottroff, "Die Heilsgabe, das lebendige Wasser, das der johanneische Jesus gibt, ist also das ewige Leben" ("Johanneischen Dualismus," 208). She is however more specific, and in that specificity it becomes clear that there is not agreement on what the living water means, even where it seems to be the case. Jesus "kann das Heil nur zeigen, indem er sagt, was es *nicht* ist. Ewiges Leben heißt für Johannes, sich in den Gegensatz zur Welt zu begeben (17:15f.), heißt, alle innerweltlichen Dinge als irrelevant für das Heil erkennen . . . . Ewiges Leben ist also für Johannes ein bestimmtes negatives Verhältnis zur Welt. Das Ja zur himmlischen Offenbarung ist das Nein zur Welt" (ibid).

See also Zahn, "Diese *dōrea tou theou* oder dieses *hydōr zōn* kann . . . nicht seine eigene Person sein. . . . Das Wasser, welches 1, 33 einen Gegensatz zum Geist bildet und 3, 5 mit demselben zu einem Paar von Faktoren gleicher Wirkung zusammengefaßst ist, wird 7, 37-39 als Bild des Geistes gebraucht und gedeutet, welchen Jesus den an ihn Glaubenden geben wollte. Daß nach jener Stelle der Geist in der Bestimmtheit als Ausfluß der Person Jesu zur Zeit seines Erdenwandels noch nicht existirte und noch nicht mitteilbar war, schließt nicht aus, daß schon damals die Frommen um den heil. Geist als die unentbehrliche Gabe des Vaters bitten sollten (Lc 11, 13). Um so weniger kann in Sätzen wie V. 10 oder 3, 5 ein Hinweis auf den heil. Geist befremden, als dessen Spender Jesus van Anfang an bezeugt worden war (1, 33), obwohl er erst als der Auferstandene und Erhöhte ihn den Glaubenden mitteilen konnte und sollte (7, 39; 15, 26; 20, 22)" (*Das Evangelium des Johannes*, 237-38).

Note what is in some respects a parallel in 6:27, " 'Work not for food that perishes, but for food which remains to eternal life, which the Son of Man will give you. For him God the Father sealed.' Then they said to him, 'What must we do to perform the works of God?' Jesus replied and said to them, 'This is the work of God, that you believe in the one he sent.' " This is in agreement with our passage; the recognition of Jesus as savior of the world does mean eternal life for the Samaritan villagers, but, as we shall see, the story makes what that means more specific.

Note also the remark of Olsson, "The first verses are particularly related to the

portant ingredient, and therefore, symbol, for life in arid areas of the world.[36] According to Isa 49:10, "they will not hunger, nor will they thirst" in the time of salvation, a view quoted in Rev 7:16. But what does that mean concretely? One might refer to the statement in 5:25, "The hour is coming and now is when the dead will hear the voice of the son of God, and those who hear will live." Jesus is obviously trying to get through to the woman, but her level-headedness prevents him from succeeding. It is the villagers who do hear in the end, which evidently means salvation for them, "We have heard and we know that he is the savior of the world" (v 42). But that the ending does not include the woman — they say it partly as a criticism of her — seems to indicate that what Jesus was driving at with her may have been something different. The woman never comes to such a full expression of faith in Jesus, but plays the role of mediatress between Jesus and the villagers.

Furthermore, if one takes into consideration the parallel[37] image of Jesus' other food — which he interprets for his disciples as doing the will of his father and completing his work (v 34) — it appears probable that the water of life which Jesus offers the woman meant something more than her consciously hearing the voice of the son of God when Jesus speaks to her.[*15] As the story unfolds it becomes clear that she had a decisive contribution to make in the doing of the work of the Father. What is remarkable about the story is that in making the contribution she is never said to have clearly understood who Jesus was.

In the woman's reply she unwittingly speaks the truth far beyond her own comprehension. Ironically it is Jesus' hopeless condition — sitting tired at the well in need of a drink, but without the means of drawing water — and the fact that he offers

---

context, 3:22ff and 4:43ff and give a special perspective to the Samaritan narrative: the old order with its water and purifications is disappearing and a new one is coming into being through Jesus who is the Messiah" (*Structure and Meaning*, 138). Also, ". . . the remarkable conclusion of the text, vv. 39-42, not only refers to vv. 5ff but also to the opening verses with their connection with 3:22ff" (ibid.).

[36] For the importance of water as a symbol of life in the Hebrew Scriptures and other ancient near eastern literature, see the numerous references in Barrett (*The Gospel according to St. John*, 233-34).

[37] Cf., however, Bultmann, "Offenbar kann mann das Motiv des *brōma* nicht mit dem des *hydōr* von V. 10-15 zusammenbringen; denn das *hydōr* dort war die Gabe, die er spendet; das *brōma* hier ist, wovon er selbst lebt" (*Das Evangelium des Johannes*, 144; *The Gospel of John*, 195). The differences are there indeed, and should be noted, but that does not exclude the parallel which is decisive.

[*15] 114, 120-21, 127, 151

her living water, which aids her in this insight.[38] He would have to be "greater than our father Jacob"[39] to provide water under these circumstances. The woman has imagination. She does not ask him how he thinks he is going to get her the water, but mocks him with the image of Jacob's miraculous provision of water.[40] By posing the question in this way, not merely expressing skepticism, but formulating it in terms of Jesus' lack of a particular ability, she focuses more on Jesus himself, than on the expected performance. In this way she brings into focus the central Christological question concerning the identity of Jesus.

The woman evidently has in mind an incident such as the one alluded to in the Targum of Gen 28:10, "After our father Jacob had lifted the stone from the mouth of the well, the well rose to its surface and overflowed and was overflowing twenty years." It is an image of which Jesus makes use in his answer, when he affirms that he is indeed capable of something greater than Jacob, "Whoever drinks the water I give to him/her will not thirst in eternity; the water I give will become in him/her a fountain of water springing[41] up to eternal life" (v 14).[42]

The reader who is too well informed may miss the woman's mockery. She finds what Jesus says incredible. By referring to

[38] Cf. O'Day, ". . . the woman's *pothen* actually reflects a much deeper ignorance on her part, as she asks one of the most ironically charged questions in the gospel — the whence of Jesus and his gifts. . . . In 1:48, Nathanael raises a related question about the source of Jesus' knowledge (*pothen me ginōskeis;*)" ("Irony," 151; *Revelation*, 61).

According to Schottroff, "Die Frau stellt damit die richtige Frage, denn das Woher Jesus ist der entscheidende Inhalt der Offenbarung. Sie impliziert in ihre Frage jedoch die falsche Antwort (etwa diese: 'auf wunderbare Weise aus diesem tiefen Brunnen')" ("Johanneischen Dualismus," 207).

[39] A similar challenge is addressed to Jesus by the Jews in 8:53, "Are you greater than our father Abraham?"

Cf. Lagrange, "Mais quel était donc celui qui pouvait donner une parreile eau? — Philon a dit plus d'une fois que la fontaine de la Sagesse c'était le Logos de Dieu, par exemple *De Fuga*, 97 . . . : *protrepei dē ton men ōkydromein hikanon synteinein apneusti pros ton anōtatō logon theion, hos esti pēgē, hina arysamenos tou namatos anti thanatou zōēn aidion athlon heurētai*" (*Évangile selon saint Jean*, 108).

[40] Cf. O'Day, "The juxtaposition of *pas ho pinōn* with the woman's list of those who drank from Jacob's well, including Jacob himself (*kai autos ex autou epien*), clearly places Jacob among those who continue to thirst because they have not drunk the water offered by Jesus" ("Irony," 155; *Revelation*, 63).

[41] Note, however, the comment by Bernard, "The verb *hallomai* does not seem to be applied elsewhere to the action of water. But water in this passage is symbolic of the Spirit (cf. 7:38f)" (*The Gospel according to St. John*, 1.141). Similarly, Zahn, "Da *hallesthai* keine übliche Bezeichnung für das springende, hüpfende Dahinströmen des Baches ist, kann es auch nicht für sich ein Attribut des Wassers sein, . . . sondern bedarf der seinen Begriff erst vervollständigenden Näherbestimmung durch *eis z.*

Jacob's miracle she gives expression to her incredulity. This will be confirmed by her challenge to Jesus after his next reply, when she continues her mockery: "Sir, why don't you give me this water so that I won't need to come here anymore to draw water" (v 15).[43] To reinforce her disbelief she challenges him to a performance for which she is convinced he does not have the ability.

Actually Jesus would have had to be only the equal of Jacob

---

ai" (*Das Evangelium des Johannes*, 239). The image of water rising up to the surface may nevertheless have been called to mind.

Cf. Strathmann, "Manche erinnern hier an die Stelle 7,38f., wo es mit Bezug auf den Geist, den der erhöhte Christus den Gläubigen verliehen wird, heißt, daß vom Leibe des Gläubigen Ströme lebendigen Wassers ausgehen. Aber dort ist die Vorstellung eine ganz andere als in 4,14. Denn dort handelt es sich um die Wirkung des Gläubigen auf andere, hier dagegen darum, daß er selbst das ewige Leben gewinnt. Dieses gewinnt er aber durch den christlichen Heilsglauben" (*Das Evangelium nach Johannes*, 85).

Excellent is the comment of Haenchen, "Meist versteht man dieses Wort so, daß dieses Wasser den Empfänger zum ewigen Leben führt. Dabei wird *eis* final afbgefaßt (vgl. *Schnackenburg* I 466; *Braun* 342; *Brown* I 171). Aber eigentlich steht doch da: Dieses Quellwasser wird im Empfänger zu einer Quelle. Das legt eine andere Deutung nahe: Wen Jesus durch seinen Geist zu Gott führt, der wird selbst zur Quelle, zum Heilbringer für andere. Das erfüllt sich tatsächlich bei der Samaritanerin: selbst zum Glauben gekommen, führt sie Samariter zum Glauben (vgl. auch 7, 38)" (*Das Johannesevangelium*, 241; *A Commentary on the Gospel of John*, 221-22).

[42] Cf. O'Day, ". . . the give and take between Jesus and the woman is essential to John's portrait of Jesus as revealer. The woman's struggle to move from her vantage point to Jesus', to understand fully Jesus' words and thereby discover who Jesus is, enables the reader to experience Jesus and his revelation in a way that would be impossible if reading straight discourse" ("Irony," 157; *Revelation*, 63-64).

[43] Note Lagrange's excellent remark: "*dierchōmai* . . . est beaucoup plus pittoresque, comme on dirait familièrement : pour que je n'aie plus à faire le voyage. Et cette expression souligne la pointe d'incrédulité qui dut apparaitre aussi sur la physionomie et détermina Jésus à prendre un autre ton" (*Évangile selon saint Jean*, 109). So also Bernard, "She speaks half in irony; for she does not believe in any *pēgē hydatos* such as Jesus had incomprehensibly spoken of as being 'in' the recipient of His gift" (*The Gospel according to St. John*, 1.142).

Note, however, Strathmann, "Abergläubig wie sie ist, hält sie alles für möglich: 'Gib mir solches Wasser.' Denn schwerlich wird das im Sinne spöttischer Ironie gemeint sein" (*Das Evangelium nach Johannes*, 85).

See also O'Day, "With v. 15 we therefore end up where we began — with a request for water. The request with which the dialogue opened, *dos moi pein*, is now ironically placed in the mouth of the other dialogue partner, *dos moi touto to hydōr*" ("Irony," 158; *Revelation*, 64). Also, "Although by her request for water the woman is ostensibly doing exactly what Jesus had earlier said she should do, she does not know what she is asking for nor of whom she is asking it. Her ignorance highlights the irony of her response, for the comprehending reader knows that the woman is making the correct request in spite of herself" ("Irony," 159; *Revelation*, 65).

to provide water from the well, but the woman challenged him with claiming to be even greater than Jacob.[*16] Jesus affirms this by pointing out the inferiority of Jacob's water compared with the water he will provide — "everyone who drinks of this (Jacob's) water will thirst again." What Jesus says reminds one of the Wisdom statement that whoever tastes wisdom continues to hunger for it, and whoever drinks from wisdom continues to thirst for it (cf. Eccl 24:21).[44] As far as the metaphors themselves are concerned the difference between "will not ever thirst again" and "continues to thirst" are insignificant. In both cases the water is self-replenishing.[45]

There is however a difference in the polemical function which the saying has in our text; the water about which Jesus speaks stands in opposition to drinking water, as provided by Jacob and available from the well. When Jesus says, "whoever drinks the water I give will not thirst in eternity," the meaning is that one will also not thirst for drinking water, parallel to Jesus having no need for the disciples' food when engaged in doing the will of the Father (v 34).[46] Our analysis has shown that the meaning of drinking water and the disciples' food in the story is not to be taken primarily as nourishment, but in opposition to the water of life and Jesus' other food. The negative evaluation of drinking water and the disciples' food is not an affirmation of asceticism, but as values that are opposed to doing the will of God, represented by the water of life and Jesus' other food.[*17] It is, after all, Jesus who requests a drink of water, until it comes to stand in opposition to doing the will of God, i.e., the task in which he engages when the woman challenges him with the convention of non-association of Jews and Samaritans.[*18] This becomes clear subsequently in the conversation with the disciples.

---

[44] For further references see Lindars (*The Gospel of John*, 183-84), Lagrange (*Évangile selon saint Jean*, 107-108), Schnackenburg (*Das Johannesevangelium*, 465-66; *The Gospel According to St. John*, 430-31).

[45] Note, however, correctly Lagrange, "Deplus le don de Jésus ne procéde pas, comme la Sagesse du Siracide, par addition d'eau rafraîchissante : c'est le don même de la source, de sorte qu'on a pas à désirer une autre eau : on n'éprouve même plus la soif, puisque l'eau jaillit, et jusqu'à la vie éternelle" (*Évangile selon saint Jean*, 108).

[46] Cf. Zahn, "Wie ihm über dem Gespräch mit der Sam. der Durst vergangen ist, zu dessen Stillung er jene um einen Trunk Wassers gebeten hatte, so auch der Hunger, zu dessen Stillung er die Jünger beauftragt hatte, in der Stadt Nahrungsmittel zu kaufen" (*Das Evangelium des Johannes*, 254).

[*16] 62-67
[*17] 118-20, 160-61
[*18] 119

Whether the reference to the water "springing up" to eternal life in Jesus' reply is intended as a contrasting parallel to the legend that when Jacob lifted the lid off the well the water sprang up to the top of the well is not clear, but if it is, it would enhance the contrast between Jesus and Jacob. The involvement of Jacob and his miraculous provision of spring water function to bring to expression the meaning of who Jesus is by placing Jesus' provision of the water of life in opposition to Jacob's provision of spring water, playing on the ambiguity of the meaning of "living" water.[*19]

The woman, without realizing it, once more speaks the truth when she says that if Jesus gave her this water she would not thirst and have to come to the well to draw water. Of course, she does not understand the truth of what she says. As with the reference to Jacob, she expresses the complete incredibility of Jesus' statement. The first round in the conversation ends in complete failure. The woman remains level-headed, incredulous. If that is recognized it becomes clear that Jesus' next remark, that she call her husband, does not constitute a break in the flow of the discussion, but responds to a need which he attempts to satisfy in his next program of action.[*20] The woman's remark demands an almost desperate change in Jesus' attempt to get through to her, which brings the reader to the second round in the conversation.

3. *Jesus Becomes Credible (4:16-26)*

For the naive reader Jesus' demand that the woman call her husband constitutes a sharp change in topic in order to break through to her.[47] The critical reader is aware that Jesus has no real expectation of seeing the husband. His demand functions as

---

[47] Note, however, O'Day, "In v. 15 the woman asks for water so that she will not have to return to the well (*mēde dierchomai enthade*). In v. 16, however, Jesus asks her to do that very thing — he sends her away after her husband, but then tells her to come back to the well (*elthe enthade*)" ("Irony," 162; *Revelation*, 66). Cf. also, Rebell, "Beim Übergang von V. 15 zu V. 16 fällt '*enthade*' eine Schlüsselfunktion zu. Das Wort 'hooks up the section on water and the woman's private life' " ("Gemeinde als Gegenwart," 174). The quotation is from P.S.-C. Chang, *Repetitions and Variations in the Gospel of John* (Dissertation; Strassburg, 1975, 162). In the footnote reference Rebell adds the following, which may also come from Chang, "Daß in V. 15 ein Abschnitt beendet wird, zeigt sich formal durch eine Inklusion; die Bitten '*dos moi pein*' (V. 7) und '*dos moi touto to hydōr*' (V. 15) korrespondieren miteinander und stellen Anfang und Ende einer Sinneinheit dar." Cf. also the remark of Lagrange, above, footnote 43.

[*19] 104-105
[*20] 18, 28-30

a transition to revealing his miraculous knowledge about her, similar to the knowledge he reveals to Peter in 1:42 and to Nathanael in 1:47-49. At the surface level there seems to be a break, but at the deeper level Jesus' command prepares for the revelation of his miraculous ability which the woman mockingly denied him by challenging him with Jacob's miracle.*[21] The connection is not text-syntactical, where the break appears, but paradigmatic, through the repetition of an image, in this case of miraculous power. Jesus failed to demonstrate it in connection with water; now he is about to succeed by means of his knowledge of the woman's husbands. In the conversation concerning the water of life Jesus had moved beyond the level of Jacob's miraculous power. Because of his failure he now has to backtrack to where the woman is by demonstrating his miraculous knowledge.

When he tells the woman to fetch her husband she replies that she does not have a husband,[48] upon which Jesus responds,

---

[48] See Lindars, "the woman simply tells a white lie; there is no suggestion that she is hiding the truth out of shame" (*The Gospel of John*, 185).

Duke sees irony in this for someone who is aware of this kind of a story as a type-scene, the term he took over from Robert Alter: "When Jesus therefore ventures into a foreign territory and meets a woman at a well, the properly conditioned reader will immediately assume some context or overtone of courtship and impending marriage. Such an assumption is rewarded here, for not only do narrative and dialogue keep well within the structure outlined above, but the author has placed this account closely following a story in which *water* transformed into wedding wine is attributed to the *bridegroom* (2:1-11), and almost immediately after John the Baptist has talked about hearing the *Bridegroom's voice* (3:29). The reader knows that Jesus is not only the Christ, the Logos of God, but that he is the Bridegroom who will shortly win this woman to himself. Her initial resistance, her questions, evasions, and gradually unfolding faith in him become occasions for the rich laughter of irony" (*Irony in the Fourth Gospel*, 101). "The next exchange now has new interest. Jesus asks her to go get her husband, and she replies that she has none. A woman with no husband is precisely what we expect in such a type-scene, for that is the role to be filled by the traveler. What is surprising is Jesus' sudden revelation that contrary to both the reader's expectation and the woman's implication, her unmarried status is not because she is a maiden but because she is a five-time loser and currently committed to an illicit affair. This is situational irony par excellence. The Old Testament well scenes invariably feature a *naarah*, a girl whose virginity is assumed and sometimes made explicit (Gen. 24:16). When the heavenly Bridegroom Jesus plays this scene, however, his opposite turns out to be a tramp. He weds himself not to innocence but to wounded guilt and estrangement" (102-103).

The "type-scene" as a frame of reference sheds interesting light on the way the scene could have been understood by readers who were aware of them. Duke, however, over-interprets by taking this as the story of a betrothal in somewhat bi-

---

*[21] 67

not only by revealing that he knows that she now lives with a man who is not her husband, but that she had previously had five men.[49] There is almost a consensus in the commentaries that she had actually been married to the previous five, who could have died or divorced her. The reason for this consensus is probably because the text reads, "You had five *men*, and the one you have is not your *man*" (v 18). The parallel between "you had" and "you have," i.e., now, however, may suggest that none of the other men were her husbands either. The fact that she *has* a man does not have to mean he is her husband. The question is not important for the story. The purpose of the reference to the woman's husbands is to reveal Jesus' miraculous knowledge, not to give information about the woman or her husbands. The figure is of no further significance once Jesus has disclosed his miraculous knowledge to the woman.

It may be worth noting that none of the Fourth Evangelist's women are dependent on husbands, except possibly Jesus' mother (but note her knowing persistence in 2:5). The Samaritan woman in our text, Martha and Mary (11:1-53; 12:1-8), and Mary Magdalene (19:25; 20:1-2, 11-18) are independent.[50] Even though this may not be intended by the evangelist, the effect of

zarre details. The meaning of the story is in tension with what may be expected because of its closeness to such stories.

[49] Zahn remarks, "Sie mußte die Ironie verstehen, mit welcher Jesus, ihre Aussage wörtlich wiederholend, dieselbe als eine zutreffende lobt und seine Erwiderung denn noch mit den Worten abschließt: *touto alēthes eirēkas* d.h. im Unterschied von deinen bisherigen leichtfertigen Reden ist dieses Wort ein wahres Bekenntnis des Sachverhaltes: einen Ehemann hast du in der Tat nicht" (*Das Evangelium des Johannes*, 241). Similarly, O'Day, "Jesus and the reader have heard/read the same statement and interpreted it to mean completely different things. From Jesus' perspective, and in retrospect for the reader, the woman's statement is a masterful example of ironic understatement. What she says is true, but is at odds with what she means. Similarly, Jesus' own response begins as an affirmation of the reader's original interpretation of the woman's statement. Is is not until Jesus indicates *why* the woman has spoken truthfully that the reader is able to see the full significance of both speeches. If the woman's statement is ironic understatement, Jesus' is ironic overstatement — his words are also true, but their manifest meaning is in conflict with their intended meaning" ("Irony," 163; *Revelation*, 66-67).

[50] Cf. Sandra M. Schneiders ("Women in the Fourth Gospel and the Role of Women in the Contemporary Church," *BTB* 12 [1982] 44), "These women do not appear dependent on husbands or other male legitimators, nor as seeking permission for their activities from male officials. They evince remarkable originality in their relationships within the community. They are the privileged recipients of three of Jesus' most important self-revelations . . . ." Indeed, in John Mary Magdalene far overshadows the disciples. Even after Peter and John had gone to the grave (20:3-10), it is to Mary that he appears; she who announces to the disciples, *hoti heōraka ton kyrion.*

the woman's statement that she does not have a husband, is that
Jesus continues his conversation with her, not with the husband
he asked her to call. It is to her that he reveals the nature of true
worship in the story. The reader does not even know what transpires between Jesus and the villagers. As far as communication
with the readers is concerned, the woman remains far more important than the villagers. That this is so is certainly in character
with this feisty woman. If the evangelist is not indeed a woman,
the Fourth Gospel certainly reveals a remarkable understanding
of a woman's point of view.

A more important question may be whether the husbands
are metaphors for the gods worshipped by the Samaritans
before they returned to the worship of Yahweh, as has frequently been proposed.[51] Such a conception would be of some
significance for the interpretation of the story. If the reference
to the husbands is an allusion to the gods of the Samaritans the
story would at this point already polemicize against the Samaritans' form of worship, in agreement with verse 22, "you do not
know what you worship; we worship what we know." There are,
however, serious difficulties with this view. According to 2 Kings
17:30-31, five nations returned to Samaria, each with its gods,
but two of them had two gods each, adding up to seven. On the
other hand, according to Josephus "each nation brought its own
god to Samaria, there being five" (*Ant.* 9.14.3 § 288). It is not
clear whether the "five" refers to the nations only, or also to the
gods, but that distinction does not seem to have occurred to
Josephus. A more serious problem is how well the reference to
the woman's present husband, who "is not your husband," could
serve as a metaphor for the Samaritan worship of Yahweh.

In any case in the further development of the story such allusions do not play a part,[52] except possibly, in a vague way, the
statement in verse 22. When the woman asks whether the correct place to worship is on "this" mountain or in Jerusalem (v
20), there is not the slightest hint that her question has anything
to do with the god who is worshipped; neither is it an issue in
Jesus' reply (vv 21, 23); in both cases the issue is the correct
place to worship. The assumption is that it is the same God.
Only in that way would Jesus' reply be appropriate.

The effect of Jesus' disclosure of his knowledge about the wo-

---

[51] For a discussion see, for example, Barrett, *The Gospel according to St. John*, 235.

[52] Cf. Lagrange, "En se lançant dans une allégorie, et aussie obscure, le Sauveur
eût manqué son but qui était d'éveiller dans la femme la conscience morale au
contact d'un homme de Dieu; enfin et surtout elle n'aurait pu dire *à ses compatri-
otes* : il m'a dire tout que j'ai fait (29)" (*Évangile selon saint Jean*, 110).

man's private life is that she recognizes him as a prophet (v 19).[53] For the first time she sanctions his performance by recognizing his ability, not as a miracle worker but as a prophet. With that it becomes clear that he has finally broken through to her, and, remarkably, to a point beyond Jacob' miraculous provision of water.[54] Now it is the woman who raises what is evidently a

[53] Cf. Siegfried Schulz (Das Evangelium nach Johannes [NTD 4; Göttingen: Vandenhoeck & Ruprecht, 1983] 75), "Die Anrede 'Herr' ist Höflichkeitsanrede, nicht aber im Sinne der Erzählung als christologische Hoheitsprädikat (wie in der sogenannten Kyrios-Christologie) zu verstehen. Ihr Ausruf ist auch nicht eine Schuldbekenntnis, sondern Ausdruck der Verwunderung."

Schottroff sees in this part of the story already a change from what she considers the theme of the original legend. "Ganz im Stile einer Wundergeschichte akklamiert die Frau: ich sehe, Du bist ein Prophet, ein göttlicher Mann mit übernatürlichem Wissen. Hier wird die Frau nun als Frau und nicht mehr als Samaritanerin — und Jesus nicht mehr als Durchbrecher jüdischen Samariahasses, sondern als Wundermann gesehen" ("Johanneischen Dualismus," 204).

Zahn remarks, "Gewiß ist dies ein Anfang der Überwindung ihrer Unwissenheit in bezug auf das *tis estin ho legōn autē* (V. 10 cf 9, 17). Aber anstatt sich von dem Propheten lehren zu lassen, . . . legt sie dem Propheten eine seit Jahrhunderten zwischen Samaritern und Juden strittige Streitfrage vor, die zu ihrer Person und ihren Sünden keine näheren Beziehung hat. Sie lenkt also das Gespräch von diesem peinlichen Gegenstand ab auf eine den volkstümlichen Kultus betreffende konfessionelle Frage" (Das Evangelium des Johannes, 242).

According to O'Day, "One could compare the woman's response to that of Nathanael in 1:47f. — from an unexpected demonstration of knowledge on Jesus' part comes a profession of Jesus' identity. There is an important difference between this scene and the Nathanael scene, however. John does not just provide the reader with a demonstration of Jesus' omniscience as is the case in 1:47ff.; instead he involves the reader in every step from naive ignorance to enlightenment, so that the reader can make the discovery for himself or herself" ("Irony," 164-65; Revelation, 67).

[54] So Adolf Schlatter (Der Evangelist Johannes, Wie er spricht, denkt und glaubt, Ein Kommentar zum Neuen Testament [3rd ed.; Stuttgart: Calwer Verlag, 1960] 123), "Damit ist der Umkreis der natürlichen Anliegen überschritten und das Verhältnis der Frau zu Jesus religiös geworden." However, he understands this in the sense of moral guilt. Cf. also idem, Das Evangelium nach Johannes, 68-79. So also Edwyn Clement Hoskyns (The Fourth Gospel [ed. Francis Noel Davis; London: Faber & Faber, 1947] 246), "Since the water of salvation is for sin and for uncleanness (Zech. xiii. 1), it was necessary that Jesus should lay bare the woman's sin . . . ."

The woman's moral life is not the issue. So Walter Bauer (Die Evangelien II: Johannes [HNT 2; Tübingen: Mohr [Siebeck], 1912] 45), "Seelsorgerische Feinheiten sind in dem Vorgehen Jesu nicht zu rekognoszieren. Die Frau zeigt sich auch keineswegs beschämt oder zum Sündenbekenntnis betrieben." Also Schmid, "Auf keinem Fall aber geht es an, den Schlüssel zum Verständnis der Gedankenführung im Gespräch mit der Samariterin in psychologischen Einzelheiten zu suchen. . . . Es ist nämlich mit Recht aufgefallen, daß bei der Frau keine spur von Schuldgefühl oder Reue zeige, die ihr das lebendige Wasser Jesu etwa begreiflich oder begehrenswert gemacht hätte. Einzig die Allwissenheit Jesu macht ihr Eindruck (vgl. auch V. 20) und der Erfolg der Worte Jesu ist einzig der, daß sie in ihm einen Propheten sieht. Dagegen bleibt der Erfolg der angeblichen

relevant question, "Our fathers worshipped on this mountain,[55] but you (Jews) say Jerusalem is the place where one should worship" (v 20).[56] She assigns to Jesus the task of responding to the question concerning the right place to worship; recognizing his qualification for the task, she assigns it to him.[*22] She may not yet be fully aware of who Jesus is, but she has evidently raised a

seelsorgerischen Einwirkung offenbar vollkommen aus" ("Komposition der Sama-ria-Szene," 155). Furthermore, Bultmann, "So wenig wie in der Nikodemus-Ges-chichte Kap. 3 will der Evangelist hier eine Bekehrungsgeschichte erzählen. Auf die Gestalt der Frau ruht kein selbständiges Interesse" (*Das Evangelium des Johannes*, 142; *The Gospel of John*, 193). To the point is Schnackenburg's remark, "Die ältere Exegese hat dabei die pädagogische Meisterschaft Jesus bewundert; aber Jesu Bemühen richtet sich zuerst nicht darauf, die Frau von ihrem sündhaften Lebenswandel abzubringen, sondern sie für seine Offenbarung empfänglich zu machen" (*Das Johannesevangelium*, 467; *The Gospel According to St. John*, 432). More strongly, "Dem Evangelisten geht es nicht um eine pädagogisch-seelsorger-ische Einwirkung Jesu auf die Frau, sondern um die stufenweise Selbstoffenbarung Jesu" (456).

So also Strathmann, *Das Evangelium nach Johannes*, 81-82, and 85. Exaggerated is his statement, "Die Frau ist berhaupt keine Gestalt von Fleisch und blut. Sie ist . . . ein Symbol des Samaritertums, eine Personifikation der samaritanischen Gemeinde" (82). That is the way in which he then also interprets the meaning of the woman's husbands.

55 Although the temple built on Mount Gerizim by Sanaballetēs for his son-in-law, Manasse, the brother of the High Priest Jaddus, after he had been expelled from Jerusalem, with the approval of Alexander the Great (Josephus *Ant*. 11.7.2 § 302-303; 8.2-4 § 306-324) was destroyed by John Hyrkanus around 128 B.C.E. (Josephus *Ant*. 13.9.1 § 254-56; cf. *Bell. Iud*. 1.2.6 § 62-63), the Samaritans evidently continued to worship on the site, where it was claimed holy vessels had been deposited by Moses and buried (Josephus *Ant*. 18.4.1 § 85). It was a long-standing controversy between Jews and Samaritans (Josephus *Ant*. 13.3.4 § 74-79). Cf. Emil Schürer, *Geschichte des jüdischen Volkes im Zeitalter Jesu Christi* (Leipzig: Hinrichs, 1907), 2.21-22; see the revised English edition, *The History of the Jewish People in the Age of Jesus Christ (175 B.C. - A.D. 135)*. (ed. Geza Vermes, Fergus Millar, Matthew Black; Edinburgh: T. & T. Clark, 1979), 17-19; also Lagrange, *Évangile selon saint Jean*, 111; Schnackenburg, *Das Johannesevangelium*, 469-70, fns 2 and 3; *The Gospel According to St. John*, 434-35, fns 44 and 45; Bauer, *Johannes*, 45. The atmosphere of the woman's question is reflected in the following passage from *Gen. Rab.* 81: "R. Jishmael (born around 180) went up to Jerusalem to pray; he passed a plane-tree (on Mount Gerizim) where a Samaritan who saw him asked, 'Where are you going?' He replied, 'I go up to Jerusalem to pray.' The other said to him, 'Would it not be better for you to pray on this holy place and not on that dungheap?'" Quoted from Paul Billerbeck (and Hermann L. Strack), *Kommentar zum Neuen Testament aus Talmud und Midrash* (3rd ed.; Munich: Beck, 1961) 1.549, which has other interesting rabbinic passages as well.

56 Haenchen notes, "Die Überzeugung, daß die Gottheit an einem bestimmten Ort verehrt werden wolle, den sie durch ihr Erscheinen dort kundgetan hat, ist alt: Sie reicht von dem brennenden Dornbusch bis Lourdes" (*Das Johannesevange-lium*, 243; *A Commentary on the Gospel of John*, 222).

___

*22 32, 36

question which is at the center of the meaning of the narrative and of Jesus' activity in it. The issue, for which the geographic setting provided the context and which had been hinted at with the woman's questioning the appropriateness of Jesus asking her for a drink of water, has now come fully into focus.[57] It is obvi-

---

[57] According to Bernard, "The woman diverts the conversation to another subject, and proceeds to raise a theological difficulty, either to evade the personal issue, or because she was honestly anxious to learn what a prophet with such wonderful insight would say about the standing controversy between Jews and Samaritans. Probably both motives affected her" (*The Gospel according to St. John*, 1.145). This is a naive reading which takes the meaning at the most concrete level. It has value in highlighting the contrasting critical reading which makes clear that the woman's question was raising an issue to which the conversation was steering. Cf. also Lagrange, "Mais le terme même de prophète, dont elle se sert, lui permet de dètourner une conversation qui n'est pas à son avantage. Puisque ce Juif est un prophète, c'est une bonne occasion de traiter avec lui une question religieuse" (*Évangile selon saint Jean*, 110-111). Also, "Mais elle se jette rapidement hors de cette pent scabeuse. Le terrain de la religion lui parait plus solide" (*L'Évangile de Jésus Christ*, 105-106). In the case of Lagrange this should be seen in the light of the following, "L'agréable verbiage de la Samaritaine est assurément moins émouvant que les larmes silencieuses de la pécheresse ou le cri de Marie-Magdeleine au tombeau vide, mais quelle vivacité, que d'ésprit et d'art! Et un coeur droit, en dêpit d'égarements qu'elle n'a sûrement pas été embarrassée de justifier aux yeux des autres, sinon à elle-meme. Quand Jésus a parlé avec autorité, son armature de fierté nationale et de dédain tombe avec sa dernière réplique. Le premier acte de sa contrition est d'avouer sa faute, le second est un apostolat qui la confesse encore : une merveille incomparable de l'ascendant de Jésus" (107).

To the point are the observations of Heitmüller, "Man sieht in dieser Frage meist ein Ausweichen oder Abbrechen der Frau, die sich in ihrem Gewissen getroffen fühle und das heikle Thema ihrer Schuld vermeiden wolle. Das beruht auf der herkömmlichen Meinung, daß Jesus in diesem Gespräch der Samariterin eine kunstvoll angelegte, psychologisch feine seelsorgerliche Behandlung angedeihen lasse, daß er sie fleischlicher Sicherheit und sorgloser Oberflächlichkeit durch die Tiefe des Schuldgefühls zum Glauben führe. Diese Auffassung ist kaum richtig, sie trägt zu viel in den Text hinein. Im Mittelpunkt des Interesses steht nicht die Frau, sondern, wie immer im vierten Evangelium, Jesus, sein Reden und Verhalten, seine Messias-Persönlichkeit (bem. das wuchtige Schlußwort V. 26); die Samariterin ist nur Hilfsperson, um deren Inneres der Verfasser sich wenig kümmert. Auch verät sie ja keine Spur von Reue oder Scham oder Schuldgefühl in V. 17 und 19. . . . Das Gespräch soll gipfeln in der Aussprache Jesu über die wahre, geistige Gottesverehrung, v: 21ff. Die Frage der Samariterin gibt die Gelegenheit gerade zu dieser Aussprache, und deshalb läßt der Schriftsteller sie stellen" (*Die Johannes-Schriften*, 77). So also well-stated by Schmid, "Davon aber, daß der Frau das Thema peinlich wäre, und daß sie deshalb durch eine allgemeine Frage abzulenken sucht, steht jedenfalls keine Silbe im Text. Vielmehr ist nach der Meinung des Textes offenbar einzig das Prophetentum Jesu das Motiv dafür, daß die Frau die religiöse Streitfrage vorbringt, nicht die Peinlichkeit der Situation. Letztes Motiv für das Aufwerfen dieser und zwar gerade dieser Frage ist nach unserer Auffassung allerdings ihre Eignung für den Evangelisten als Sprungbrett zur Erreichung der letzten Etappe des Gesprächs, der Feststellung des Messianität Jesus. Übrigens geht Jesus ja auch sehr bereitwillig auf die Frage nach der rechten *proskynēsis* ein,

ously of great concern for the woman; she asks it not merely as a personal question, but as one that concerns her people as well.

Important to note is the non-polemical way in which she asks the question. Before him whom she recognized as a prophet she poses her question with complete openness. Unlike the challenging rejoinder with which she responded to Jesus' request for a drink, reminding him of what separated Jews and Samaritans, she now looks forward to him, a Jew, saying something concerning a problem that was at the heart of that separation. A slight provocation may still be in her remark, but also an openness; she had already recognized him as a prophet.

For the woman the question does not go further than the concrete issue of the controversy between Jews and Samaritans concerning the correct place to worship. In the story that issue brings to expression a meaning which lies deeper, namely, the true meaning of worship beyond the immediate dispute, and through it, resolution of the social-religious opposition between Jews and Samaritans. Here it already becomes clear that the religious issue of the right place to worship is intricately intertwined with the social issue of the opposition between rival national groups.*[23]

Jesus' reply is obviously not what she may have expected; he does not choose either alternative. "Trust me,[58] Lady, an hour comes when neither on this mountain nor in Jerusalem will you worship[59] the Father,[60] . . . but the true worship-

---

ohne dabei weitere seelsorgerische Absichten zu verfolgen" ("Komposition der Samaria-Szene," 155).

[58] Cf. Dodd, "Here *pisteue moi* no doubt means 'trust me'; but the trust is exhibited in the intellectual judgement that the words of Jesus are credible, exactly as Socrates 'trusted' his *daimonion*, which trust was exhibited in 'believing' its promptings. That is, it means 'believe me'; and the content of belief is given in the *hoti*-clause. We might translate 'Take my word for it: a time is coming . . .' " (*Interpretation*, 182).

[59] Cf. O'Day, "Jesus' words in v. 21 reflect a technique that we have seen before in the dialogue — the words of one speech are repeated in another (vv. 7, 9, and 10; 7 and 15; 15 and 16; 17 and 18). Here Jesus repeats the woman's statement in order to refute it: . . . *oute en tō orei toutō oute en Ierosylymois proskynēsete tō patri*" ("Irony," 168; *Revelation*, 68). Cf. also Rebell, "Eine typische joh 'Spiralbewegung' liegt in VV. 23f vor. Die zentralen Aussagen von V. 23 werden in V. 24 wiederholt, wobei vertiefend — gleichsam als Begründung — hinzugefgt wird: *pneuma ho theos*" ("Gemeinde als Gegenwart," 175).

[60] On the significance of the term "father," cf. O'Day, " 'Father' is first introduced indirectly in the narrative when the evangelist describes Sychar as near the land which *edōken Iakob (tō) Iōsēph tō hyiō autou*. The Samaritan woman explicitly mentions Jacob as father in v. 12, and his 'children' are expanded from his own

---

*[23] 68-70, 123-27, 175-76, 187-88

pers[61] will worship the Father in spirit and truth" (vv 21, 23).[62]
The second person plural, "you will worship," is specific, anticipating the villagers' recognition of Jesus as the savior of the
world at the end of the story. Its meaning is of course not limited to that, but is certainly intended primarily to draw in the
reader as well.[63] The formulation is somewhat clumsy with the

flesh and blood to include all the Samaritans. The next use of *patēr* (v. 20) expands
the meaning in a different way. Jacob, and all the Samaritan ancestors, are included
under the rubric *hoi pateres hēmōn*. John subtly changes the meaning of father in
this text — from the father of one son to the collective Samaritan fathers. All the
referents for *patēr* are dramatically undercut, however, by the one expression of
Jesus — you will worship *the Father*. By repetition and juxtaposition John has ironically shown that the Samaritan woman has no idea who the Father is" ("Irony,"
169; *Revelation*, 69).

Also Duke, "That Jacob is 'our father' will shortly be undercut by the reminder
of another Father who calls his children to move beyond this venerated site and all
the others to the realm of spirit and truth. Jacob is defined as the one 'who gave us
the well'; but 'the gift of God,' Jesus has already said, is 'living water,' a gift the
woman will shortly ask to be given her. The superiority of Jesus as gift and giver is
unconsciously emphasized further when the woman elaborates upon the sufficiency of the well, which satisfied Jacob, 'and his sons, and his cattle' — a bountiful
well indeed! '*You* aren't greater than such a provider, are you?' she asks the stranger — whose own gift is a spring of water 'welling up to eternal life' (vs. 14)" (*Irony
in the Fourth Gospel*, 70).

[61] According to Dodd, ". . . as a rule (John) reserves *alēthinos* . . . for its more usual
sense of 'real', e.g. *phōs alēthinon, artos alēthinos, ampelos alēthinē, ho alēthinos
Theos*, and so, surely, *hoi alēthinoi proskynētai* (iv. 23) — not 'sincere worshippers',
but 'real worshippers', i.e. those whose religious exercises are in actual fact and
reality an approach to God, and not a shadowy ritual which either counterfeits or at
best merely symbolizes the approach to God" (*Interpretation*, 170).

[62] Lagrange asks, "Est-ce à dire que la religion ne comprendra ni rites, ni
symboles?" only to reply, "Ce serait contraire à la pensée de Jo. (iii, 3)" (*Évangile
selon saint Jean*, 114). More to the point is Bultmann's statement, "Dieser Satz
begründet die Forderung eines *proskynein en pneumati kai alētheia* insofern, als
er zu verstehen gibt: jeder Kult, der menschliches Unternehmen (im besten Falle
Frage nach Gott) ist, ist illegitim; die angemessene Gottesverehrung kann nur die
sein, die Antwort auf Gottes wunderbare Kundgebung und also selbst wunderbar
ist" (*Das Evangelium des Johannes*, 141; *The Gospel of John*, 191-92).

According to Büchsel, with Jesus' reply "gibt er ihr das lebendige Wasser. Nach
der Ort der Anbetung war gefragt, von der Art der Anbetung redet Jesus" (*Das
Evangelium nach Johannes*, 65).

See also Zahn, "Jesus verschmäht es nicht, ihr Antwort zu geben, tut es aber so,
daß sie eine Ahnung davon bekommen muß, daß die konfessionell-nationalen
Gegensätze zwischen Juden und Samaritern nur eine untergeordnete Bedeutung
zukommt, und daß nur das innerliche persönliche Verhältnis zu Gott für alle Menschen, die Gott verehren wollen, das Entscheidende sei" (*Das Evangelium des Johannes*, 243).

[63] See, however, Zahn, "Daß Jesus in dem 'ihr', anstatt dessen man ein 'man' oder
dgl. erwarten möchte, Sam. und Juden zusammengefaßt haben sollte, ist angesichts
der scharfen Gegensatz von 'ihr' (Sam.) und 'wir' (Juden) V. 22 undenkbar" (*Das
Evangelium des Johannes*, 243). So also Barrett, but more cautiously: "In view of

redundant "true worshippers will worship in truth." This clum-
siness is not helped by the unneeded explanations, "for the Father seeks such to worship him" and "God is spirit, and those
who worship him should worship in spirit and truth" (vv 23c-
24).[64]

It should be noted first of all that with Jesus' reply the second
round in his conversation with the woman comes to a successful
culmination. What follows is further clarification of what had
been said. When the woman responds with what appears to be a
negative sanction by saying that Messiah,[65] when he comes —

the *hymeis* of the next verse this second person plural must be taken seriously: You
Samaritans who are about to believe (vv. 39, 41) will worship; but John no doubt
thinks also of his readers" (*The Gospel according to St. John*, 236).

[64] Schnackenburg (*Das Johannesevangelium*, 475; *The Gospel According to St.
John*, 440) refers to *The Gospel of Truth*, 21: "But those who are to receive teaching
[are] the living who are inscribed in the book of the living. They receive teaching
about themselves. They receive it (pl.) from the Father, turning again to him. Since
the perfection of the all is in the Father, it is necessary for the all to ascend to him."
The quotation is from the translation by George W. MacRae in *The Nag Hammadi
Library in English* (ed. James M. Robinson; New York: Harper & Row, 1977) 40.
Schnackenburg adds, "Alles ist hier im Sinne der gnostischen Geheim- und Ex-
klusivlehre entfaltet; dem Erwählten gibt der 'Geist' die rettende Gnosis: 'Was die
Erkenntnis des Vaters und die Offenbarung seines Sohnes betrifft, so gab er (der
Geist) ihnen (den Gnostikern) die Fähigkeit, sie zu erfahren' (30). Der Abstand der
gnostischen von der christlichen Erlösungslehre wird gerade in der Begegnung mit
der Samariterin deutlich: Hier spricht ein wirklicher Offenbarer and Heilsmittler"
(ibid.). It is not clear on what basis Schnackenburg makes his judgement that it is a
"real revealer and mediator of revelation," contrary to the gnostic understanding,
who speaks in our text.

Cf. Dodd, "The life of man lies in the sphere of *ta katō*, of *sarx*. God on the other
hand is *pneuma*, and can properly be worshipped only *en pneumati kai alētheia*,
'in spirit, that is, in reality' " (*Interpretation*, 258). He also points out that "in iv. 23
we have the virtual hendiadys *en pneumati kai alētheia*. . . . *alētheia* has in the
Fourth Gospel in general its Hellenistic sense of reality, reality as apprehended, or
knowledge of reality. Thus *pneuma* has some very close relation to reality, unseen
or eternal. It is (as for Philo) the vehicle by which knowledge of such reality is given
to men. But also, it is so conjoined with *alētheia* that it appears as if for John
pneuma could itself stand for the world of ultimate reality, as can *nous* (or *kosmos
noētos*) in Hellenistic writers" (223-24).

According to Zahn: "Erst derjenigen Anbetung, welche von dieser Bindung an
Örtlichkeiten und Äußerlichkeiten befreit ist und also *en pneumati* sich vollzieht,
geschieht auch *en alētheia*. Dazu soll es dereinst kommen. Daß der im Fleisch
lebende Mensch nicht anders als an einem bestimmten Ort der Erde beten kann,
sei es ein Tempel oder sein Kämmerlein (Mt 6, 6); und daß gemeinsame Anbetung
nicht möglich ist ohne dafür bestimmte Orte, Zeiten und Formen, ist so selbstverständlich, daß Jesus nicht nötig hatte, das *en pneumati* durch Erinnerung and diese
Trivialitäten abzuschwächen" (*Das Evangelium des Johannes*, 247).

[65] The Samaritans expected a messiah-like figure, Ta'eb, "the one who returns, or
restores," according to *Memar Markah* 4.12, a Samaritan source from the 3rd-4th
century. Cf. Zahn, *Das Evangelium des Johannes*, 250, fn. 35; Schnackenburg, *Das*

and thus not Jesus — will clarify these matters, she nevertheless, in terms of the story, gives Jesus the opportunity to confirm that, indeed, the hour has come,*24 for "It is I, who speak to you!" (v 26).66 In many respects, thus, Jesus' reply is the culmination of the entire narrative,67 because what now follows, the coming to the full realization of faith by the Samaritans, makes what he said a concrete reality. His explanation to the disciples that his food is to do the will of his Father, for which their inability to understand why he declines their food gives him the opportunity (vv 31-38), clarifies the entire incident. It points to the centrality of Jesus' statement about true worship, and its

---

Johannesevangelium, 475-76; *The Gospel According to St. John*, 441. According to Zahn, "Nicht aus Davids Haus und Judas Stamm, sondern aus dem Stamm Josephs (Ephraim und Manasse), auf welchem die Sam. ihre Herkunft zurückführten, muß er vorgehen. . . . Nach wahrscheinlichster Deutung heißt dies nicht 'der Zurückkehrende oder sich Bekehrende', sondern der 'Wiederbringer, Wiederhersteller' " (*Das Evangelium des Johannes*, 250). Cf. also Schnackenburg, ibid. Furthermore, according to Zahn, he is "der von Gott gelehrte, mit der Gabe der Prophetie ausgestattete Wiederhersteller Israels in jeder Beziehung. . . . Er wird ferner alle im Gesetz Mosis Verborgene offenbar machen" (251). Except possibly for the last feature, the precise identity of this figure is of little significance here. He is the equivalent of the Jewish expectation in the story, and provides Jesus with the opportunity to reveal that he is the one who is expected. Cf. Zahn, "Auch hier, an der entscheidende Stelle des Gesprächs, will Jo den originalen Laut der Rede festhalten. . . . Dies scheint aber vorauszusetzen, daß das Weib wirklich dieses jüdisch-aramäischen Wort und nicht irgend ein bei den Samaritern übliches Synonym gebraucht habe" (*Das Evangelium des Johannes*, 249).

66 So Bauer, "Die Frau antwortet, wie sie tut, weniger aus Ratlosigkeit und um das Gepräch zu beenden, als um Jesus Gelegenheit zu seinem Selbstzeugnis . . . zu geben. Und zwar birgt sich hinter diesem weder das samaritische, noch das jüdische Messiasideal, sondern der Anspruch *sōtēr tou kosmou* zu sein (42)" (*Johannes*, 47-48). Cf. also Bernard, "Her words are almost a query; they invite a further declaration on the part of Jesus, which he gives forthwith" (*The Gospel according to St. John*, 1.151). Also Heitmüller, "Auch das soll nicht als ein Ausweichen aufgefaßt werden. Das Wort ist im Zusammenhang nötig, um das die Krone bildende unumwundene Bekenntnis Jesus zur messianischen Würde (V. 26) zu ermöglichen" (*Die Johannes-Schriften*, 78).

67 Cf. Haenchen, "Sachlich hat Jesu Unterredung mit der Samariterin ihr Ziel erreicht" (*Das Johannesevangelium*, 245; *A Commentary on the Gospel of John*, 224). Cf. Dodd, "The main dialogue then ends with an express avowal by Christ that He is the 'Messiah' — with the implication that 'Messiah' means not only the messenger who will 'announce' certain religious truths (iv. 25), but inaugurator of a new era in religion, of which it may be said, not only *erchetai hōra* (iv. 21), but *erchetai hōra kai nyn estin* (iv. 23). This introduces what is to be the central theme of the dialogue which forms the conclusion of the whole scene (iv. 27-42)" (*Interpretation*, 314). Remarkably, though, he states, "iv. 27-42 forms an appendix to the dialogue with the Samaritan woman" (387).

---

*24 33-36

concretization in the Samaritans coming to the full realization of faith in him as a savior, of neither specifically the Samaritans nor the Jews, but of the world. Their faith implies a salvation that is beyond the controversies which separate Jews and Samaritans, a separation which is highlighted by the very location of the incident, i.e., its spatialization in Samaria which stands in opposition to Judea/Galilee.

The essence of Jesus' reply is a conception of worship in which the religious discord between Jews and Samaritans is overcome in a new community of believers who worship in spirit and truth.[68] This is confirmed by the villagers in their recognition of him as the savior of the world. Jesus does not say on this mountain as well as in Jerusalem, uniting Samaritans and Jews, but "neither on this mountain nor in Jerusalem," "in spirit and truth." It is certainly not in agreement with the meaning of the passage that Christianity became one more religious community over and against all the others, claiming for itself the right way of worship, and so once more establishing the alternatives, "this mountain or Jerusalem."[69]

All that still is needed is the sanction that "the hour which is coming" is already present.[70] The woman's expressing her expectation that the hour is still coming — "I know that Messiah is coming; when he comes he will explain everything" — is what

[68] Note the interpretation given to this by Schottroff, "Die johanneische Jesus, und d.h. Johannes, antwortet auf dieses Problem: eure Alternative der Kulturplätze ist ein vordergründiges, ein innerweltliches Problem. Die Alternative ist überhaupt falsch, jüdische und samaritanische Gottesverehrung liegen auf *einer*, der falschen, Ebene. Weder auf dem Garizim noch in Jerusalem wird der Vater verehrt, die wahre Gottesverehrung ist die in 'Geist und Wahrheit', und d.h. für Johannes: wahre Gottesverehrung ist Glaube an den himmlischen Offenbarer, der die Freiheit von den irdischen Bindungen, auch von den religiöson Bindungen des Juden- oder Samaritanertums, schenkt" ("Johanneischen Dualismus," 205). But note also the following, "Aus dem Bisherigen ist klar geworden, was Johannes *nicht* will — er will nicht wie die ihm vorliegende Legende gegen die Schranke innerweltlichen Hasses kämpfen, er will nicht Bezug nehmen auf die für ihn vordergrundigen und irdischen Probleme, wie sie sich im Verhältnis von Juden und Samaritanern zeigen" (ibid).
[69] Heitmüller interprets, "das Christentum ist rein geistige, von allen nationalen und lokalen Schranken befreite Menschheits-Religion" (*Die Johannes-Schriften*, 80). This would be true for Christianity only if it takes this story as an essential element in the definition of its identity.
[70] Jesus already announced this in verse 23, *alla erchetai hōra kai nyn estin*. Cf. Schnackenburg, "Die joh. Wendung (vgl. 5, 25 28; 16, 2 25 32) hat einen religiösen eschatologischen Sinn und wird durch das folgende *nyn estin* (V 23) näher bestimmt: Diese Stunde bricht mit Jesu Person bereits an; in ihm kündigt sich eine neue Art der Gottesverehrung an, für die der Ort des Kultus unwichtig ist" (*Das Johannesevangelium*, 470; *The Gospel According to St. John*, 435).

gives Jesus the opportunity to reaffirm that it is already present — "It is I, who speaks to you."[71] Highly significant is the temporalization introduced by Jesus' statements: "an hour is coming when neither on this mountain nor in Jerusalem" (v 21) and "an hour is coming, and now is, when the true worshippers

---

[71] O'Day, "Vv. 25 and 26 bring Jesus' actual conversation with the woman to a close — v. 25 is the last word spoken directly by the woman to Jesus and v. 26 is the last word spoken directly by Jesus to her. The dialogue is formally brought to its conclusion, however, by the return of the disciples" ("Irony," 134; *Revelation*, 53).

According to Strathmann, "In dieser Selbstoffenbarung Jesu wird das Ziel und der Höhepunkt des Gesprächs erreicht (nicht in den Sätzen über die Anbetung Gottes in Geist and Wahrheit)" (*Das Evangelium nach Johannes*, 87). He misses the intricate relationship between the two, in which each clarifies the meaning of the other.

Schlatter thinks that with that Jesus gave her the living water, but once more in the sense of the admission of moral guilt. "Während sich aber Nikodemus noch besinnen muβ, ob er kommen will oder nicht, eilt sie zu Jesus hin und ergreift seine Hand, und er reicht sie ihr. Was macht den Unterschied? Die Sünde, Schande und Not der Frau war ihre kranke Liebe, des Nikodemus Sünde, Schande und der Not seiner kranke Weisheit" (*Das Evangelium nach Johannes*, 74). "Die Wendung vom falschen zum wahren Licht ist schwerer als die von der Finsternis zum Licht" (75).

Cf. also Rebell, "Der Ausklang des Gesprächs zwischen Jesus und der Samariterin ist vom Thema Christologie bestimmt. Bei der Frau bahnt sich eine christologische Erkenntnisbereitschaft an (V. 25), mit welcher eine Selbstoffenbarung Jesu im Ego-eimi-Stil korrespondiert (V. 26). Vom Thema der Proskynese Gottes bewegt sich der Gedankengang also zum Thema Christologie. Beide Themen gehören sachlich eng zusammen: die wahre Anbetung, die 'in Geist und Wahrheit' (vgl. VV. 23f), ist christologisch qualifizierte, aus der Begegnung mit Jesus erwachsende Anbetung. Anders gesagt: die Erkenntnis Jesu als Christus und die wahre Anbetung Gottes fallen in eins" ("Gemeinde als Gegenwart," 175). Furthermore, "Da nun für das Joh-Ev Jesus nicht nur der Geber des Lebens ist, sondern das Leben selbst (vgl. 1, 4; 11, 25; 14, 5), ist die personale Erschließung Jesu für den Glaubenden als solche das Angebot der Lebensübermittlung. Jesus eröffnet der Samariterin also in V. 26 durch seine personale Selbsterschließung des 'Leben' " (178).

With regard to the literary nature of the passage O'Day, remarks, "Jesus answers the woman with his most direct statement of the dialogue: *egō eimi, ho legōn soi*" ("Irony," 176; *Revelation*, 72). "Throughout the dialogue, John let stand, often without explicit comment, two contradictory perceptions of the same event. The 'correct' view is never allowed to stand in isolation. When Jesus makes an explicit statement (e.g., vv. 13 and 14, 23 and 24), John immediately undercuts it with the woman's response. The reader is left to decipher the relationship between the two perspectives and to choose between them. The ironic 'double exposure' of Jesus' statements and the woman's responses allows for reader participation in the revelatory process in a way that declarative statements could not. It is for this reason that the *egō eimi* of v. 26 has such tremendous impact on the reader. The distance which John has allowed throughout the dialogue for the woman's and the reader's free movement toward Jesus is removed with this absolute statement of self-revelation. The reader is faced with a direct, definitive revelation of Jesus which calls for a type of decision different from that of the ironic interplay of the rest of the dialogue. Now the decision is only to affirm or deny" ("Irony," 178; *Revelation*, 73).

will worship the Father in spirit and truth" (v 23).[25] The woman
tries to hold time back: "Messiah is coming . . ." (v 25), but her
attempt gives Jesus the opportunity to reaffirm that the future
for which she is waiting has come, "I am he!" (v 26). The story of
Jesus and the Samaritan woman is not just another incident in
the life of Jesus. It is an incident in which the end, the goal of
the Father's revelation, is achieved.

This level-headed woman, who jestingly mocked Jesus because of his incredible claims, to whom Jesus was totally unable
to get through in the first round of the conversation, has now
become the one who raises the right issues for Jesus to respond
to, the fundamental need which calls for a resolution, i.e., the
religious and social issues which separate Jews and Samaritans.
It is noteworthy that in the first round, in which Jesus made the
proposals, they all ended in a failure of communication, whereas
in the second round, when the woman raises the issues, Jesus'
responses lead to increasing insight, culminating in the woman
leaving her jar (which signified her need for water from Jacob's
well) to become the essential mediatress between Jesus and the
villagers, a mediation on which depends the realization of what
Jesus had proclaimed as the form of worship that overcomes the
alternatives, "either this mountain or Jerusalem." Unlike Nico-
demus in the previous chapter, who quietly disappears from the
scene as Jesus' partner in conversation, allowing Jesus to turn
the conversation into a revelatory monologue, the woman here
remains Jesus' partner in a conversation in which true worship is
revealed; moreover, she becomes Jesus' co-worker in bringing
the villagers to sanction the end of time which Jesus had
announced.[26]

4. *The Water of Life (4:27-30)*

The woman dropping the jar is highly significant.[27] If Jesus
interprets what he does in terms of having other food for nourishment, which is to do the will of the one who sent him and to
complete his work, there should be little doubt that his co-
worker in this work partakes of the living water which he offered her, signified by the dropping of her jar.[72] The jar repre-

---

[72] An excellent suggestion in that direction is Brown's comment: "This detail
seems to be John's way of emphasizing that such a jar would be useless for the type
of living water that Jesus has interested her in" (*The Gospel according to John*, 173).

[25] 100-101
[26] 45-46
[27] 118-21, 138-39, 154, 160-61, 170-72

sents the contrary of his living water, as the food offered by the disciples represents the contrary of his "other" food. In so far as the jar represents the means of satisfying the need for drinking water, dropping it must mean the negation of that need, not in a general way, but in terms of the semantic structure of the story as the implication of affirmation of the quest for the water of life.

There is no need to take the woman's exited announcement that the man she met, who told her everything about herself, "is maybe the messiah" (v 29), as the expression of a mere remote possibility, or even scepticism.[73] Her statement was sufficient to

Cf. also Schlatter, *Das Evangelium des Johannes*, 75; *Der Evangelist Johannes*, 129; and Hoskyns, "The Evangelist says that the woman left her waterpot behind her, . . . in order to show how completely the purpose for which she had come to the well had been driven out of her mind" (*The Fourth Gospel*, 245-46). Their interpretations nevertheless remain fundamentally within the framework of the woman's recognition of her sinfulness. Cf. also Schnackenburg, "Hinter dem Zurücklassen des Kruges braucht man nicht mehr zu vermuten, als daß die Frau schnell und ungehindert in den Ort gelangen will, um mit ihren Landesleuten zurückzukehren. Dem Erzähler kommt es nur auf die Kunde an, die sie in der Orstschaft verbreitet" (*Das Johannesevangelium*, 478; *The Gospel According to St. John*, 443). Furthermore, "Die Frau ist von dem Gedanken beseelt, auch andere zu jenem geheimnisvollen Mann am Brunnen herauszurufen (*deute, idete*); ein Rückschluß auf ihre eigene Glaubenshaltung is darum nicht am Platze" (ibid). Especially strong is Olsson's suggestion, "The waterpot and the drawing of water could to some extent be symbols of her old life, or of her old religion" (*Structure and Meaning*, 156, fn. 31).

See also Schneiders, "We should not fail to note the feminine version of the standard Gospel formula for responding to the call to apostleship, namely to 'leave all things,' especially one's present occupation, whether symbolized by boats (e.g., Mt 4:19-22), or tax stall (cf. Mt 9:9), or water pot" ("Women in the Fourth Gospel," 40).

For a variety of other interpretations of the meaning of the incident, some highly improbable, cf. Barrett, *The Gospel according to St. John*, 240.

[73] Cf. Lagrange, "En général *mē* ou *mēti* supposait une réponse négative, mais dans la *koinè* on trouve le sens de 'ne serait-ce pas?' " (*Évangile selon saint Jean*, 116). Cf. Blass, Friedrich, *Grammatik des neutestamentlichen Griechisch* (8th ed. Albert Debrunner; Göttingen: Vandenhoeck & Ruprecht, 1949), § 427.2; *A Greek Grammar of the New Testament and Other Early Christian Literature* (ed. Robert W. Funk; Chicago: University of Chicago Press, 1961) § 427.2. So also Schnackenburg, "der *mēti*-Satz erfordert nicht unbedingt eine negative Antwort, sondern kann auch eine vorsichtige Vermutung äußern" (*Das Johannesevangelium*, 478; *The Gospel According to St. John*, 444). Zahn interprets the woman's call as follows: " 'Kommt her, sehet einen Menschen, der mir alles gesagt hat, was ich getan habe, (und prüfet) ob dieser etwa der Christ sei' " (*Das Evangelium des Johannes*, 253). Cf. Lindars, "The Samaritan woman's testimony corresponds with the two stages of argument in the preceding discourse. First she adduces the evidence of Jesus' insight, which had led her to believe that he was a prophet (verses 16-19); then she makes the further suggestion, which really goes beyond this evidence, that he might be the Christ (25-6)" (*The Gospel of John*, 193). Also Haenchen, "Jesu wunderbares Wissen dient hier als Hinweis darauf, daß er vielleicht der Messias

let the villagers go in haste to see for themselves (v 30),[74] and
they themselves subsequently give recognition to the fact that it
was through her that they came to their preliminary insight into
who Jesus was (v 42).[75] She is the sower,[76] who is not identical

sein könne" (*Das Johannesevangelium*, 246; *A Commentary on the Gospel of John*,
224). That she grounds her presumption in this is surprising, as Haenchen comments, "Merkwürdigerweise begründet die Frau in V. 29 ihre Vermutung, Jesus sei
der Messias, nicht mit Jesus Selbstbezeugung als Messias (V. 26), sondern mit
seinem wunderbaren Wissen (V. 18)" (249; *A Commentary on the Gospel of John*,
227).

O'Day points out, "The last words spoken by the woman in the narrative contain her tentative confession of Jesus — *mēti houtos estin ho Christos*;. The *mēti*
with which this statement begins is difficult to pin down — it is not a denial, but
neither is it a full affirmation. In light of the bold *egō eimi* of v. 26, it is difficult to
see how anyone could respond so tentatively" ("Irony," 184-85; *Revelation*, 76-77).
Thus, according to her, "The invitation to come and see Jesus is . . . an important
step in understanding who Jesus is — it is the invitation to participate. It is an ironic
invitation in the mouth of the Samaritan woman, because she was able to see so
little in the course of her conversation with Jesus. It is the correct invitation, but
she offers it unknowingly" ("Irony," 183-84; *Revelation*, 76).

Cf. Rebell, "Sie legt den Dorfgenossen ihre aufkeimende Erkenntnis vor, daß
Jesus der Messias sei, und möchte sich dieser Erkenntnis bei ihnen vergewissern.
Damit es bei ihr zur vollen christologischen Erkenntnis kommt, bedarf sie also
einer Interpretationsgemeinschaft. Die Begegnung eines *einzelnen* mit Jesus mün-
det — wenn man das Gefälle der Aussagen von VV. 7-26 über VV. 28-30 zu VV. 39-
42 folgt — ein in die Begegnung einer *Gemeinschaft* mit Jesus; erst *eine solche*
Begegnung mit Jesus scheint vollgültigen Charakter zu haben" ("Gemeinde als
Gegenwart," 186). This is certainly read into the text. The reason why she com-
municates her knowledge about Jesus is to lead the villagers to Jesus, not to find
social affirmation of her "budding" faith.

[74] According to Olsson, "In the first part of the text, she is the Samaritan woman,
drawing water from Jacob's well, while in the second, from v. 26, she is the Samaritan woman bearing witness to the Samaritans about Jesus" (*Structure and Meaning*,
156).

[75] Note Olsson, "There is no clear statement in the text that there is a *qualitative*
difference in the belief on the two occasions. The wording would rather suggest
that on both occasions the belief was complete. Thus it seems a question of a
change in the basis of belief from one occasion to another. At first the belief was
based on *the woman's testimony*, then on *Jesus' words*. Here we find no designation
of the contrast 'Jüngerwort und Herrenwort' or 'Glaube aus zweiter — Glaube aus
erster Hand' but rather the comparison of 'Zeugenwort' and 'Jesuswort' " (*Structure and Meaning*, 159).

[76] Bernard is willing to concede that "the seed was sown there by Jesus Himself,
and in some measure by the Samaritan woman" (*The Gospel according to St. John*,
1.159). Also, "The first believers at Samaria were won, not by visible miracles or
signs (cf. 2:23; 7:31; 10:42; 11:45; 12:42), but by the woman's report of what Jesus
had said to her" (160). But he has to interpret it in the sense of Jesus having sown
the seed through the woman. With regard to the harvest which is already ripe in
the fields he writes: "The allusion is to the spiritual receptiveness of the Samaritan
woman, the measure of faith which she has already exhibited (v. 29), and the eager-
ness with which her friends and neigbours were even now coming to inquire of

with him who is about to reap the harvest that is ripe in the fields, but she rejoices with him in the harvest.[77] This woman does not say like Mary after the annunciation, "Behold, the servant of the Lord. Let it be with me according to your word" (Lk 1:38). She is Jesus' co-worker in an unprecedented way,[*28] more concretely even than John the Baptist, in the sense that John merely pointed to Jesus as "the Lamb of God who takes away the sins of the world" (1:92).[78] The woman participates actively with Jesus in doing the will of his Father; here, with her question about the right place to worship, she provided him with the opportunity to reveal the nature of true worship.

The significance of the parallel between John and the woman is highlighted by John's statement, when he was told, "Rabbi, he who was on the other side of the Jordan with you, concerning whom you witnessed — look, he is baptizing and

Jesus for themselves" (157). Since he takes Jesus as the sower, he interprets the disciples as the reaper: "Jesus, who was here the Lord of the Harvest, had Himself done the sowing, while He permitted His servants to gather the fruits" (159). There is of course nothing like that in the text.

A remarkable formulation is that of R.H. Lightfoot (*St. John's Gospel: A Commentary* [ed. C.F. Evans; Oxford: Clarendon, 1957] 135), "With regard to 4:36, the woman may be said to be both sowing (4:29) and reaping (4:30, 39-42); and, as we have seen (4:28), she is already gathering fruit to issue in eternal life."

There is one comment, quoted previously, that is worth repeating partially here, by Haenchen: "Wen Jesus durch seinen Geist zu Gott führt, der wird selbst zur Quelle, zum Heilbringer für andere. Das erfüllt sich tatsächlich bei der Samaritanerin: selbst zum Glauben gekommen, führt sie die Samariter zum Glauben (vgl. auch 7, 38)" (*Das Johannesevangelium*, 241; *A Commentary on the Gospel of John*, 220-21).

[77] With regard to rejoicing together, cf. Zahn, "Nicht die Gleichzeitigkeit der beiderseitigen Freude, die ja allerdings damit gegeben ist, . . . sondern die Gemeinsamkeit der Freude am Erfolg trotz der Verschiedenartigkeit der Arbeit; daß der Eine sich nicht ohne den Andern freut" (*Das Evangelium des Johannes*, 259).

[78] Cf. Barrett, "The woman joins with John the Baptist as witness, and in fact precedes the apostles" (*The Gospel according to St. John*, 243). Also R. Walker ("Jüngerwort und Herrenwort. Zur Auslegung von Joh 4:39-42," *ZNW* 57 ([1966] 50), "Das samaritische Weib steht mit ihrem *martyrein* neben keinem Geringeren als neben Johannes dem Täufer — Johannes gab Zeugnis (vgl. 1:15. 32. 34; 3:26) —, was bei der Auslegung von 4:41f. wohl zu beachten ist." Furthermore, Olsson, "The role of the testimony may suggest a comparison with John the Baptist, the great witness in Jn, he who reveals Jesus to 'Israel', the children of God throughout the world. Indeed his testimony is mentioned in the context, 3:27ff. Moreover, when the bridegroom's voice is heard he stands there rejoicing. He disappears but Jesus gathers crowds of people around him" (*Structure and Meaning*, 159). See also Schneiders, "In John's perspective the witness of a believing disciple brings a person to Jesus but then the disciple fades away as the prospective believer encounters Jesus himself (cf. Jn 1:35-41)" ("Women in the Fourth Gospel," 40).

[*28] 92-94, 120

everybody is flocking to him" (3:26). John replied, "It is the
bridegroom who has the bride. The friend of the bridegroom
who stands there[79] and hears his voice rejoices because of the
bridegroom's voice. Thus my joy (*chara*) is complete. He must
grow (in significance), I diminish" (3:29-30). What John says is
the other side of what Jesus says about the sower and the reaper,
"The reaper receives the reward[80] and gathers the fruit for eternal life,[81] in order that the sower rejoice (*chaire*) together with
the reaper. For this reason the word is true, 'It is one who sows,
another who reaps' " (4:36-37). Jesus could have made this statement equally well about John's relationship to him. The parallel
should leave no doubt that it is the woman about whom he says
it here; she is confronted with a remark similar to what John
encountered when he was told that everyone was flocking to
Jesus (3:26). The villagers tell her, "We no longer believe
through your word, for we have heard and we know that he is
the savior of the world" (4:42). Her reaction is not given, but,
like John, she may have thought, "That is the way it should be.
He must grow (in significance), I diminish."

5. *The Hour which Now Is (4:31-38)*

When the disciples return[82] they provide Jesus with the op-

---

[79] Cf. 1:35, "The next day John was *standing* there again, and [with him] two of his
disciples; and seeing Jesus walk by he says, 'Behold the Lamb of God.' "

[80] The reward is not a wage that is paid out, but the fruit of the harvest. So, for
example, Zahn, "Der Lohn, welchen der Erntende empfängt, kann nach der
Reihenfolge der Sätze nichts anderes sein, als das Korn, welches er erntet, und
nicht etwa ein Taglohn für die anstrengende Erntearbeit" (*Das Evangelium des
Johannes*, 259). Cf. also Schnackenburg, "Das 'Lohn-Empfangen' bezieht sich hier
schwerlich auf das Bild von der Lohnauszahlung (vgl. Mt 20, 8ff); vielmehr dürfte
der 'Lohn' eben im 'Frucht-Einsammeln' bestehen, das *kai* also die nähere
Erläuterung bringen" (*Das Johannesevangelium*, 483; *The Gospel According to St.
John*, 450).

[81] Lindars remarks, "But by specifying eternal life, John has dropped the metaphor and provided the application" (*The Gospel of John*, 196).

[82] Cf. O'Day, "The temporal reference in v. 31 (*en tō metaxy*) indicates that vv. 28-
30 are to be perceived as background activity to the central activity of the narrative. Vv. 27-30 is thus a highly developed transition scene which has its own important role in the narrative. It is a narrative hinge which serves both to end the first
dialogue and to provide a context out of which the second can operate" ("Irony,"
135; *Revelation*, 53). Also, "Set against the background of the Samaritan woman's
activity in the village, the dialogue proper between Jesus and his disciples begins,
as did the first dialogue, with a request/demand. In v. 31 the disciples say to Jesus,
rabbi phage" ("Irony," 135; *Revelation*, 53-54).

It is noteworthy that their surprise is not that Jesus speaks with a Samaritan
woman, but with a *woman*. *P. Aboth* 1:5 gives expression to the undesirability of a
rabbi conversing with a woman: "Let your house be opened wide and let the needy

portunity to clarify further the nature of what is about to happen,[83] but as far as the actual incidents are concerned they
remain uninvolved. Notwithstanding Jesus' statement in verse
38, they are not participants in this harvest;[84] the Samaritans invite only Jesus to stay with them (v 40) — the disciples have
once more disappeared from the scene — and only he stays the
two days (v 40).[85] The role they play in the story is to show their
ignorance, providing Jesus with the opportunity to comment on

be members of your household; and do not talk much with womankind. They said
this of a man's wife: how much more of his fellow's wife! Hence the Sages have said:
He that talks much with womankind brings evil upon himself and neglects the
study of the Law and at the last will inherit Gehenna." (Quoted from Barrett, *The
Gospel according to St. John*, 240, who also quotes an even more crude rabbinic
example.) This attitude adds interesting contemporary flavor to the story, but does
not make good sense of the statement in the story, since Jesus habitually conversed
with women in the gospel. Is it intended to express the distance which the disciples
maintain from the woman?

Note also O'Day, "Although the disciples are amazed that Jesus is conversing
with a woman, they do not make their amazement known (*oudeis mentoi
eipen . . .*). This is quite a contrast from the behavior of the woman, who voiced her
thoughts when anything was startling or incongruous" ("Irony," 179-80; *Revelation*, 74). O'Day also makes the following relevant observation, "The question *ti
zēteis* has an additional irony in its context. Jesus has just told the Samaritan woman
that the Father seeks those who worship him in spirit and truth, and now the disciples are somewhat incredulous that Jesus could be seeking anything from this woman" ("Irony," 181; *Revelation*, 75). Is there not a hint in this that Jesus did need
something from the woman? If the entire story was subject to divine necessity the
appearance of the woman at the well should be understood in the same way.

[83] O'Day notes, "This dialogue between Jesus and his disciples is one of Jesus' few
private conversations with them outside of the farewell discourses" ("Irony," 186;
Revelation, 77). Nevertheless, "A careful reading of the scene between Jesus and
his disciples reveals that no genuine dialogue has occurred between the parties"
("Irony," 193; *Revelation*, 80-81).

Rebell remarks, "Während zwischen Jesus und der Samariterin ein Dialog mit
mehreren Redebeiträgen beider Gesprächspartner abläuft, sind die Jünger nur
einmal — mit einer kurzen Aufforderung — am Gespräch beteiligt (V. 31). Der
erste Dialog wird von Jesus, der zweite von seinen Gesprächspartnern eröffnet. Mit
der Frau spricht Jesus über Wasser, mit den Jüngern über Speise; die Gegenüber-
stellung von Wasser und Speise findet sich bereits in VV. 7f. Im ersten Gespräch ist
das Gegenüber Jesu eine Frau und in der Einzahl, im Zweiten handelt es sich um
Männer in der Mehrzahl. Die Frau bietet nichts an, und Jesus will etwas von ihr
haben; die Jünger bieten etwas an, und Jesus will es nicht nehmen . . ." ("Gemeinde
als Gegenwart," 172).

[84] Cf. Zahn, "Weder in diesem Augenblick noch während des zweitägigen
Verweilens Jesu in Sychar tuen die Jünger irgend etwas bemerkenswertes . . ." (*Das
Evangelium des Johannes*, 260).

[85] Cf. Olsson, "The text has a striking conclusion, which binds vv. 5-42 together. In
this conclusion we encounter only Jesus, the woman and the Samaritans, not Jesus'
disciples" (*Structure and Meaning*, 138).

the meaning of the story.*29 The ignorance they show is high-lighted by their presumption that someone else must have pro-vided him with something to eat.[86] Ironically, someone did, the woman through her conversation with Jesus, but it was not the type of food they had in mind.

In his commentary on the story — in the form of a discussion with the disciples[87] — Jesus first clarifies the difference between food as physical nourishment and food as the doing of God's will.[88] In as much as the second part of his conversation is com-

---

[86] Cf. O'Day, "The *mē* with which this question begins indicates that the disciples already have their answer in mind, and thus ironically marks the false assumption that they are making" ("Irony," 188; *Revelation*, 78).

[87] Rebell ("Gemeinde als Gegenwart," 184-85) quotes the following from J. Blank concerning the conversation with the disciples; it contains "die eigentliche johan-neische Interpretation des Gesprächs Jesu mit der Samariterin und steht daher auch mit Absicht an dieser Stelle, ehe vom 'Missionserfolg' bei den Samaritanern die Rede ist" (*Das Evangelium nach Johannes* [Geistliche Schriftlesung, Erläuterungen zum Neuen Testament; Düsseldorf: Patmos, 1977] 1.304).

Cf. Lightfoot, ". . . the Lord's teaching to His disciples in 4:31-38 is inserted between His conversation with the woman and its results on her (4:7-30) and its further results on others, through her word and work (4:39-42). In this way the past (4:7-10) and the future (4:39-42) are seen as a unity, a single whole, and the teach-ing of 4:31-38 explains and illustrates this unity" (*St. John's Gospel*, 135).

See also Heitmüller, "Im Zusammenhange dient die Aufforderung, zu essen, offensichtlich nur dazu, das Wort von der geistigen Speise einzuführen" (*Die Jo-hannes-Schriften*, 78). Furthermore, Schnackenburg, "Aber ähnlich wie die Bitte Jesus an die Samaritanerin dient hier die Aufforderung der Jünger zu essen nur als Anlaß zu einem tieferen Offenbarungswort Jesu" (*Das Johannesevangelium*, 479; *The Gospel According to St. John*, 445). Also Haenchen, "Auch dieser Zug dient, wie oben die Bitte um Wasser, nur zur Anknüpfung einer Rede Jesu, diesmal einer Lehrrede an die Jünger und die Leser" (*Das Johannesevangelium*, 246; *A Com-mentary on the Gospel of John*, 224).

[88] Cf. Zahn, "Jesus sagt nicht, was durch *to emon br.* ausgedruckt würde, daß er irdische Nahrungsmittel überhaupt nicht nötig habe, sondern nur, daß die Ausrich-tung des göttlichen Willens für ihn ein Nahrungsmittel, ein Mittel der Erquickung und Stärkung sei, welches unter Umständen auch für sein leibliches Leben ein Er-satz der irdische Speise sei" (*Das Evangelium des Johannes*, 255). This interpreta-tion makes a reservation similar to the one he makes about the place of worship.

Cf. also O'Day, "Jesus' description of his food is a crystallization of Johannine Christology — *brōma* appears as a metaphorical manifestation of Jesus' divine com-mission and of the working relationship of Jesus and God" ("Irony," 190; *Revela-tion*, 79). Furthermore, "Jesus directly supplies the disciples with the information necessary to understand his identity, thereby eliminating the possibility of pro-longed ironic interplay. When compared with the interplay of vv. 7-26, one won-ders if a different communicative mode is being used here" ("Irony," 193; *Revelation*, 80). Indeed, here we have commentary on what preceded and on what is about to follow.

Note the parallel from the Hermetic Corpus to which Dodd (*Interpretation*, 50)

---

*29 4, 40-49, 95

mentary on what is in the process of happening, there is good reason to understand the first part in a similar sense. "That I do the will of the one who sent me, and that I complete his work" (v 34) is in the first place a clarification that Jesus was engaged in doing his Father's work.*30 Doing the will of his Father must refer to his activity in general in the story, engaging in conversation with the woman, which leads to her mediating the information to the villagers which prompts them to go out to see Jesus for themselves. This process is similar to the testimony of John the Baptist and the series of disciples who lead acquaintances to Jesus in chapter 1. Completing his work must mean that which is about to happen, which he clarifies further with the metaphor of the harvest.[89]

draws attention, "*hai dynameis hai en emoi . . . to son thelēma telousin*" (C.H. 13.19).

[89] Bultmann points to 5:36 and 17:4 to argue "daß *ergon* nicht das von Gott gewirkte, sondern das von Gott dem Offenbarer aufgetragene Werk ist, zweitens daß *teleioun* nicht das Zu-ende-führen eines Angefangenen zu bedeuten braucht, sondern auch das Ausführen oder Erledigen des Aufgetragenen bedeuten kann" (*Das Evangelium des Johannes*, 143, fn 3; *The Gospel of John*, 194, fn 3). Here, however, the coordination of "that I do the will of the one who sent me" and "that I complete his work" suggests work that has started and needs completion. See Heitmller, "Jesus hatte gesagt, es sei ihm Speise, den Willen Gottes zu tun und sein Werk zu 'vollenden'. Das letztere kann er sagen. Eben erst hat er an der Samariterin Gottes Werk getan, und schon zeigt sich die Vollendung, der Erfolg — in den aus Sychars Toren herausströmenden Samaritern" (*Die Johannes-Schriften*, 79). See also Schnackenburg, "Das Singular *to ergon* meint das gesamte auf Erden von Jesus auszurichtende 'Werk' und ist von den *erga*, den einzelnen von ihm zu vollbringende Werken, zu unterscheiden. Freilich habe sowohl 'die Werke' als auch 'das Werk' des gesamten Erdenwirkens Jesu ihren Einheitsgrund im Willen des Vaters. *Teleioun* hat darüber hinaus aber den Sinn, daß Jesus das vom Vater begonnene Werk zur Vollendung bringen soll, so daß beide im vollkommener Einheit 'zusammenarbeiten' (vgl. 5, 17 19)" (*Das Johannesevangelium*, 481; *The Gospel According to St. John*, 447). On that basis he concludes, "Wenn man *teleioun* auf diese Weise versteht, ergibt sich ein guter Zusammenhang mit V 36: der 'Säende' is dann der Vater, der 'Erntende' der Sohn" (481, cf. 484).

Cf., on the other hand, Zahn, "Denn erstens heißt *teleioun* mit *ergon*, *erga* als Objekt nicht, wie *poiein* (5, 36; 7, 3; 10, 25) oder *ergazesthai* (3, 21; 6, 28; 9, 4), eine Handlung vollziehen, ein Werk produciren, sondern ein bereits im Gang befindliches Wirken und Werk vollenden, zum Abschluß bringen cf 5, 36; 17, 4; Hb 7, 19; AG 20, 24. Zweitens zeigt die Voranstellung von *autou* vor *ergon*, daß Jesus das, was zu Ende zu führen ihm Speise für Leib und Seele ist, mit gegensätzlichem Nachdruck als Gottes, seines Auftraggebers, Werk bezeichnet. Das Werk, welches Jesus zu vollenden hat, wird dadurch nicht etwa nur als ein von Gott gebotenes, im Dienste und Interesse Gottes auszuführenendes, Gottes gehöriges und wohlgefälliges charakterisirt (cf 6, 28f.; Ap 2, 25; 1 Kr 15, 58; 16, 10), sondern Gott ist dadurch als der *ergazomenos* vorgestellt cf 5, 17. 19-21. 36; 9, 3f.; Rm 14, 20; 1 Kr 3,

*30 pp. ???????

Furthermore, the contrast between Jesus' other food and the disciples' food, which he declines, clarifies the distinction between the living water which Jesus offers the woman and drinking water.*[31] In what she does she participates in Jesus' activity of doing his Father's will. In this way a powerful unity in the story becomes manifest, including the function of the setting in Samaria near the mountain where the Samaritans' central place of worship was located. This unity is strengthened by Jesus' statement in which he ties the first part of the story to the second as *"doing* the will of the one who sent me, and *completing* his work."

The fact that Jesus comments on the story demands that we look for all the elements of his clarification in the story itself. Thus the sower and the reaper should be found in the story itself, which alone already makes it almost obvious that the woman must be the sower who prepared the villagers for the harvest which Jesus was about to reap as the completion of his Father's work.[90] Jesus' statement, that his food is to do the will of

---

7-9. Das längst von Gott begonnene und vor der Erscheinung Christi betriebene Werk und Wirken ist es, welches Jesus als der zu diesem Zweck von Gott in die Werk Gesandte vollenden soll durch seine Berufsarbeit wirklich zum Abschluß bringt" (*Das Evangelium des Johannes*, 255). Thus he interprets the situation with the woman, "bei diesem Weib von unsittlichem Leben und leichtfertigen Sinn hat er doch vorgefunden, was nur Gott im Menschen wirken kann" (ibid.). Also, "Aus sich selbst hat sie jene Voraussetzungen des Glaubens an Jesus den Christ auch nicht erzeugt, sondern Gott hat dies in ihr gewirkt. Die Aufgabe Jesu ist nur gewesen, die vorhandenes Keime zu entwickeln" (256).

Schlatter states, "Er hat dem elenden Weibe geholfen, weil er den Willen dessen tut, der ihn sandte, und Gottes Werk vollbracht, indem er ihr mit Geist und Wahrheit half" (*Das Evangelium des Johannes*, 77).

[90] Barrett thinks "it is best to take as the basis of exegesis the parabolic interpretation (which corresponds to v. 35 — seed-time and harvest paradoxically coincide), though it is not wrong to see here and there (as in the synoptic parables) fleeting allegorical allusions. Thus in this verse sower and reaper are identical; Jesus himself has sown the seed in conversation with the woman, and the believing Samaritans (v. 39) are his harvest . . ." (*The Gospel according to St. John*, 242). Thus, he has to understand the "principle" of the next verse that "it is one who sows another who reaps," to be contradicted by verse 36 (ibid.), notwithstanding the fact that Jesus introduces the "principle" with "for this reason the word is true" (ibid.). So also Bauer, "so kann nur Jesus, wie er Säemann war, auch Schnitter sein . . . ." (*Johannes*, 48); similarly Strathmann, "Da aber hier bei den Samaritern der Erfolg so unmittelbar eintritt, fühlt er sich als Säemann und Schnitter in einer Person — beide Begriffe beziehen sich also auf Jesus selbst . . ." (*Das Evangelium nach Johannes*, 88). Such statements, as already mentioned, do not take into account the remark which introduces the saying, *"en gar touto ho logos estin"* (v 37).

According to Zahn, "Schon vor Eintritt in die parabolische Darstellung hat Jesus

---

*[31] 104-107

the one who sent him and to complete his work, makes sense only if the woman is recognized as the sower who prepared the harvest which Jesus was about to reap. Only in that way would there be coordination between doing the will of his Father and completing his (the Father's) work.

In this way everything Jesus does, except the request for a drink of water, but including the necessity of passing through Samaria in the sense of divine necessity (*edei*, v 4), can be recognized as figures which bring to expression the value /obedience/[91] as "doing the will of the one who sent me and completing his work" (v 34) which stands in opposition to the value /sustenance/. Jesus' actions transform the abstract value into concrete reality in the narrative. This applies to the woman as well in a more dramatic way. Jesus' abandonment of his quest for a drink of water, the moment water comes to represent the value /sustenance/ in its opposition to /obedience/, is almost imperceptible. Slightly more dramatic is his abandonment of the quest for food for the same reason, i.e., when he declines the disciples' offer (vv 31-32). In contrast, the woman's move is highly dramatic.[*32] To begin with, she persists in the quest for objects which, in the development of the story, have already been recognized as representing the negative values: /factional security/ — Jews and Samaritans do not associate (v 9), /sustenance/ — water in the sense of Jacob's miracle (vv 11-12), and /partisan salvation/ — the conflict between Jews and Samaritans concerning the right place to worship (v 20). Even though she unmistakably moves in the direction of an affirmation of the positive values, for example, /human solidarity/, by allowing herself to be drawn into a conversation with Jesus, a Jew, this does not diminish the dramatic impact when she abandons her jar (v 28), signifying her abandonment of the quest for physical nour-

---

bekannt, daß es seine Aufgabe sei, das längst im Gang befindliche Werk Gottes zur Vollendung zu bringen; daß also sein Wirken an jenem Tage, das ihn Essen und Trinken vergessen ließ, nicht eine grundlegendes und bahnbrechendes, sondern ein vollendendes sei, und daß es darum auch nicht seines, sondern des göttlichen Willens Verwirklichung, nicht sein, sondern Gottes Werk sei, welches er treibt. Ungesucht und unverhofft, fast ohne Mühe und zu freudiger Überraschung erntet Jesus, was nicht er, sondern Gott gesät hat . . ." (*Das Evangelium des Johannes*, 261). Remarkably, he nevertheless does not fail to notice, "Schon die Mitteilung des Weibes . . . hat viele Einwohner der Stadt zu einem gewissen Glauben an Jesus geführt (cf 2, 23) . . ." (262).

[91] For an explanation of the meaning of values and their identification with slash marks, see Part One, Chapter 1, B.2, "The Values Expressed by the Themes."

[*32] 151

ishment, representing the value /sustenance/ in its opposition to the value /obedience/, which she now affirms in her action of witnessing to the villagers concerning Jesus. The success of her mission is sanctioned by Jesus when he tells the disciples that the sower rejoices with the reaper in the fruit of the harvest (v 36).

What is important about this is that the meaning of the water of life which springs up to eternal life now becomes concrete. As far as the woman is concerned, it means to participate in Jesus' doing of his Father's work. Jesus said to her, "If you knew the gift of God and who it is that says to you, 'Give me to drink,' you would ask him and he would give you living water" (v 10). In that first round of the story the woman in her level-headedness remained oblivious of Jesus' identity. It is an indication of the story-teller's skill that he does not say explicitly, as the woman becomes increasingly aware of Jesus' identity in the second round of her conversation with him, that she becomes persuaded that she should ask him for the living water; as she becomes aware of Jesus' identity she receives the living water from him. At the beginning of the second round of the conversation Jesus tells her to go call her husband, which she does not do; after she begins to recognize who Jesus is, she does not bring just one man to Jesus but a large part of the village. Compared with the one man Jesus tells her to call, it is a great harvest.

The statement to the disciples that he sent them to reap where they did not work places the story in a more distant past.[92] It now presupposes not merely the story itself, but others who had also worked in the "Samaritan mission" prior to the disciples going in to reap the fruits of that activity.[*33] There is no way in which one can interpret that comment as part of the story without breaking its temporal integrity; the disciples who are told that they are being sent to reap where they did not work cannot be the disciples in the story. There are no "others" who worked where they are about to reap — except the one woman — but neither do they do any of the harvesting in the story. Jesus alone is invited to the Samaritan village; it is only he who stays over for the two days. The final statement of the villagers also leaves no place for any activity of other intermediaries, such as harvesting disciples. The point of their

---

[92] Cf. Olsson, "When the proverb is later applied in what follows, there is an obvious shift. Now the parties involved are no longer the Father and the Son but 'the disciples' and 'others' " (Structure and Meaning, 230).

[*33] 100

comment is the immediacy of their relationship to Jesus, "We no longer believe through your talk,[93] for we ourselves have seen, and we know that he is the savior of the world" (v 42).

It is understandable how a subsequent redactor could adapt the story to a later situation, in the sense of verse 38, on the basis of Jesus' statement that "it is one who sows and another who harvests" (v 37).[94] There is no harm in such a contemporizing of the story, making it relevant to a new situation. Less harmless is the other contemporizing comment in verse 22, which could come from the same redactor. It reintroduces religious polemic against the Samaritans with the remark that "you worship what

[93] There is not necessarily anything disparaging in the usage of the term *lalia* for the woman's witness. Cf. Bauer, "*lalia* bei den Klassikern gewöhnlich 'Geschwätz' oder 'Schwatzigkeit', im NT nicht im üblen Sinn" (*Johannes*, 49). It is used here to contrast with the *logos* of Jesus (v 41). Her word is also referred to as *logos* in verse 39. Schnackenburg, "Ihre *lalia* verblaßt vor dem *logos* Jesu, nicht als ob es bloßes 'Geschwätz' gewesen wäre, aber als ein nur menschliches, äußerliches Reden über etwas, was sich in der Selbstoffenbarung Jesus wirklich erschließt" (*Das Johannesevangelium*, 489-90; *The Gospel According to St. John*, 456-57). Cf. Schulz, ". . . der Evangelist fügt V. 41f. an: die vermittelnde Rolle der Frau wird anerkannt, aber auch nicht mehr" (*Das Evangelium nach Johannes*, 78).

Cf. Walker, "Viele Samariter glaubten an ihn! Dieser Glaube 'um des Wortes des Weibes willen' ist bei Joh nichts Zweitrangiges, Minderwertiges, nicht etwa 'nur Vorstufe . . . zum Glaube der Worte Jesu'. (Gottlob Spörri, *Das Evangelium nach Johannes*, Zürich 1950, 86.) Denn mehr und besseren Glauben als diesen *pisteuein eis auton* umschriebenen gibt es bei Joh nirgends" ("Jüngerwort und Herrenwort," 49-50). He recognizes: "Das Herrenwort löst den Glaubenden vom Wort des Zeugen und bindet ihn an sich selbst, macht den Glauben 'selbständig', 'unmittelbar' und das Wort des Zeugen überflüssig (4:42)" (51). Nevertheless, he maintains, "Man darf aber *lalia*, 'Rede', nicht als 'weniger wichtiges', nur 'in menschlicher autorität' gesprochenes und für sich selbst bedeutungsloses Menschenwort mißverstehen. . . . Auch Jesu Wort wird bei Joh — im Wechsel mit *logos!* — ohne jede abschätzige Nuance *lalia* genannt (8:43). Warum versteht ihr meine Rede nicht? Weil ihr mein Wort nicht hören könnt" (52-53). Thus he concludes, "Zeugenwort und Herrenwort sind im Sinne des Evangelisten in ihrem Ergebnis sachlich kongruent, wenn sich auch der Glaube aus zweiter Hand vom Glauben aus erster Hand nach 'Ausdehnung' und Art des 'Grundes' kräftig unterscheidet" (54).

[94] Cf. Schnackenburg, "Das missionarische Interesse schlägt unverkennbar in dem Zwischenstück 4, 35-38 durch. So wäre ein 'Sitz im Leben' (der Gemeinden) für diesen Traditionsstück gefunden" (*Das Johannesevangelium*, 455; *The Gospel According to St. John*, 419). Also, "Jesus setzt sich im Geiste in die Zukunft, da er die Jünger bereits ausgesandt hat" (485).

Note also Bultmann, "Da V. 38 nicht wie V. 35-37 *sub specie* des Eschatologischen, sondern des Historischen geredet wird, so gehört zu den *alloi* allerdings Jesus als der Vorbereiter der christlichen Mission; aber die, mit denen er sich zusammenfaßt, sind die jeweiligen Vorgänger in der Missionsarbeit. Das *apesteila*, das ja durch die bisherige Erzählung ganz unbegründet ist, ist vom Standpunkt der späteren Missionsarbeit gesprochen, innerhalb deren jeder Missionar schon auf Vorgänger zurückblickt" (*Das Evangelium des Johannes*, 147-48; *The Gospel of John*, 199-200).

you do not know; we worship what we know, for salvation is from the Jews," now no longer from a Jewish, but from a Christian point of view.[95] The salvation which is from the Jews obvi-

[95] So Bultmann, *Das Evangelium des Johannes*, 139, fn 6; *The Gospel of John*, 189, fn 6. Brown's retort that "such an exegesis, of course, does not take seriously the setting given to the episode" (*The Gospel according to John*, 1.172), lacks recognition of the historical question. Note, however, his recognition of another historical setting for certain elements in the story, the disciples being sent to reap where they did not work (v 38): "the whole passage takes on new meaning when we think of its being narrated in Johannine circles familiar with the story of the conversion of Samaria in Acts viii" (184). In that case "the sower of the Christian faith was Philip, . . . the reapers were Peter and *John* who came down to confer the Spirit" (184).

Brown wants it both ways with a formula that does not serve the interests of historical inquiry, but the affirmation of a maximum of historicity: "If, as we suspect, there is a substratum of traditional (read historical) material, the evangelist has taken it and with his masterful sense of drama and the various techniques of stage setting, has formed it into a superb theological scenario" (176, cf. 184). Exact is Bauer's comment, "Die . . . am Brunnen sich abspielende Szene ist jedenfalls als Ganzes literarisches Produkt des Evangelisten, mögen auch gewisse, nicht mehr feststellbare, Erinnerungnen an Jesu Leben und Lehre hinein verflochten sein" (*Johannes*, 49-50).

Barrett brings to expression precisely such a reassertion of (Christian) religious superiority, in the process correctly relating it to the metaphoric interpretations of the woman's husbands. "Here, if not already in v. 18, the unsatisfactory religion of the Samaritans is brought to light. Religion without, or apart from the main stream of revelation, may be instinctive but can be neither intelligent nor saving" (*The Gospel according to St. John*, 237). His interpretation is correct from the point of view of verse 22, but is contrary to that of the story. So also Zahn, "Dem nun erst betonten 'ihr' (*hymeis*), d.h. ihr Samariter, tritt ein *hēmeis* gegenüber, in welchem Jesus sich mit seinen Volksgenossen zusammenfaßt. *Er bekennt sich als Juden* nicht nur der Abstammung nach, sondern auch in religiöser Beziehung" (*Das Evangelium des Johannes*, 244). The worship in "spirit and truth," in the sense of God belonging equally to all, is still future according to Zahn, "Dies ist um so auffälliger, als Jesus vorher und nachher (21. 23) Gott *ho patēr* nennt . . . im Sinn der allgemeinen Vaterschaft Gottes im Verhältnis zur ganzen Menschheit (Lc 3, 38; AG 17, 28f.; Hb 12, 9). So aber redet Jesus von Gott nur im Hinblick auf die im Kommen begriffene neue Zeit, in welcher Menschen aus allen Völkern den allein wahren Gott als ihren Vater erkennen (Jo 17, 3)" (ibid.). He certainly runs into difficulty when he recognizes, "daß (Jesus) durch das zu *erchetai hōra* hinzutretende *kai nyn estin* erklärt, die geweissagte Zukunft sei auch schon Gegenwart," but nevertheless maintains, "Diese parenthetische *Contradictio in adjecto* . . . soll selbstverständlich nicht den futurische Charakter der Hauptaussage wieder aufheben, welcher auch durch das *proskynēsousin* in dem Nebensatz festgehalten wird, sondern will besagen, daß die Keime und Ansätze der geweissagten zukunftigen Ereignisse und Zustände schon in der Gegenwart vorhanden sind, und daß der Glaube an die geweissagte Zukunft das Verhalten in der Gegenwart zu regeln habe" (246).

Zahn reaffirms the distinction between the future worship in "spirit and truth" and the presence with the following, "Geist bildet auch hier den Gegensatz zum Fleisch und zu allem, was des Fleisches Art hat, zu bestimmten Örtlichkeiten,

ously refers to the Christian savior. Such an understanding is as contrary to the intention of the story as is the controversy between Samaritans and Jews concerning the right place to worship.*[34] Indeed, the comment not only reasserts religious discord between Christians and Samaritans, but represents the central bone of contention between Christians and *Jews*![96]

The sayings "Do you not say it is four months and the harvest comes" (v 35)[97] and "It is one who sows and another who harvests" (v 37) provide excellent material for reflection on the contemporary situation of the story. Such considerations are by no means irrelevant for its meaning, but do not contribute fundamentally to it. If they did, it would be difficult to uncover the meaning, since the contemporary understanding of these smaller units of meaning remains unclear. It is similar to looking up the possible meanings of a word in a dictionary and not finding a single one which fits the sentence one is trying to understand, but realizing that with the aid of the meanings provided by the dictionary and the syntactic context of the term in the sentence it is possible to recognize the sense in which it is used.

wohin man wallfahren, zu Gebäuden, in denen man sich einfinden, zu sinnlich wahrnehmbaren Handlungen, die man vollziehen muß. *Zur Zeit* ziehen auch die frommen Israeliten, denen es mit ihrer Anbetung ein Ernst ist, wie Jesus selbst, nach Jerusalem zu den hohen Festen, 'um anzubeten' (12, 20; AG 24, 11) . . ." (246. The emphasis is mine. Cf. also, 247).

More to the point is the observation of Schulz, "Im 'Wir' melden sich dagegen die Christen zu Wort, die um den wahren Gottesdienst wissen. Die heilsgeschichtliche Begründung allerdings, die dafür gegeben wird: 'denn das Heil stammt von den Juden' ist ganz unjohanneisch und dürfte auf eine spätere Bearbeitung zurückgehen" (*Das Evangelium nach Johannes*, 76).

[96] The numerous interpretations which take the statement as an affirmation of the relative correctness of Jewish worship compared with Samaritan obviously miss this point.

[97] Bernard points out (*The Gospel according to St. John*, 1.156), "The words of this proverbial saying, with a trifling change, form a line of iambic verse:
tetramēnos esti chō therismos erchetai."

He nevertheless concludes "that the rhythm of *ho therismos* is an accident, and that we are to regard the whole phrase as the Greek rendering of an Aramaic agricultural proverb" (ibid.). The trifling change is that the "fourth evangelist has simplified *chō* into its component elements *kai ho*, just as Paul in quoting an iambic line from Menander at I Co 15. 33 has simplified *chrēth' homiliai* by writing *chrēsta homiliai*" (A.W. Argyle, "A Note on John 4:35. *(eti) tetramēnos estin cho therismos erchetai,*" *ExpTim* 82 [1971] 247). Argyle questions scepticism about the Fourth Evangelist having quoted the iambic verse with the following excellent argument, "If Menander's poem from which the line is taken had perished, as thousands of Greek poems have, would commentators have insisted that this iambic line was accidental?" (ibid.).

---

*[34] 154

Whatever the contemporary meaning of these two expressions may have been, it is clear that Jesus uses the first to contrast a waiting period of four months before harvest time with the harvest which is already "white for reaping" (v 35), possibly having a similarity to "the hour is coming, and now is" (v 23, cf., 5:25) in mind.[98] It is not necessary to envision that, when the disciples "lifted up their eyes" (v 35), they could actually see the Samaritans approaching from the village (v 30). The comment is intended more for the reader who can imagine, not only the villagers approaching, but the entire harvest which is about to take place.[99] As has already been suggested, the expression about the sower and the harvester not being identical serves as a comment on the statement that "the sower rejoices with the one who reaps" (v 36),[100] which may more often than not have been true in the contemporary setting.

6. *The Harvest (4:39-42)*

That the woman's activity was not incidental is emphasized when the thread of the actual story, which had been left in verse 30, "many went out from the village and came to him," is taken

[98] According to Bultmann, "Demgegenber aber gilt hier: *idou legō hymin ktl*: die Zeit der Ernte ist schon da; für die Arbeit der Verkündigung, für den Dienst am Offenbarungsgeschehen gibt es immer nur entscheidende Gegenwart; sie gehört nie erst in ein Dann, sondern immer Jetzt, — und zwar deshalb, weil sie, wie die Bezeichnung dieser Arbeit als *therismos* andeutet, und wie V. 36 weiter klar macht, eschatologisches Geschehen ist" (*Das Evangelium des Johannes*, 145; *The Gospel of John*, 196-97). Similarly Schulz, "Es heißt gerade nicht: jetzt wird das Evangelium ausgerichtet, jetzt wird gepredigt, und dann kommt die Zeit des Wartens bis zur Ernte, d. h., der endgültigen Annahme oder Verwerfung, sondern vielmehr; angesichts des Wortes des gegenwärtigen Offenbarers fällt die endgültige Entscheidung, fallen Annahme oder Verwerfung eschatologisch zusammen. Denn wo das Wort erklingt (5, 19ff.), empfängt der Hörer ewiges Leben oder wird definitiv gerichtet" (*Das Evangelium nach Johannes*, 77-78).

[99] Cf. O'Day, "Jesus has earlier invited his interlocutors to see things correctly, but this invitation has always been implicit — the invitation itself often has to be discerned. The double exhortation here stands in sharp contrast to those implicit invitations, because now Jesus gives an explicit charge to see" ("Irony," 196; *Revelation*, 82). Furthermore, "The arrival of the Samaritan townspeople begins the conclusion of the narrative. Like the preceding two dialogues, this exchange begins with a request/command (although in this case the request is reported as indirect speech) — the Samaritans ask Jesus to stay with them" ("Irony," 135; *Revelation*, 54).

[100] There is an interesting twist in who it is that rejoices with whom in Schneiders' remark, "Jesus is evidently filled with joy at the woman's work (4:35), which he recognizes as a realization of his own mission to do the will of the one who sent him (4:34), and as an anticipation of the later work of the disciples (4:38)" ("Women in the Fourth Gospel," 40).

up again by the narrative in verse 39, "From the village many Samaritans believed in him through the word of the woman,[101] who witnessed that 'he told me all I did.' " They ask him to stay with them.[102] It is remarkable that the author on the one hand does emphasize that many *believed in him* through the word of the woman," but then brings out the very elementary level of their faith with the comment that it was based on her witness that "he told me everything I did" (cf. v 29). Her witness, nevertheless, it should be remembered, did not revert back to the recognition of him as merely a prophet. She wonders in her witness, "Maybe he is the messiah" (v 30).[103] On the other hand, there is no suggestion that she mentioned to them the discussion concerning the right place to worship. The statement in verse 39 interprets their faith as based on his knowledge of the private life of the woman.

In this way the distinction between the sowing and the harvesting is maintained.[*35] The woman could have told the villagers about the conversation concerning the right place to worship, but that is not the way the story is conceived. For the villagers, as for the woman, but possibly even more importantly for them, there is a progression from a lesser understanding of the significance of Jesus to a full understanding, as their final statement makes clear (v 42).[104]

---

[101] Cf. Schneiders, "The force of this expression (*dia ton logon*) as apostolic identification of the woman appears when we compare it with Jesus' prayer in 17:20 describing, in essence, the apostolic mission: 'I do not pray for these only (i.e., those present at the supper) but also for those believing through their word' (*dia tou logou*)" ("Women in the Fourth Gospel," 40).

[102] O'Day, remarks, "For the first time in the narrative, a request is complied with: *kai emeinen ekei dyo hēmeras*" ("Irony," 206; *Revelation*, 87).

[103] Cf. Bernard, "The question is put tentatively, with just a shade of hope that the answer may turn out to be in the affirmative" (*The Gospel according to St. John*, 1.152).

[104] Bultmann observes, "Der Evangelist hat durch seine Bildung V. 39. 41f. den Bericht zu einer symbolischen Darstellung des Problems der Hörer 'zweiter Hand' gemacht. Er konnte ja nicht wohl eine Szene bilden, in der Hörer der Boten Jesu zu diesem selbst vordringen, denn nach seinem Plane werden die Jünger ja erst vom Auferstandenen entsandt. Sie werden deshalb hier von der Frau vertreten; diese repräsentiert die vermittelnde Verkündigung, die den Hörer zu Jesus selber führt. Dieser Gedanke ist stark betont: wohl war das Zeugnis der Frau für die Leute die notwendige Voraussetzung ihres Glaubens. Aber es bedeutet nichts für sich, sondern seine Bedeutung ist die, daß es zu Jesus führt, sodaß der Glaube zu einem Glauben *dia ton logon autou* wird, demgegenber das menschliche Zeugnis zur *lalia*, zu bloßen Worten, die die Sache nicht mit sich führen, herabsinkt. Damit ist gesagt: der Glaube darf nicht auf die Autorität Anderer hin glauben, sondern

---

[*35] 80-81

But not only that; what Jesus told the woman was not something to which the Samaritan villagers' faith would be a response. What Jesus explained to the woman was to be realized in the very fact of the villagers' coming to a full understanding of faith in him as the savior of the world. There is a sense, thus, in which what Jesus told the woman was commentary on the event that was about to happen, i.e., on what was to take place when the villagers came to their faith in Jesus as the savior of the world. Here once more the extraordinarily compact unity of the story comes to expression, not only through the coordination of commentary (vv 21, 23-24) and event (vv 39-42), but also of the woman's moving from the recognition of Jesus as a prophet, because he told her everything about her (vv 16-19), to her reaction to his clarification of true worship (vv 20-26, 28-30), and the villagers' moving from a faith in Jesus on the basis of the woman's witness, that Jesus told her everything about herself (v 39, cf. 30), to the full recognition of him as the savior of the world (v 42).[105]

On the other hand, the actualization of that to which Jesus points forward with his comment on true worship (vv 21, 23) in the event of the villagers coming to the understanding of faith in him as savior of the world (v 42),[106] in turn adds meaning to

muß selbst seinen Gegenstand finden; er muß durch das verkündigte Wort hindurch das Wort des Offenbarers selbst vernehmen" (*Das Evangelium des Johannes*, 148-49; *The Gospel of John*, 201-202).

To this Haenchen responds incisively, ". . . es fragt sich, ob damit die Verse 39-42 adäquat erklärt werden. Was die Frau ihren Landsleuten verkündigte, war ja die Botschaft von dem Prophet-Messias Jesus. Was die Hörer erst aus Jesu Botschaft erfahren, ist, daß Jesus der 'Retter der Welt' ist. Damit wird die Auffassung Jesu als eines *sōtēr*, die im Grunde die Ganze Vorlage durchzieht, ebenso korrigiert, wie die Bezeichnung der Frau als einer 'Hörers erster Hand' durch die Botschaft Jesu selbst berichtigt ist: Er selbst it der Weg. . . . Das Zeugnis eines Gläubigen kann einem anderen oder Späteren zur Veranlassung werden zu der Entscheidung für oder gegen Christus; das hat Johannes in 20, 20 angedeutet (vgl. Gerdes, *Das Christusbild Sören Kierkegaards*, 1960). Aber da es zuletzt darauf ankommt, Gott im Worte der Zeugen zu hören, werden die Unterschiede von Jüngeren erster und zweiter Hand belanglos" (*Das Johannesevangelium*, 251-52; *A Commentary on the Gospel of John*, 228).

105 Note Olsson, ". . . one point is sure: the author who gave our text its present form is not primarily interested in *her* belief in Jesus but in that of the Samaritans" (*Structure and Meaning*, 153).

106 Schnackenburg points out, "Rein historisch gesehen ist es unwahrscheinlich, daß die Samariter diesen *geprägten Ausdruck* wählten, wenn sie auch nach der Auffassung des Evangelisten über ihre beschränkte Messiaserwartung hinausgewachsen sind. Der Titel *ho sōtēr* ist dem Judentum als Messias-bezeichnung nicht geläufig" (*Das Johannesevangelium*, 490; *The Gospel According to St. John*, 457). Furthermore, "Aber der Titel 'Heiland der Welt' spielt auch im hellenisti-

the worship in spirit and truth. True worship of the Father is in the spirit, not in identifiable religious claims, "neither on this mountain nor in Jerusalem."

And so the meaning our passage becomes clear as the process of revelation of Jesus as the savior of the world in two moves, first in Jesus' encounter with the woman, repeated in his encounter with the villagers, manifested concretely in the villagers' overcoming the divisiveness of their claim to true worship over and against that of the Jews.*[36] Jesus, the messiah, is neither the savior of the Samaritans nor of the Jews — "an hour comes when neither on this mountain nor in Jerusalem will you worship the Father" (v 21) — but the savior of the world — "the true worshippers will worship the Father in spirit and truth" (v 23). True worship, worship in the spirit, constitutes a community beyond all earthly religious communities,*[37] a community of worship in which all of humanity is united.[107] That is what the

schen Bereich eine nicht geringe Rolle, und der Evangelist wird ihn bewußt als 'Verkundigungswort' aufgenommen haben" (491; *The Gospel According to St. John*, 458).

According to Bernard, "That the Samaritan villagers rose to the conception of Jesus as not only the Messiah, but as 'the Saviour of the world,' is not probable. This great title reflects the conviction of a later moment in Christian history, and of a more fully instructed faith. Jn. in writing the story of Jesus at Sychar tells it in his own phraseology . . ." (*The Gospel according to St. John*, 1.161). The understanding is similar to Brown, above, who also tries to maintain the historicity of the story, and admits the much later stage which the narrative represents. The historical location of the story is that of the author. Questions of actual earlier events on which it may have been based, or to which it alludes, are secondary.

Cf. Zahn, "Grundlos ist die Annahme, daß Jo hier den Sam. eine ihnen fremde, seiner eigenen theologischen Denkweise entlehnte Benennung Jesu (cf 1 Jo 4. 15; Jo 1, 29; 3, 16-17 etc.) in den Mund lege. Gerade diese Bezeichnung entsprach der Tatsache, daß der Jude Jesus, ohne im geringsten sein Judentum zu verleugnen oder die Sam. als Juden gelten zu lassen, sie eingehender Belehrung gewürdigt und zu der Überzeugung geführt hatte, daß er die Erfüllung der auch von ihnen gehegten Hoffnung auf einen Wiederbringer alles Heils sei, daß er dies also nicht nur für die Juden, sondern für alle nach Gott und seinem Heil verlangenden Menschen sei. Auch der Taheb, den die Sam. erwarteten, sollte ein Bekehrer und Heiland der Sam., der Juden und der Heiden sein . . . . Ein kleiner Bruchteil dieses Volks hat in jenen Tagen seinen Taheb in Jesus gefunden" (*Das Evangelium des Johannes*, 263-64). However mistaken this may be historically, it certainly is the sense of the story. It was in Jesus, "Messiah," who had been expected to "announce everything" (v 25), cf. his affirmation, "I am, who speaks to you" (v 26), that the Samaritans recognized the savior of the world.

[107] Cf. Schulz, "Mit diesem Bekenntnis der Samaritaner am Schluß dieser kunstvollen und eindrücklichen Komposition will der Evangelist unüberhörbar sage: es geht hier weder um den Garizim noch um den Zion, weder um Samaritaner noch

*[36] 109-10, 121-23
*[37] 142-43

villagers recognize; it is the point of the story.

The realization of worship of the Father in spirit and truth, in opposition to either on this mountain or in Jerusalem, when the Samaritan villagers, having invited Jesus to stay with them, recognize him as the savior of the world, reinforces the integration of the values /human solidarity/ and /universal salvation/. These values, in turn, are integral to /obedience/ in the overall structure of the story. Everything that happens in it is a transformation of the value /obedience/ into a concrete figure of the story,[38] represented at the most general level by Jesus "doing the will of the one who sent him and completing his work" for which the woman is his indispensable co-worker. In that way it becomes possible to recognize all the figures in the story as transformations of the system of values into concrete reality, revealing its remarkable semantic unity notwithstanding what appear to be breaks in its surface text-syntactic structure.[39]

Judäer, sondern Jesus ist insofern für den gesamten Kosmos da, als er die 'Seinen' errettet" (*Das Evangelium nach Johannes*, 78).

Note also the interpretation of Schottroff, formulated as a radicalization of Bultmann's existentialist understanding, "Von der Welt der heillosen Menschen, die die Glaubenden mit Haß verfolgen, wird der johanneischen Christ befreit, nicht von sich selbst wie bei Bultmann" ("Johanneischen Dualismus," 213).

[38] 143-48
[39] 155-57

BIBLIOGRAPHY ON JOHN 4

Argyle, A.W. "A Note on John 4:35. *(eti) tetramenos estin cho therismos erchetai.*" *Expository Times* 82 (1971) 247-48.

Balague, M. "Hacia la religion del espiritu." *Cultura biblica* 18 (1961) 151-66.

Baldermann, I. *Die Bibel - Buch des Lernens. Grundzüge biblischer Didaktik.* Göttingen, Vandenhoeck & Ruprecht, 1980.

Barrett, C. K. *The Gospel according to St. John: An Introduction with Commentary and Notes on the Greek Text.* London: S.P.C.K., 1958; 2nd ed.; London: S.P.C.K. and Philadelphia: Westminster, 1978.

Bauer, Walter. *Die Evangelien.* Vol. 2. *Johannes.* Handbuch zum Neuen Testament 2. Tübingen: J.C.B. Mohr (Paul Siebeck), 1912.

Becker, J. *Das Evangelium nach Johannes, Kapitel 1-10.* Ökumenischer Taschenbuchkommentar zum Neuen Testament. Gütersloh /Würzburg: Gerd Mohn/Echter, 1979.

Bernard, J.H. *A Critical and Exegetical Commentary on the Gospel according to St. John.* 2 Vols. New York: Charles Scribner's Sons, 1929.

Blank, J. *Das Evangelium nach Johannes.* 2 vols. Geistliche Schriftlesung, Erläuterungen zum Neuen Testament. Düsseldorf: Patmos, 1977.

Bligh, J. "Jesus in Samaria." *Heythrop Journal* 3 (1962) 329-346.

Boers, Hendrikus. "Discourse Structure and Macro-Structure in the Interpretation of texts: John 4:1-42 as an Example." In *SBL 1980 Seminar Papers*, edited by Paul J. Achtemeier, 159-182. Chico, California: Scholars Press, 1980.

Bonneau, N.R. "The Woman at the Well. John 4 and Genesis 24." *Bible Today* 67 (1973) 1252-59.

Brown, Raymond E. *The Gospel according to John*. Anchor Bible. Garden City, New York: Doubleday & Co., Inc., 1966; Vol. 2, 1970.

Brown, Raymond E. *The Community of the Beloved Disciple*. New York: Paulist, 1979.

Bull, R.J. "An Archaeological Context for Understanding John 4:20." *Biblical Archaeology* 38 (1975) 54-59.

Bultmann, Rudolf. *Das Evangelium des Johannes*. 10th rev. ed. Kritisch-exegetischer Kommentar über das Neue Testament. Göttingen: Vandenhoeck & Ruprecht, 1941; reprinted 1959. ET: *The Gospel of John: A Commentary*. Translated by G.R. Beasley-Murray, R.W.N. Hoare, and J.K. Riches. Philadelphia: Westminster, 1971.

Bultmann, Rudolf. *Das Evangelium des Johannes. Ergänzungsheft*. Rev. ed. Kritisch-exegetischer Kommentar über das Neue Testament. Göttingen: Vandenhoeck & Ruprecht, 1957.

Büchsel, Friedrich. *Das Evangelium nach Johannes*. Das Neue Testament Deutsch 4. Göttingen: Vandenhoeck & Ruprecht, 1934.

Cahill, P.J. "Narrative Art in John IV." *Religious Studies Bulletin* 2 (1982) 41-48.

Cantwell, L. "Immortal Longings in Sermone Humili: A Study of John 4:5-26." *Scottish Journal of Theology* 36 (1983) 73-86.

Carmichael, C.M. "Marriage and the Samaritan Woman." *New Testament Studies* 26 (1980) 332-46.

Chappuis, J.-M. "Jesus and the Samaritan Woman. The Variable Geometry of Communication." *Ecumenical Review* 34 (1982) 8-34.

Dagonet, P. *Selon saint Jean une femme de Samarie*. Epiphanie. Paris: Cerf, 1979.

Daube, David. "Jesus and the Samaritan Woman: The Meaning of *syngraomai*." *Journal of Biblical Literature* 69 (1950) 137-147.

De Boor, W. *Das Evangelium des Johannes*. Wuppertal: Brockhaus, 1968.

De la Potterie, I. "Structura primae partis Evangelii Johannis (capita III et IV)." *Verbum domini* 47 (1969) 130-40.

De la Potterie, I. " 'Nous adorons, nous, ce que nous connaissons, car le salut vient des Juifs': Histoire de l'exégèse et interprétation de Jn 4,22." *Biblica* 64 (1983) 74-115.

De Vries, E. "Johannes 4:1-42. In geest en hoofdzaak." *Gereformeerd Theologisch Tijdschrift* 78 (1978) 93-114.

Díaz, José Ramón. "Palestinian Targum and New Testament." *Novum Testamentum* 6 (1963) 75-80.

Dodd, C.H. *The Interpretation of the Fourth Gospel.* Cambridge: Cambridge University Press, 1960.

Dodd, C.H. *Historical Tradition in the Fourth Gospel.* Cambridge: Cambridge University Press, 1963.

Duke, Paul D. *Irony in the Fourth Gospel.* Atlanta: John Knox, 1985.

Fenton, J.C. *The Gospel According to John.* Oxford: Clarendon Press, 1970.

Galbiati, E. "Nota sulla struttura del 'libro dei segni' (Gv. 2-4)." *Euntes Docete* 25 (1972) 139-44.

Graf, E. "Theology at Jacob's Well. Chapters from the Gospel of St. John." *Homiletic and Pastoral Review* 59 (1959) 1099-1104.

Grundmann, W. *Das Evangelium nach Johannes.* Theologischer Handkommentar zum Neuen Testament. Berlin: Evangelischer Verlagsanstalt, 1968.

Gryglewicz, F. "Ein rätselhaftes Fragment des 4. Evangeliums (4,31-38)." *Biblica* 64 (1983) 74-115.

Guardini, R. *Jesus Christus. Sein Bild in den Schriften des Neuen Testaments. Das Christusbild der Johanneischen Schriften.* Würzburg: Werkbund-Verlag, 1940.

Hall, D.R. "The meaning of *sygchraomai* in John 4:9." *Expository Times* 83 (1971) 56-57.

Haenchen, Ernst. *Das Johannesevangelium. Ein Kommentar.* Aus den nachgelassenen Manuskripten herausgegeben von Ulrich Buss. Göttingen: Vandenhoeck & Ruprecht, 1980. ET: *John 1. A Commentary on the Gospel of John Chapters*

1-6. Translated by Robert W. Funk. Philadelphia: Fortress, 1984.

Heitmller, Wilhelm. *Die Johannes-Schriften*. Die Schriften des Neuen Testaments neu übersetzt und für die Gegenwart erklärt. Göttingen: Vandenhoeck Ruprecht, 1918.

Horgan, M.P. "The Woman at the Well (John 4:1-42)." *Bible Today* 82 (1976) 663-69.

Hoskyns, Edwyn Clement. *The Fourth Gospel*. Edited by Francis Noel Davis. London: Faber and Faber, 1947.

Howard, Wilbert F. *The Gospel According to St. John: Introduction and Exegesis*. Interpreters Bible 8. New York, Nashville: Abingdon Cokesbury Press, 1952.

Hudry-Clergeon, C. "De Judée en Galilée. Étude de Jean 4, 1-45." *Nouvelle revue théologique* 103 (1980) 818-30.

King, J.S. "Sychar and Calvary. A Neglected Theory in the Interpretation of the Fourth Gospel." *Theology* 77 (1974) 417-22.

Kracauer, S. *Geschichte - Vor den letzten Dingen*. Frankfurt/M: Suhrkamp, 1973.

Lagrange, M.-J. *Évangile selon saint Jean*. Études bibliques. Paris: Gabalda, 1923; 8th ed., 1948.

Lagrange, M.-J. *L'Évangile de Jésus-Christ*. Études bibliques. Paris: Gabalda, 1928.

Leidig, E. *Jesu Gespräch mit der Samaritanerin und weitere Gespräche im Johannesevangelium*. Theologischen Dissertationen 15. Basel: Reinhardt, 1979.

Lightfoot, R.H. *St. John's Gospel: A Commentary*. Edited by C.F. Evans. Oxford: Clarendon, 1957.

Lindars, Barnabas. *The Gospel of John*. New Century Bible. Greenwood, S.C: Attic, 1972; reprinted, 1977.

MacRae, G.W. *Invitation to John*. New York: Doubleday, 1978.

Marshall, I.H. "The Problem of New Testament Exegesis." *Journal of the Evangelical Theological Society* 17 (1974) 67-73.

Neyrey, J.H. "Jacob Traditions and the Interpretation of John 4:10-26." *Catholic Biblical Quarterly* 41 (1979) 419-37.

O'Day, Gail Radcliffe. "Irony and the Johannine Theology of

Revelation. An Investigation of John 4." Ph.D. dissertation, Emory University, 1983.

O'Day, Gail Radcliffe. *Revelation in the Fourth Gospel.* Philadelphia: Fortress, 1986.

Olsson, Birger. *Structure and Meaning in the Fourth Gospel: A Text-Linguistic Analysis of John 2:1-11 and 4:1-42.* Lund: CWK Gleerup, 1974.

Perkins, Pheme. *The Gospel According to St. John: A Theological Commentary.* Herald Scriptural Library. Chicago: Franciscan Herald, 1978.

Pollard, T.E. "Jesus and the Samaritan Woman." *Expository Times* 92 (1981) 147-48.

Potin, J. "Jesus chez les Samaritains." *Bible et terre sainte* 44 (1962) 4-5.

Prete, B. "La Samaritana (Giov. 4:1-42)." *Sacra Doctrina* 9 (1964) 252-68.

Rebell, Walter. "Gemeinde als Gegenwart. Ein didaktischer und wissenssoziologischer Zugang zum Johannes-Evangelium mit einer Auslegung der Kapitel 3 und 4." Habilitationsschrift, Universität-Gesamthochschule-Siegen, 1985.

Roustang, F. "Les moments de l'Acte de Foi et ses conditions de possibilité. Essai d'interprétation du dialogue avec le Samaritaine." *Recherches de science religieuse* 46 (1958) 344-78.

Sabugal, S. "El titulo *Messias-Christos* en el contexto del relato sobre la actividad de Jesus en Samaria: Jn 4,25.29." *Augustinianum* 12 (1972) 79-105.

Sanders, J.N. *A Commentary on the Gospel According to St. John.* Edited and completed by B.A. Mastin. New York: Harper & Row, 1968.

Schenke, H.-M. "Jacobsbrunnen-Josephsgrab-Sychar. Topographische Untersuchungen und Erwägungen in der Perspektive von Joh. 4,5.6." *Zeitschrift des deutschen Palästina-Vereins* 84 (1968) 159-184.

Schlatter, Adolf. *Das Evangelium nach Johannes.* Schlatters Erläuterungen zum Neuen Testament 3. Stuttgart: Calwer, 1908; 3rd ed., 1947.

Schlatter, Adolf. *Der Evangelist Johannes, Wie er spricht, denkt und glaubt, Ein Kommentar zum Neuen Testament*. 3rd ed. Stuttgart: Calwer Verlag, 1960.

Schmid, Lothar. "Die Komposition der Samaria-Szene Joh 4.1-49." *Zeitschrift für die neutestamentliche Wissenschaft* 28 (1929) 148-158.

Schnackenburg, R. "Die 'Anbetung in Geist und Wahrheit' (Joh 4,23) im Lichte von Qumran-Texten." *Biblische Zeitschrift* 3 (1959) 88-94.

Schnackenburg, Rudolf. *Das Johannesevangelium*. Vol. 1. Herders theologischer Kommentar zum Neuen Testament 4. Freiburg: Herder, 1965. ET: *The Gospel According to St. John. Volume One, Introduction and Commentary on Chapters 1-4*. Translated by Kevin Smyth. New York: Herder and Herder, 1968.

Schneider, J. *Das Evangelium nach Johannes*. Theologischer Handkommentar zum Neuen Testament. Berlin: Evangelische Verlagsanstalt, 1976.

Schneiders, Sandra M. "Women in the Fourth Gospel and the Role of Women in the Contemporary Church." *Biblical Theology Bulletin* 12 (1982) 35-45.

Schottroff, L. "Johannes 4:5-15 und die Konsequenzen des johanneischen Dualismus." *Zeitschrift für die neutestamentliche Wissenschaft* 60 (1969) 199-214.

Schürer, Emil. *Geschichte des jüdischen Volkes im Zeitalter Jesu Christi*. 3 Vols. Leipzig: J.C. Hinrichs'sche Buchhandlung, 4th ed., 1901-1909. ET: 5 Vols., *The History of the Jewish People in the Age of Jesus Christ*. Translated by John MacPherson. New York: Charles Scribner's Sons, 1891. Revised and edited edition: *The History of the Jewish People in the Age of Jesus Christ (175 B.C. - A.D. 135)*. 4 Vols. Edited by Geza Vermes, Fergus Millar, Matthew Black. Edinburgh: T. & T. Clark, 1973-1986.

Schulz, Siegfried. *Das Evangelium nach Johannes*. Das Neue Testament Deutsch 4. Göttingen: Vandenhoeck & Ruprecht, 1983.

Stanley, D.M. "Interlude samaritain." *Bible et terre sainte* 28 (1960) 2-3.

Stolt, B. "B. Olsson, *Structure and Meaning in the Fourth Gospel*," *Linguistica Biblica* 34 (1975) 110-123.

Strack, Hermann L. und Billerbeck, Paul. *Kommentar zum Neuen Testament aus Talmud und Midrash*. Munich: C.H. Beck'sche Verlagsbuchhandlung, 1922; 3rd ed. 1961.

Strathmann, Hermann. *Das Evangelium nach Johannes*. Das Neue Testament Deutsch 2. Gttingen: Vandenhoeck & Ruprecht, 1963.

Thyen, H. "Auf neuen Wegen dem Rätsel des vierten Evangeliums auf der Spur? Überlegungen zu dem Buch von Birger Olsson." *Svensk Exegetisk Årsbok* 40 (1975) 136-43.

Vellanickal, M. "Drink from the source of the Living Water." *Biblebhashyam* 5 (1979) 309-18.

Walker, R. "Jüngerwort und Herrenwort. Zur Auslegung von Joh 4:39-42." *Zeitschrift für die neutestamentliche Wissenschaft* 57 (1966) 49-54.

Watson, W.G.E. "Antecedents of a New Testament proverb." *Vetus Testamentum* 20 (1970) 368-70.

Windisch, Hans. "Der Johanneische Erzählungsstil." In *EYXAPISTHPION: Studien zur Religion und Literatur des Alten und Neuen Testaments, Hermann Gunkel zum 60. Geburtstags, den 23 Mai 1922, dargebracht von seinem Schülern und Freunden*. Edited by Hans Schmidt, pp. 174-213. Göttingen: Vandenhoeck & Ruprecht, 1923.

Zahn, Theodor. *Das Evangelium des Johannes*. Kommentar zum Neuen Testament. Leipzig: A. Deichert'sche Verlagsbuchhandlung, 1912.

APPENDICES

1.   LIST OF SUBJECTS

S_1	=	the woman
S_{1a}	=	whoever drinks water of life
S_2	=	Jesus
S_3	=	Jewish men
S_{3a}	=	a particular Jewish man
$S_{3'}$	=	Jews and Samaritans
S_4	=	water of life
S_5	=	Jacob
S_6	=	worshippers
S_7	=	Messiah
S_8	=	disciples
S_9	=	fields
S_{10}	=	the reaper
S_{11}	=	the sower
S_{12}	=	the villagers

2. LIST OF OBJECTS

O_1 = drinking water

O_{1a} = F1 = the program of providing Jesus with drinking water

$O_{1'}$ = spring water

O_{1b} = water of life

$O_{1b'}$ = understanding of water of life

$O_{1b''}$ = practical understanding of water of life

O_{1c} = /obedience/

$\bar{O}_{1c}$ = /sustenance/

O_2 = thirst for drinking water

$\bar{O}_{2'}$ = quenching of thirst for drinking water

O_{2a} = thirst for water of life

$\bar{O}_{2a}$ = quenching thirst for water of life

O_{2b} = F3 = the program to provide the Samaritan woman with water of life

O_3 = association of Jews and Samaritans

$O_{3'}$ = /human solidarity/

$\bar{O}_{3'}$ = /factional security/

O_{3a} = association with Samaritan women

$O_{3a'}$ = association with a particular Samaritan woman

O_4 = means of drawing water

$O_{4'}$ = water jar

O_{4a} = miraculous ability to provide drinking water

$O_{4a'}$ = miraculous knowledge of the woman's husbands

$O_{4a''}$ = duplication of Jacob's miracle

O_{4b} = ability to provide water of life

$O_{4b'}$ = understanding Jesus' ability to provide water of life

O_5 = Jesus' identity

$O_{5'}$ = recognition of Jesus' identity

O_{5a} = ability of a prophet

$O_{5a'}$ = recognition of Jesus as a prophet

O_6 = messianic ability to reveal the truth

$O_{6'}$ = misconceived messianic ability to reveal the truth

O_{6a} = recognition of Jesus' ability to reveal the truth

O_7 = identity of the messiah

O_{7a} = Jesus' identity as the messiah
$O_{7a'}$ = recognition of Jesus as the messiah
O_{7b} = misconception of Jesus as the messiah
$O_{7b'}$ = the woman's testimony about Jesus
O_{7c} = belief in Jesus in the sense of the woman's testimony
O_8 = the alternatives, worshipping either on this mountain or in Jerusalem.
$O_{8'}$ = worship on this mountain or in Jerusalem
$O_{8''}$ = discussion of the right place to worship
O_{8a} = worship of the Father in spirit and truth
O_{8b} = revelation of the truth about worship
$O_{8b'}$ = the announcement of "everything"
O_9 = the company of Jesus
$O_{9'}$ = engagement in discussion with Jesus
O_{9a} = presence in the village
O_{10} = food
$O_{10'}$ = food brought by another
$O_{10''}$ = food as nourishment
O_{10b} = Jesus' other food
$O_{10b'}$ = understanding of Jesus' other food
O_{11} = hunger for food
$\bar{O}_{11'}$ = satisfaction of hunger
O_{11a} = hunger for Jesus' other food
$\bar{O}_{11a'}$ = satisfaction of hunger for Jesus' other food
$\bar{O}_{11a''}$ = doing the will of the one who sent Jesus
O_{12} = readiness of the fields for harvesting
O_{12a} = the harvest
O_{12b} = rejoicing in the fruit of the harvest
$O_{12b'}$ = rejoicing with the reaper in the fruit of the harvest
O_{13} = invitation to stay with the Samaritan villagers
$O_{13'}$ = staying with the Samaritan villagers for two days
O_{14} = identity of the savior of the world
O_{14a} = ability of the savior of the world
$O_{14a'}$ = recognition of Jesus as the savior of the world
O_{15} = /universal salvation/
$\bar{O}_{15}$ = /partisan salvation/

3. LIST OF NARRATIVE PROGRAMS

(The * indicates assumed programs that are not actually presented in the discussion.)

F_1 $[S_1 => (S_2 \geq O_1) -> (S_2 \leq O_1)]$ = the woman providing Jesus with a drink of water

*F_{1a} $[S_2 => (S_1 \geq O_{1a}) -> (S_1 \leq O_{1a})]$ = Jesus asking the woman to give him a drink of water

F_{1b} $[S_2 => (S_2 \geq \bar{O}_{2'}) -> (S_2 \leq \bar{O}_{2'})]$ = Jesus quenching his thirst for drinking water

*F_{1c} $[S_1 => (S_1 \geq \bar{O}_{2'}) -> (S_1 \leq \bar{O}_{2'})$ = the woman quenching her thirst for drinking water

F_2 $[S_2 => (S_2 \geq O_{3a'}) -> (S_2 \leq O_{3a'})]$ = Jesus associating with the Samaritan woman

F_3 $[S_2 => (S_1 \geq O_{1b}) -> (S_1 \leq O_{1b})]$ = Jesus providing the Samaritan woman with water of life

*F_{3a} $[S_1 => (S_1 \geq O_{2b}) -> (S_2 \leq O_{2b})]$ = the woman asking Jesus to provide her with water of life

F_{3b} $[S_1 => (S_1 \geq \bar{O}_{2a}) -> (S_1 \leq \bar{O}_{2a})]$ = the woman quenching her thirst for the water of life

*F_{3c} $[S_2 => (S_1 \geq O_{1b'}) -> (S_1 \leq O_{1b'})]$ = Jesus explaining to the Samaritan woman the nature of the water of life

*F_{3d} $[S_1 => (S_1 \geq O_{1b''}) -> (S_1 \leq O_{1b''})]$ = the woman achieving a practical understanding of water of life

F_{3e} $[S_4 => (O_{1b} \geq S_{1a} \geq \bar{O}_{2a}) -> (O_{1b} \leq S_{1a} \leq \bar{O}_{2a})]$ = water of life becoming a fountain continuously quenching thirst for it

*F_{3f} $[S_1 => (S_2 \geq O_{4b})]$ = the woman not recognizing Jesus' ability to provide water of life

F_4 $[S_5 => (S_y \geq O_{1'}) -> (S_y \leq O_{1'})]$ = Jacob miraculously providing spring water for himself, his sons and their livestock

F_{4a} $[S_2 => (S_1 \geq O_{4a'}) -> (S_1 \leq O_{4a'})]$ = Jesus revealing to the woman his miraculous knowledge about her husbands

*F_5 $[S_1 => (S_1 \geq O_{5a}) -> (S_1 \leq O_{5a})]$ = the woman attributing the identity of a prophet to Jesus

*F_6 $[S_1 => (S_2 \geq O_{8''}) -> (S_2 \leq O_{8''})]$ = the woman suggesting to Jesus the right place of worship as a topic for discussion

F_7 $[S_2 => (S_1 \geq O_{8b}) -> (S_1 \leq O_{8b})]$ = Jesus revealing the truth about worship to the woman

F_{7a} $[(S_6 => (O_8 \leq S_6 \geq O_{8a}) -> (O_8 \geq S_6 \leq O_{8a})]$ = worshippers worshipping, not on this mountain nor in Jerusalem, but the Father in spirit and truth

*F_{7b} $[S_2 => (S_{3'} \geq O_3) -> (S_{3'} \leq O_3)]$ = Jesus resolving the issue of Jews and Samaritans not associating

F_8 $[S_7 => (S_y \geq O_{8b'}) -> (S_y \leq O_{8b'})]$ = Messiah announcing everything

*F_9 $[S_2 => (S_1 \geq O_{7a}) -> (S_1 \leq O_{7a})]$ = Jesus telling the woman that he is Messiah

F_{9b} $[S_1 => (S_2 \geq O_{6'}) -> (S_2 \leq O_{6'})]$ = the woman attributing to Jesus a misconceived messianic ability

*F_{10} $[S_1 => (S_1 \leq O_{4'}) -> (S_1 \geq O_{4'})]$ = the woman abandoning her jar

F_{11} $[S_1 => (O_9 \leq S_1 \geq O_{9a}) -> (O_9 \geq S_1 \leq O_{9a})]$ = the woman leaving Jesus to go to the village

F_{12} $[S_8 => (S_8 \geq O_{9'}) -> (S_8 \leq O_{9'})]$ = the disciples engaging in discussion with Jesus

F_{13} $[S_8 => (S_2 \geq O_{10}) -> (S_2 \leq O_{10})]$ = the disciples offering Jesus food

F_{13a} $[S_2 => (S_2 \geq \bar{O}_{11'}) -> (S_2 \leq \bar{O}_{11'})]$ = Jesus satisfying his hunger for food

*F_{14} $[S_2 => (S_8 \geq O_{10b'}) -> (S_8 \leq O_{10b'})]$ = Jesus explaining to the disciples the nature of his other food

F_{14a} $[S_2 => (S_2 \geq \bar{O}_{11a'}) -> (S_2 \leq \bar{O}_{11a'})]$ = Jesus satisfying his hunger for his other food

*F_{14b} $[S_2 => (S_2 \geq \bar{O}_{11a''}) -> (S_2 \leq \bar{O}_{11a''})]$ = Jesus doing the will of the one who sent him

F_{15} $[S_9 => (S_9 \geq O_{12}) -> (S_9 \leq O_{12})]$ = the fields' getting ready for the harvest

F_{15a} $[S_{10} => (S_{10} \geq O_{12a}) -> (S_{10} \leq O_{12a})$ = the reaper bringing in the harvest

F_{15b} $[S_{10} => (S_{10} \geq O_{12b}) -> (S_{10} \leq O_{12b})]$ = the reaper rejoicing in the fruit of the harvest

F_{15c} $[S_{11} => (S_{11} \geq O_{12b'}) -> (S_{11} \leq O_{12b'})]$ = the sowers rejoicing with the reaper in the fruit of the harvest

F_{16} $[S_1 => (S_{12} \geq O_{7b'}) -> (S_{12} \leq O_{7b'})]$ = the woman testifying about Jesus to the villagers

F_{16b} $[S_{12} => (S_{12} \geq O_{7c}) -> (S_{12} \leq O_{7c})]$ = the villagers believing in Jesus in the sense of the woman's witness

F_{17} $[S_{12} => (S_{12} \geq O_9) -> (S_{12} \leq O_9)$ = the villagers going to meet Jesus

F_{18} $[S_{12} => (S_2 \geq O_{13}) -> (S_2 \leq O_{13})]$ = the villagers inviting Jesus to stay with them

F_{18a} $[S_2 => (S_2 \geq O_{13'}) -> (S_2 \leq O_{13'})]$ = Jesus staying with the villagers for two days

F_{19} $[S_{12} => (O_{7c} \leq S_{12} \geq O_{14a'}) -> (O_{7c} \geq S_{12} \leq O_{14a'})]$ = the villagers no longer believing in Jesus in the sense of the woman's testimony, but recognizing him as the savior of the world

4. LIST OF NARRATIVE PROGRAMS IN THE GENERATIVE TRAJECTORY

(These descriptions refer to the concrete expressions through which the values come to expression)

A. *Expressing the value /obedience/*

$F_{1a'}$ $[S_2 => (S_2 \le \bar{O}_{1c})]$ = Jesus affirming the value of drinking water as /sustenance/ by asking the woman for a drink

$F_{10'}$ $[S_1 => (S_1 \le \bar{O}_{1c}) -> (S_1 \ge \bar{O}_{1c})]$ = the woman negating the value of drinking water as /sustenance/ by dropping her jar

$F_{13'}$ $[S_8 => (S_2 \le \bar{O}_{1c})]$ = the disciples attributing to Jesus the value /sustenance/ for food

$F_{13b'}$ $[S_2 => (S_2 \le \bar{O}_{1c}) -> (S_2 \ge \bar{O}_{1c})]$ = Jesus declining the disciples offer of /sustenance/

$F_{14a'}$ $[S_2 => (S_2 \ge O_{1c}) -> (S_2 \le O_{1c})]$ = Jesus having other food, /obedience/, of which the disciples do not know

$F_{14a''}$ $[S_2 => (\bar{O}_{1c} \le S_1 \ge O_{1c}) -> (O_{1c} \le S_2 \ge \bar{O}_{1c})]$ = $F_{13b'}$ and $F_{14a'}$ as a single parformance

$F_{16'}$ $[S_1 => (S_1 \ge O_{1c}) -> (S_1 \le O_{1c})]$ = the woman partaking of the water of life by witnessing concerning Jesus in the village

$F_{16''}$ $[S_1 => (\bar{O}_{1c} \le S_1 \ge O_{1c}) -> (O_{1c} \le S_1 \ge \bar{O}_{1c})]$ = $F_{10'}$ and $F_{16'}$ as a single performance

B. *Expressing the value /human solidarity/*

$F_{2a'}$ $[S_2 => (S_2 \le \bar{O}_{3'}) -> (S_2 \ge \bar{O}_{3'})]$ = [by associating with the Samaritan woman] Jesus violates the convention of non-association between Jews and Samaritans

$F_{2a''}$ $[S_1 => (S_1 \le \bar{O}_{3'}) -> (S_1 \ge \bar{O}_{3'})]$ = by associating with Jesus the woman negates the convention of non-association

$F_{2b'}$ $[S_2 => (S_2 \ge O_{3'}) -> (S_2 \le O_{3'})]$ = Jesus associating with the Samaritan woman by asking her for a drink of water

$F_{2b''}$ $[S_1 => (O_1 \ge O_{3'}) -> (S_1 \le O_{3'})]$ = the woman associates with a Jew by entering into conversation with Jesus

$F_{2c'}$ $[S_2 => (\bar{O}_{3'} \le S_2 \ge O_{3'}) -> (O_{3'} \ge S_2 \le \bar{O}_{3'})]$ = $F_{2a'}$ and $F_{2b'}$ as a single performance

$F_{2c''}$ $[S_1 => (\bar{O}_{3'} \le S_1 \ge O_{3'}) -> (O_{3'} \ge S_1 \le \bar{O}_{3'})]$ = $F_{2a''}$ and $F_{2b''}$ as a single performance

$F_{7a''}$ $[S_{3'} => (S_{3'} \leq \bar{O}_{3'}) -> (S_{3'} \geq \bar{O}_{3'})]$ = Jews and Samaritans negate the convention of non-association by worshipping the Father neither on this mountain nor in Jerusalem

$F_{7b''}$ $[S_{3'} => (S_{3'} \geq O_{3'}) -> (S_{3'} \leq O_{3'})]$ = Jews and Samaritans worshipping the Father in spirit and truth

$F_{7c''}$ $[S_{3'} => (\bar{O}_{3'} \leq S_{3'} \geq O_{3'}) -> (O_{3'} \leq S_{3'} \geq \bar{O}_{3'})]$ = $F_{7a''}$ and $F_{7b''}$ as a single performance

$F_{18a'}$ $[S_{12} => (S_{12} \leq \bar{O}_{3'}) -> (S_{12} \geq \bar{O}_{3'})]$ = the assumed affirmation of the convention of non-association negated by the Samaritans' invitation that Jesus visit them

$F_{18b'}$ $[S_{12} => (S_{12} \geq O_{3'}) -> (S_{12} \leq O_{3'})]$ = the Samaritans associating with Jews by inviting Jesus to stay with them

$F_{18c'}$ $[S_{12} => (\bar{O}_{3'} \leq S_{12} \geq O_{3'}) -> (O_{3'} \leq S_{12} \geq \bar{O}_{3'})]$ = $F_{18a'}$ and $F_{18b'}$ as a single performance

C. *Expressing the value /universal salvation/*

$F_{7a'}$ $[S_{3'} => (S_{3'} \leq \bar{O}_{15}) -> (S_{3'} \geq \bar{O}_{15})]$ = Jews and Samaritans negating the value /partisan salvation/ by worshipping neither on this mountain nor in Jerusalem

$F_{7b'}$ $[S_{3'} => (S_{3'} \geq O_{15}) -> (S_{3'} \leq O_{15})]$ = Jews and Samaritans affirming /universal salvation/ by worshipping the Father in spirit and truth

$F_{7c'}$ $[S_{3'} => (\bar{O}_{15} \leq S_{3'} \geq O_{15}) -> (O_{15} \leq S_{3'} \geq \bar{O}_{15})]$ = $F_{7a'}$ and $F_{7b'}$ as a single performance

$F_{7d'}$ $[S_{6} => (\bar{O}_{15} \leq S_{6} \geq O_{15}) -> (O_{15} \leq S_{6} \geq \bar{O}_{15})]$ = worshippers' negating /partisan salvation/ and affirming /universal salvation/ by worshipping the Father in spirit and truth

$F_{19a'}$ $[S_{12} => (S_{12} \leq \bar{O}_{15}) -> (S_{12} \geq \bar{O}_{15})]$ = the villagers reject /partisan salvation/ in their rejection of the woman's testimony

$F_{19b'}$ $[S_{12} => (S_{12} \geq O_{15}) -> (S_{12} \leq O_{15})]$ = the villagers affirm /universal salvation/ by recognizing Jesus as the savior of the world

$F_{19c'}$ $[S_{12} => (\bar{O}_{15} \leq S_{12} \geq O_{15}) -> (O_{15} \leq S_{12} \geq \bar{O}_{15})]$ = $F_{19a'}$ and $F_{19b'}$ as a single performance

INDEX OF BIBLICAL AND OTHER ANCIENT TEXTS

Patristic

Philo

Josephus

Rabinnic Literature

Samaritan

Targum

Corpus Hermeticum

Nag Hammadi

INDEX OF TOPICS

INDEX OF MODERN AUTHORS